Couple Schema Therapy

Couple Schema Therapy

The Two-Legged Dimensional Model

Daniel Aurelio Ceballos Peña

WILEY

This edition first published 2027

Registered Offices
John Wiley & Sons, Inc., 111 River Street, Hoboken, NJ 07030, USA
John Wiley & Sons Ltd, New Era House, 8 Oldlands Way, Bognor Regis, West Sussex, PO22 9NQ, UK

For details of our global editorial offices, customer services, and more information about Wiley products visit us at www.wiley.com.

The manufacturer's authorized representative according to the EU General Product Safety Regulation is Wiley-VCH GmbH, Boschstr. 12, 69469 Weinheim, Germany, e-mail: Product_Safety@wiley.com.

Wiley also publishes its books in a variety of electronic formats and by print-on-demand. Some content that appears in standard print versions of this book may not be available in other formats.

Library of Congress Cataloging-in-Publication Data has been applied for:

Print ISBN: 9781394444564
ePDF ISBN: 9781394444588
ePUB ISBN: 9781394444571
oBook ISBN: 9781394444595

Cover Design: Wiley
Cover Image: Sileno/stock.adobe.com

Printed and bound by CPI Group (UK) Ltd, Croydon, CR0 4YY
C9781394444564_240826

Contents

List of Figures *xii*
List of Tables *xiii*
Preface *xiv*
Acknowledgments *xvi*
Explanatory Note *xvii*
Prologue *xix*
Introduction *xxi*

Part I Theoretical Foundations of Couple Schema Therapy *1*

1 Schema Therapy and the Contextual Model *3*
1.1 Schema Therapy *3*
1.1.1 The Schema Model *3*
1.1.1.1 Negative Schemas of the Disconnection and Rejection Domain *4*
1.1.1.2 Negative Schemas in the Domain of Impaired Autonomy and Performance *5*
1.1.1.3 Negative Schemas of the Impaired Limits Domain *6*
1.1.1.4 Negative Schemas of Dominance Directed by the Needs of Others *6*
1.1.1.5 Negative Schemas of the Overvigilance and Inhibition Domain *7*
1.1.2 Coping Behaviors *8*
1.1.3 The Process of Schema Therapy *8*
1.1.3.1 Psychoeducation Phase *9*
1.1.3.2 Change Phase *9*
1.1.4 The Work of Negative Schema Modes *10*
1.2 The Contextual Model *12*
1.3 Integration of Both Approaches in the Dimensional Model *15*
1.3.1 Integration of Schema Therapy *16*
1.3.2 The Integration of Contextual Therapies *17*

2 Theoretical Concepts of the Couple Schema Therapy Model *18*
2.1 Introduction *18*
2.2 The Three Key Concepts *18*
2.2.1 Basic Needs *18*
2.2.2 Basic and Social Emotions *21*
2.2.3 Coping Behaviors *25*
2.3 The Two-dimensional Model *28*
2.4 The Active and Blocked Sides *31*
2.5 The Balance Between the Two Needs *34*

3 The Mode Cycle *41*
3.1 Introduction *41*
3.1.1 Need for Attachment–Connection *41*
3.1.2 Need for Assertiveness–Autonomy *42*
3.2 The Moments of the Mode Cycle *42*
3.3 The Different Mode Cycles *44*
3.3.1 The Dominance–Domination Mode Cycle *45*
3.3.2 The Dominance–Avoidance Mode Cycle *47*
3.3.2.1 The Dominance–Passive Avoidance Mode Cycle *47*
3.3.2.2 The Active Dominance–Avoidance Mode Cycle *49*
3.3.3 Dominance–Submission Mode Cycle *51*
3.3.4 Avoidance–Avoidance Mode Cycle *53*
3.3.4.1 Passive Avoidance–Passive Avoidance Mode Cycle *54*
3.3.4.2 Active Avoidance–Active Avoidance Mode Cycle *55*
3.3.4.3 Active Avoidance–Passive Avoidance Mode Cycle *57*
3.3.5 Assertiveness/Cooperation–Cooperation/Assertiveness Mode Cycle *60*
3.4 Identifying Child and Coping Modes in Therapy Using Chairs *63*

4 Neurological and Cerebral Bases of Therapeutic Interventions *66*
4.1 Introduction *66*
4.2 Stimulate Executive Function to Get Out of Autopilot and Intense Emotional States *71*
4.3 Stimulate the Emotional System to Overcome Avoidance or Rational Blockage *72*
4.4 Moving from a Sympathetic State to a Parasympathetic State *75*

Part II Education *77*

5 Explanation of the Simplified "Two-leg" Model (Module I) *79*
5.1 Introduction *79*
5.1.1 General Objective of the Module *79*

5.1.2 Specific Objectives *79*
5.2 Starting the Session *80*
5.2.1 Identify the Problem to Work On *80*
5.2.2 Starting the Mode Cycle *82*
5.2.3 Stopping the Mode Cycle *83*
5.3 Cognitive Work *84*
5.3.1 Observer Team Work *84*
5.3.1.1 Identify Basic Needs *85*
5.3.1.2 Identify Coping Modes *88*
5.3.1.3 Identify Basic Emotions *92*
5.4 Closing the Session: Therapeutic Task: Awareness of Needs, Emotions, and Coping Modes *97*

6 Presentation of the Mode Cycle (Module II) *100*
6.1 Introduction *100*
6.1.1 General Objective of the Module *100*
6.1.2 Specific Objectives *100*
6.2 Beginning of the Session *101*
6.2.1 Identify the Problem to Be Worked on *101*
6.2.2 Starting the Mode Cycle *102*
6.2.3 Stopping the Mode Cycle *102*
6.3 Cognitive Work *103*
6.3.1 Observer Team Work *103*
6.3.1.1 Identify Coping Modes *105*
6.3.1.2 Identify Child Modes *107*
6.3.1.3 Display the Mode Cycle *109*
6.4 Closing the Session: Therapeutic Task: Try to Identify and Stop the Mode Cycle *110*

7 Stopping the Mode Cycle (Module III) *112*
7.1 Introduction *112*
7.1.1 General Objective *112*
7.1.2 Specific Objectives *112*
7.2 Beginning of the Session: Identify the Problem to Be Worked on and Start and Stop the Cycle *113*
7.3 Cognitive Work *114*
7.3.1 Observer Team Work *114*
7.3.2 In-session Work to Support Rebalancing *116*
7.4 Closing the Session *121*
7.4.1 Restore Coexistence *121*
7.4.2 Therapeutic Task: Stopping the Mode Cycle Themselves *124*

8 Rebalancing After Separation: Entering Healthy Adult Mode (Module IV) *126*
8.1 Introduction *126*
8.1.1 General Objective *126*
8.1.2 Specific Objectives *126*
8.2 Beginning of the Session: Identify the Problem to Be Worked on and Start and Stop the Cycle *127*
8.3 Cognitive Work *128*
8.3.1 Observer Team Work *128*
8.3.2 Analyze the Advantages of Using the Blue Leg *131*
8.4 Experiential Work: "Best Day" Exercise *133*
8.5 Closing the Session: Therapeutic Task: Identify the Active Leg, Bring a Positive Image, Reconnect with Your Partner, and Do the Best Day Activity *136*

Part III Rebalancing *141*

9 Externalizing Partner (Module V) *143*
9.1 Introduction *143*
9.1.1 General Objective *144*
9.1.2 Specific Objectives *144*
9.2 Beginning of the Session: Identifying the Problem to Be Worked on and Identifying That One of the Partners Is Too Focused on Their Red Leg *145*
9.3 Cognitive Work *146*
9.3.1 Observer Team Work *146*
9.3.2 Analyze the Advantages and Disadvantages of Using the Red Leg *149*
9.4 Experiential Work to Rebalance the Red Leg *152*
9.4.1 Gaining Access to the Vulnerable Side (Module V) *153*
9.4.1.1 Fostering Empathy Toward the Other Side *154*
9.4.1.2 Connecting with the Vulnerable Child Mode *157*
9.4.1.3 Speaking from Vulnerability *158*
9.4.1.4 Reconnection *163*
9.4.2 Reconnecting Emotionally by Floating Back to a Honeymoon Scene (Module VI) *163*
9.5 Closing the Session *167*
9.5.1 Reinforce the Benefits of Leg Switching *167*
9.5.2 Therapeutic Task: Meet with the Couple to Look at Past Photos, Remember Good Times, Give Positive Feedback, and Use the Technique Learned in Session *168*

10 **Internalizing Partners (Module VII)** *172*
10.1 Introduction *172*
10.2 Beginning of the Session: Identifying the Problem to Be Worked On and Identifying That One of the Partners Is Too Focused on Their Blue Leg *173*
10.3 Cognitive Work *175*
10.3.1 Observer Team Work *175*
10.3.2 Analyze the Advantages and Disadvantages of Using the Blue Leg *177*
10.4 Experiential Work *179*
10.4.1 Accessing the Assertive Side (Module VII) *180*
10.5 Closing the Session *184*
10.5.1 Evaluate the Benefits of Leg Switching *184*
10.5.2 Therapeutic Task: Meet with the Couple to Look at Past Photos or Remember Good Times, Give Positive Feedback, and Apply the Technique Learned in the Session *185*

11 **Facing Critical Voices (Module VIII)** *189*
11.1 Introduction *189*
11.2 Beginning Work with Critical Voices *190*
11.2.1 Identify the Activation of Critical Voices That Interfere with the Session *190*
11.3 Experiential Work *191*
11.3.1 Experiential Work with the Critical Voice in Internalizing Clients *191*
11.3.1.1 Chair Work with the Internalizing Critical Voice *191*
11.3.1.2 Chair Work with the Vulnerable Child Mode of the Internalizing Partner *194*
11.3.2 Experiential Work with the Critical Voice in Externalizing Clients *196*
11.4 Closing the Session *197*
11.4.1 Reinforce the Benefits of Partner Support in the Face of Critical Voices *197*
11.4.2 Therapeutic Task: Identifying the Critical Voice *198*
11.5 Resuming Session Work *199*

Part IV Reconnection *201*

12 **Reconnection with Joint Imagery Exercise (Module IX)** *203*
12.1 Introduction *203*
12.2 Starting the Session: Identifying the Problem to Be Worked On *204*

12.3 Experiential Work *205*
12.3.1 Detect Negative Patterns and Their Origins *205*
12.3.2 Joint Imagery Rewriting Work *209*
12.3.3 Link Between Past Experience, Coping Modes, and Child Modes of the Reparented Partner *213*
12.4 Closing the Session *218*
12.4.1 Evaluate the Benefits of Connecting with the Blue Leg *218*
12.4.2 Therapeutic Task: Remind the Partner of Their Reparenting Role, the Vulnerable Child of the Reparented Member, and Carry Out the Agreed Commitment *218*

13 Training the Healthy Adult Mode (Module X) *222*
13.1 Introduction *222*
13.2 Starting the Session: Identifying the Problem, a Member's Difficulty Speaking from Vulnerability, and Stopping the Interaction *223*
13.3 Cognitive Work: Observer Team Work: Modeling Expression From Vulnerability *224*
13.4 Experiential Work *226*
13.4.1 Rebalancing *226*
13.4.1.1 Chair Work to Facilitate the Expression of Emotions From Vulnerability *227*
13.4.1.2 Imagination Work to Facilitate the Expression of Emotions From Vulnerability *229*
13.4.2 Expressing Needs from Vulnerability *231*
13.5 Closing the Session *233*
13.5.1 Evaluate the Benefits of Expressing Emotions from Vulnerability *233*
13.5.2 Therapeutic Task: Try to Change Legs As Much As Possible *234*

14 Connection Dialogues (Module XI) *237*
14.1 Introduction *237*
14.2 Beginning of the Session: Identify the Problem and Stop the Interaction to Initiate Connection Dialogues *238*
14.3 Cognitive Work *239*
14.3.1 Explanation of the Cell Phone Metaphor *240*
14.3.2 Explanation of the Connection Dialogues Exercise *242*
14.4 Experiential Work *244*
14.4.1 Connection Dialogues: Polarization and Contradictions *244*
14.4.2 Connection Dialogue: Accept, Propose, and Reach an Agreement *246*
14.5 Closing the Session *251*
14.5.1 Evaluate the Benefits of Conducting Connection Dialogues *251*
14.5.2 Therapeutic Task: Practicing Connection Dialogues *251*

Part V Additional Modules *255*

15 Homework (Module XII) *257*
15.1 Introduction *257*
15.2 Tasks for the First Phase of Therapy: Gear Change *257*
15.3 Tasks for the Second Phase of Therapy: Nurturing the Relationship *259*

16 Preparing for Separation (Module XIII) *261*
16.1 Introduction *261*
16.2 Beginning of the Session: Raise the Possibility of Ending the Relationship *262*
16.3 Experiential Work *264*
16.3.1 Evaluate the Pros and Cons of Separating or Staying Together *264*
16.4 Closing the Session: Work Plan with Specific Objectives *266*
16.5 Beginning of the Session: Evaluate the Progress of the Work Plan Carried Out *268*
16.5.1 Positive Results of the Work Plan *268*
16.5.2 Negative Results of the Work Plan *269*
16.6 Cognitive Work: Decide Whether to Make a Last Attempt *270*
16.6.1 The Couple Decides to Make a "Last Attempt" *272*
16.6.2 The Couple Does Not Decide to Make the "Last Attempt" *273*
16.7 Closing the Session: Agreements from the Last Attempt *273*
16.8 Beginning of the Session: Review the Results of the Last Attempt *275*
16.8.1 Positive Results of the Last Attempt *275*
16.8.2 Negative Results of the Last Attempt *276*
16.9 Cognitive Work: Ending the Relationship *277*
16.9.1 Resolve the Remaining Problems *277*
16.10 Closing the Session: Farewell to the Couple *279*

References *284*
Index *289*

List of Figures

Figure 3.1 Steps in the Mode Cycle. *43*
Figure 3.2 Simplified version of the Mode Cycle. *44*
Figure 3.3 Assertiveness/cooperation–cooperation/assertiveness Mode Cycle, reflected in Andrew and Emily. *62*
Figure 3.4 Chair arrangement to represent coping modes, child modes, and the observer team in therapy. *64*
Figure 3.5 Simplified chair work to represent coping modes and active child modes in therapy. *65*
Figure 16.1 Chair work to analyze the pros and cons of ending a relationship. *265*

List of Tables

Table 5.1 Diary of needs, emotions, and coping modes that were active, as well as those that were pushed into the background, blocked, or not used. *98*
Table 7.1 Reflection questions to identify one's own needs, emotions, and active coping modes during time-out. *117*
Table 7.2 Reflective questions to identify, during the time-out, your own neglected needs, hidden or blocked emotions, and the flexible coping behaviors that could be used. *118*

Preface

This book emerged from my training in couple schema therapy and from a growing interest in understanding and applying the dimensional model used in this approach. During the process of studying and practicing the model, it became evident that many clinicians would benefit from a text that explains in detail how the modules can be applied in clinical practice, integrating practical examples, therapeutic guidance, and a clear description of the chair movements used throughout the intervention process.

Although the model has been presented in training programs and publications, many therapists experience difficulties when translating theoretical principles into concrete therapeutic interventions. For this reason, the aim of this book is to provide a practical guide that illustrates how the model can be implemented in session while preserving the flexibility required in psychotherapy.

One of the central elements of this approach is the use of spatial representations and chair movements to visualize and modify the relational dynamics of the couple. Understanding how and when to use these interventions is essential for facilitating change within the therapeutic process. Therefore, this book offers a detailed description of these procedures so that therapists can better understand the underlying logic of the interventions.

This book is not intended to serve as a rigid set of instructions. Instead, it aims to provide a structured framework that therapists can adapt according to their own clinical style and to the particular characteristics of each couple. Clarity in the description of the intervention process allows the model to be applied more consistently and also facilitates future research evaluating its clinical effectiveness.

The book is primarily intended for therapists and mental health professionals interested in working with couples. It may also be useful for clinicians who do not yet have formal training in schema therapy but wish to learn a structured model of intervention that integrates emotional, experiential, and behavioral components. Additionally, it can serve as a practical resource for students undergoing training in couple schema therapy and for researchers interested in evaluating the clinical outcomes of this model.

The book is organized into five parts. The first part presents the theoretical foundations of the approach, including the basic principles of schema therapy, the contextual framework of the model, the mode cycle in couples, and the neuropsychological foundations that support the intervention.

The second part introduces the first modules of the model, focusing on the psychoeducation of the dimensional model of needs, emotions, and behaviors. These dimensions are metaphorically represented as two "legs" that must remain balanced in order to move forward. This section explains how therapists can identify the dimension in which each partner is stuck, understand the cycle of modes that maintains the conflict, and begin the process of change.

The third part focuses on interventions designed to facilitate change in cases where the initial modules are not sufficient. In particular, strategies are described for working with individuals who show predominantly externalizing patterns (difficulty moving away from the need for autonomy and assertiveness) or internalizing patterns (difficulty moving away from the need for attachment and connection), as well as interventions aimed at addressing the influence of critical internal voices that interfere with the change process.

The fourth part describes the process of reconnection between partners once a greater balance in their emotional needs has been achieved. This section includes experiential interventions such as imagery work, reparenting processes, and structured dialogues that help partners recognize and respond to each other's emotional needs from a healthier adult perspective.

Finally, the fifth part presents therapeutic tasks that can be implemented throughout the modular process of therapy. It also addresses situations in which couples are unable to achieve sufficient change during treatment and explores how therapists can guide partners toward the possibility of a respectful and psychologically healthy separation when necessary.

Daniel Aurelio Ceballos Peña
Guadalajara, Mexico 2026

Acknowledgments

I would first like to thank my wife, Nora Serrano.

I am also grateful to those who contributed to my training as a couples schema therapist: Matías Valente, Eva Frank-Noyon, and Julia Hinrichs.

My thanks as well to Sergio Morales of the Mexican Institute of Schema Therapy.

A special thanks to Eckhard Roediger for his time, knowledge, generosity, and constant guidance throughout the writing of this book; without his help and support, this project would not have been possible.

Daniel Aurelio Ceballos Peña

Explanatory Note

Throughout this text, various clinical cases are described: none of them represent a specific individual but rather are used to illustrate typical cases related to the different concepts addressed in the book. Likewise, these cases are structured to be concrete and facilitate the reader's understanding of the model. The reactions of the partners are often more complex and less cooperative than in the cases presented throughout this text.

The work was written in a generic masculine form. However, it's important to clarify that the author advocates for inclusion and diversity, using generic writing only to facilitate the reading of the book.

This book is the product of direct training with the creator of the couples schema therapy approach based on the contextual model, Eckhard Roediger. Therefore, both the theoretical approach and the modules described in this text are his own. This text aims to describe this model in depth, providing examples, structuring the approach with steps, intervention scripts, and sample sessions to facilitate learning and implementation. However, the author of this book adds some suggestions to this structure to facilitate the completion of the stages involved in the couples therapy process.

To become certified as a couple schema therapist in English, you can contact the creator of the model, Eckhard Roediger, directly via the website: https://www.schematherapy-roediger.org/.

However, if you are looking to become certified in this model in Spanish, you can search for the author of this book, Daniel Ceballos, on the website: https://www.terapiaesquemas.com/.

Throughout the text, a guide is presented that exemplifies the "ideal" application of the model. However, it is important to note that partners and couple dynamics are unique, making the application of the model different in each case. Therefore, therapists are encouraged to internalize the processes described in the book and use them in their own unique style, focused on the needs of the couple, as long as they are based on the theoretical foundations that underpin the model presented in the book.

The same applies to the scripts presented throughout the book: these should not be considered rigid instructions but rather a guide to provide a clear reference for how to intervene in a session. Each therapist should adjust and adapt them according to their personal style and the characteristics of the partners. These scripts constitute original developments inspired by the schema therapy model for couples described by Roediger et al. (2018, 2021), as well as by subsequent developments by Roediger (2025) and joint contributions by Roediger and Valente (2025).

The exercises presented in this book are not open-ended in and of themselves, but rather are intended to guide partners along a path to connect with their needs, emotions, and impulses. Therefore, in these exercises, the therapist ends up being directive and proactive, as this facilitates the process.

This book focuses more on explaining the application of couple schema therapy, providing case examples, therapist advice, scripts, or working materials for the therapist, and a sequence of steps. However, if readers are interested in delving deeper into the theoretical foundations, readers can refer to the book "Paare bewegen" by Roediger and Frank-Noyon (2021). Also, throughout this text, an emphasis is placed on the dynamics of the couple's relationship. To learn more about the work in complementary individual sessions, where schemas or schema modes and their intervention are worked on in depth, the reader can refer to texts that address the individual schema therapy process, such as those of Young et al. (2015).

Finally, this book presents a general therapeutic process for couples using schema therapy, providing a specialized approach to difficult cases such as violence, sexual issues, infidelity, etc. You can consult the text by Roediger and Frank-Noyon (2021) or take specialized courses on this subject. In English, you can explore: https://www.schematherapy-roediger.org/; In Spanish, you can visit: https://www.terapiaesquemas.com/.

Prologue

This is actually the most comprehensive book on couple schema therapy so far since it merges the content of several preexisting books I contributed to into one concise and systematic presentation, already including the latest adjustments we made in recent years.

Besides a brief but comprehensive overview on needs, schemas, schema-coping, and modes, in the first part it lays out the neurobiological underpinnings of our simplified, dimensional "two-leg" model, beautifully illustrated with case examples depicted from the author's rich practical experience, revealing a deep connection with the model. The resulting coping mode cycles are brought to life by case vignettes covering the full range of typical maladaptive interaction patterns related to variations of the "dance" metaphor in a very creative way.

In the next step, the author continues building the interventions on a neurobiological foundation underlying the process of change, leading to a set of detailed interventions to conduct the therapeutic interaction between activating schemas and keeping the working alliance stable. This provides safety for therapists and clients while inducing corrective emotional experiences.

A second part presents the whole module system. Each chapter systematically includes an overview, objectives, how to start the session, verbatim instructions on how to convey the content to the clients, one or more case vignettes, a session transcript, and specific advice for the therapists, including summarizing tables up to how to close the session. Starting with introducing the simplified model in an easy-to-grasp manner, the author covers all modules one by one in detail. He also describes the use of the "mode cycle clashcard" as a one-page case conceptualization serving as a roadmap giving the therapy process direction. The author adds self-developed tools too e.g., to help clients access their current activation state during time-out. This shows creativity as well as a profound understanding of the processes.

A major strength of this book is the precise and step-by-step instruction throughout all the modules on how to guide the clients through our way of applying experiential techniques. We merge imagery work and chair dialogues into one unified experiential way of working in order to activate the blocked functional emotions as drivers for emotional reconnection with the partner. We broaden the bandwidth of our interventions by commuting between a metacognitive observer stance, standing up together with the clients looking down on the activated emotions and behavior on the chairs in a shared perspective, and working together in imagery states on embodied emotions in a very deep way. This is a unique feature of this approach compared to others working with couples. The book guides the readers through these exercises in a very concise way, giving clear guidance.

In a nutshell: This amazing book gives you a comprehensive and up-to-date toolbox for dealing with couples, as well as with your individual clients suffering from hard-to-challenge, maladaptive interaction patterns. For me it is the gold standard in this field. Enjoy reading and working with it!

Frankfurt (Germany), March 2025

Eckhard Roediger, MD
Director of the Frankfurt Schema Therapy Institute
Past president and honorary member of the ISST

Introduction

This book is structured in five main parts, each designed to guide the reader through the theoretical and practical foundations of the couple schema therapy model.

The first part introduces the theoretical foundations of the model. Chapter one provides a general overview of schema therapy, its main characteristics, and the contextual approach. The second chapter delves into the essential features of the model, including a holistic understanding of human nature. The third chapter focuses on couple dynamics, analyzing how each partner's behavior impacts the other's emotions, forming self-perpetuating cycles. Finally, the fourth chapter explores the neuroscientific foundations that justify the techniques used in this therapeutic approach.

Parts two through four describe the phases of work with couples. Each phase will consist of a series of "modules" designed to establish a guide for the schema therapist's direct work with couples. These parts are composed of modules geared toward achieving specific objectives.

Roediger and Frank-Noyon (2021) point out that the length of sessions depends on each case and can range from 60 to 90 minutes, so it is advisable to dedicate this amount of time to each session. Regarding frequency, the authors suggest initially establishing a session every week, especially in cases where the interaction ends up being problematic. As the emotional intensity and frequency of conflictual interactions calm down (because both partners are able to stop the mode cycle on their own), the interval between sessions increases to fourteen days. Finally, when the couple have learned to maintain constructive conversations, they move on to monthly sessions.

The second part addresses the couple education stage, in which the therapist psychoeducates the couple using the couple schema therapy model so that they can identify their needs, active childhood coping patterns, and the mode cycle that arises from their interactions.

The third part focuses on the rebalancing stage of the couple. In it, the therapist provides tools to partners who appear stuck in their search for balance in the satisfaction of their needs so that they can break free from this stagnation and become ready for reconnection.

The rebalancing phase is optional and is only used if one of the partners had difficulty switching legs at the end of the first phase. During this rebalancing phase, some partners require individual support therapy to successfully switch legs. However, the process of individual support therapy is not covered in this book. Also, this section describes how the therapist can address the emergence of an internal critical voice during the sessions.

The fourth part addresses the reconnection phase within the couple. The main objective is to facilitate both partners' ability to express themselves as individuals capable of meeting their own emotional needs and those of their partner, communicating in a balanced manner based on vulnerability. To this end, we work on how to generate attachment in the couple's relationship (blue leg) through joint imagery exercises in which, through the rewriting of images, the partners reparent each other through painful situations experienced in childhood or adolescence that generated their negative schemas. This increases empathy and connection between the two partners. Both partners are also trained to express their emotions and needs from a position of vulnerability. Finally, we work on improving communication between the partners through a strategy called "connection dialogues."

This reconnection phase is implemented only in cases where both partners have shown that they can make the leg change and are willing to connect from the blue leg, as they try to reconnect with the other partner.

The fifth part describes the additional modules that the therapist can use during couple schema therapy. It lists the tasks that the therapist can assign to couples throughout the therapeutic process. It outlines the steps to follow when the couple has finished reviewing the modules and the partners have not been able to resolve their conflicts.

The organization of these modules is not random, but rather represents a sequence of steps to achieve the objectives outlined above. Therefore, they must be completed in the suggested order. In other words, the sessions with the modules provide a structure.

During the presentation of each module, they are organized to facilitate their understanding in a suggested sequence of steps, which consists of: session start, cognitive work (awareness mode), experiential work (included starting from Module IV), and session closing. It is important to clarify that the cognitive and experiential work in the session is not "pure"; rather, it may include cognitive, emotional, and behavioral components. However, the tendency, intention, and techniques of the session tend to point more toward cognitive work or emotional activation.

The final section of the book presents the supporting references.

Part I

Theoretical Foundations of Couple Schema Therapy

Part one of this book presents some of the theoretical foundations underlying couple schema therapy. It addresses the general approach to schema therapy and the contextual model. This description is presented in a very general manner; if the reader wishes to gain a deeper understanding of these concepts, they can consult Young et al.'s (2015) book, "Schema Therapy: A Practitioner's Guide." However, if they are interested in a clearer understanding of the contextual schema therapy model, they can refer to Roediger et al.'s (2018) book, "Contextual Schema Therapy."

Below are the fundamental elements of the dimensional model, which forms the basis of couple schema therapy. This model focuses on the analysis of emotional needs, basic emotions, and coping modes, and how these influence the dynamics of the relationship. When partners fail to change their coping modes, dysfunctional cycles are generated that perpetuate conflict and emotional disconnection.

1

Schema Therapy and the Contextual Model

1.1 Schema Therapy

Young (1999) presents schema therapy as an integrative therapeutic model based on the principles of cognitive-behavioral therapy and combining elements of other approaches, such as Gestalt, attachment theory, and psychodynamic techniques. Although it was initially developed to treat personality disorders, such as borderline personality disorder (BPD), it is currently applied to a wide range of psychological problems, including anxiety disorders, depression, and difficulties in interpersonal relationships.

1.1.1 The Schema Model

This approach is based on the idea that psychological problems arise in childhood and adolescence due to the interaction between personal temperament, early environment, and the systematic frustration of some fundamental emotional needs. To survive these circumstances, people develop maladaptive schemas, which allow them to adapt to a pathological, ambivalent, or unmet environment. These so-called negative schemas ultimately manifest as a generalized pattern that includes dysfunctional and maladaptive beliefs about themselves and their relationships with others. These schemas are composed of thoughts, memories, emotions, and bodily sensations (Young et al., 2015).

Negative schemas are activated in the present when a person faces similar situations from the past, which are again perceived as a threat to the satisfaction of emotional needs. During activation, the person re-experiences the emotions, thoughts, and physical sensations associated with the memories that contributed to the creation of the negative schemas (Young and Klosko, 2012).

There are five basic needs associated with schema generation, according to the theory proposed by Young et al. (2015) and expanded by Arntz and Jacob (2013).

These needs are fundamental for healthy emotional development and, when not adequately met in childhood, can lead to dysfunctional schemas. The needs are as follows:

- **Secure Attachments to Others:** This need includes aspects such as emotional security, love, stability, attention, nurturing, and acceptance. A secure bond with attachment figures (such as parents or caregivers) fosters a solid emotional foundation, enabling the development of healthy, trusting relationships in adulthood.
- **Autonomy, Competence, and a Sense of Identity:** This refers to the development of a clear and defined sense of personal identity, accompanied by the skills necessary to function independently, face daily challenges, and be resilient in the face of adversity. This need also includes the perception of self-efficacy, that is, confidence in one's ability to cope with life situations.
- **Realistic Boundaries and Self-control:** This involves internalizing clear limits and expectations, which are necessary for developing self-discipline, self-control, and balanced emotional regulation. It also fosters a realistic perspective on oneself and relationships, which values reciprocity and achievable expectations.
- **Freedom to Express Needs and Emotions:** This need emphasizes the importance of an environment where people can freely express their emotions, needs, and opinions without fear of rejection, judgment, or criticism. It focuses on ensuring that individuals can communicate their inner experiences in a genuine and balanced manner, respecting both their own needs and those of others.
- **Play, Spontaneity, and Pleasure:** This aspect relates to the ability to enjoy life through recreation, creativity, spontaneity, and pleasurable experiences.

The frustration of these five core needs will generate negative schemas. Young et al. (2015) proposed the existence of a total of 18 negative schemas, which are presented below. Their core maladaptive beliefs are described, along with the pathological environments that stimulate their development.

1.1.1.1 Negative Schemas of the Disconnection and Rejection Domain

This domain relates to environments characterized by deprived, unstable, critical, violent, neglectful, intolerant, or exclusive personal relationships. The schemas in this domain, along with their core maladaptive beliefs, are as follows:

- **Emotional Deprivation:** Belief that one's emotional needs will never be consistently met. This includes the perception of deprivation in three main areas: nurturing (physical and emotional affection), empathy (emotional understanding), and emotional protection (feeling safe). Example: "People can't provide me with emotional connection, support, affection, or companionship."

- **Abandonment:** Belief that important people in life won't be able to consistently provide support, security, or connection because they will inevitably abandon the relationship or become emotionally unstable. Example: "The people I trust will leave me forever or for long periods of time."
- **Mistrust/Abuse:** Belief that others will intentionally or negligently take advantage of them by manipulating, mistreating, or harming them for personal gain. Example: "If people have the opportunity, they will use, manipulate, or harm me."
- **Defectiveness/Shame:** Belief that oneself is defective, inadequate, or unworthy of being loved. It may include thoughts such as, "I am imperfect, inferior, selfish, too needy, or unwanted."
- **Social Isolation:** Belief that one is different, strange, or doesn't belong to any group or community. Example: "I'm weird and don't fit in anywhere."

1.1.1.2 Negative Schemas in the Domain of Impaired Autonomy and Performance

This domain is associated with family environments characterized by overprotection or overinvolvement, which interfere with the development of the skills necessary to function independently, differentiate oneself from others, and trust in one's own abilities. These dynamics often affect the construction of a solid identity, self-determination, and personal autonomy. In some cases, the environment simply fails to provide the tools needed to foster autonomy. The schemas of this domain, along with their core maladaptive beliefs, are as follows:

- **Failure:** Belief that one is incapable of achieving success in important areas of life, such as school, work, sports, or the arts. People with this negative schema often feel inferior or incompetent compared to others. Example: "I'm a complete failure; I'll never be as talented or smart as others."
- **Dependence/Incompetence:** Belief that one lacks the necessary skills to face the challenges of daily life without excessive help from others. This can lead to constant dependence on others to make decisions or solve everyday problems. Example: "I'm not capable of doing anything alone; I need someone else to guide me."
- **Vulnerability to Harm/Illness:** Belief that one is unable to protect oneself from potential disasters or adversities (medical, emotional, economic, or external) without suffering serious harm. People with this negative schema are often in a constant state of alert for perceived risks. Example: "Something bad is going to happen soon, like an illness or disaster, and I won't be able to cope with it."
- **Enmeshment/Undeveloped Self:** Belief that one cannot function autonomously or make decisions without the constant approval, support, or

reassurance of a significant attachment figure. This negative schema is often linked to a symbiotic relationship in which the individual feels their identity is blurred or merged with that of the other. Example: “I can’t make important decisions without that person supporting or reassuring me.”

1.1.1.3 Negative Schemas of the Impaired Limits Domain

This domain relates to environments in which clear internal boundaries, responsibility for others, and skills such as self-control and self-discipline were not fostered. It often arises in contexts marked by excessive permissiveness, a lack of rules or consequences, or where caregivers idealize the child, generating an inflated sense of entitlement. People with schemas in this domain have difficulty regulating their impulses and show a lack of consideration for the needs or limits of others. The schemas in this domain are as follows:

- **Entitlement/Grandiosity:** Belief that one is superior, special, or more important than others, justifying special privileges and rights. This negative schema often leads to self-centered behavior, arrogance, and difficulty accepting the needs and rights of others. Example: “I deserve to have things done the way I want them because my opinion is more valid than others’.”
- **Low Self-control/Self-discipline:** Belief that short-term discomfort, boredom, or frustration is unnecessary, leading to avoidance of responsibilities and pursuit of immediate rewards without considering long-term consequences. People with this negative schema tend to be impulsive and lack perseverance when faced with difficult goals. Example: “I can’t stand feeling frustrated, so I’d rather avoid it now, no matter what happens later.”

1.1.1.4 Negative Schemas of Dominance Directed by the Needs of Others

This domain is linked to family environments in which there was an excessive focus on the needs, desires, and feelings of others, at the expense of one’s own needs. This pattern emerges as a mechanism to maintain love, acceptance, or avoid conflict. People with schemas in this domain often chronically neglect their own needs, which can lead to feelings of frustration, resentment, and emotional disconnection. The schemas in this domain are as follows:

- **Self-sacrifice:** The belief that it is necessary to meet the needs of others at the expense of one’s own, in order to avoid suffering or guilt for not helping them when one could. This negative schema can lead to a loss of balance between giving and receiving. Example: “It is my obligation to care for and protect those weaker than me, even if it means sacrificing my own well-being.”
- **Subjugation:** Belief that it is necessary to repress one’s needs, desires, and emotions, allowing others to take control, in order to avoid anger, retaliation,

punishment, criticism, or abandonment. This negative schema often generates frustration and repressed anger due to the lack of expression of one's needs. Example: "If I speak my mind, there will surely be a conflict and they will get angry with me, so it's better to keep quiet."

- **Approval/Recognition Seeking:** Belief that it is necessary to obtain recognition, status, beauty, or material achievements in order to gain the approval and admiration of others. People with this negative schema often base their self-esteem on external factors, which can lead to a disconnection from their internal sense of identity and values. Example: "If I can get everyone to admire me for what I do, I will finally feel valuable and loved."

1.1.1.5 Negative Schemas of the Overvigilance and Inhibition Domain

This domain is associated with environments where there was an overemphasis on the suppression of emotions, impulses, and spontaneity, or on the constant pursuit of strict goals and standards of ethical behavior. This occurs at the expense of happiness, self-expression, relaxation, friendships, and health. It often arises in rigid, controlling, or punitive environments, where constant vigilance and the fear of making mistakes or facing negative consequences generate high levels of self-control and stress. It also occurs in environments where chaos was present, and hypervigilance became a survival mechanism. Schemas in this domain include the following:

- **Unrelenting Standards:** Belief that one must constantly strive to be perfect or achieve extremely ambitious goals. People with this negative schema tend to overexert themselves, leading to chronic stress, burnout, and an inability to enjoy accomplishments. Example: "I must be the best at everything I do, no matter the effort or sacrifice involved."
- **Emotional Inhibition:** Belief that expressing spontaneous emotions is ridiculous, embarrassing, or dangerous, as it could lead to a loss of control or provoke conflict. People with this negative schema often repress their emotions and feel uncomfortable with others' emotional expressions, prioritizing reserved or controlled behavior. Example: "I must repress my emotions to avoid losing control."
- **Negativity/Pessimism:** Belief that it's necessary to constantly focus on the negative aspects of life to prevent catastrophes or avoid disappointments. People with this negative schema tend to expect the worst in all situations and distrust the positive aspects, which generates a pessimistic outlook and little enjoyment of pleasant moments. Example: "I have to prepare for the worst at all times, because that way I'll be ready when something bad happens."
- **Punitiveness:** Belief that mistakes should be punished regardless of circumstances or intentions. People with this schema tend to be extremely

self-critical, severely punish their own failures, and have little tolerance for the mistakes of others. This negative schema generates rigid and punitive relationships, as well as a lack of self-compassion. Example: "I deserve to be punished because I didn't do things the way they should have been done."

1.1.2 Coping Behaviors

When faced with the activation of a negative schema, people can respond in three main ways, known as coping behaviors (Young et al. 2011):

- **Surrender:** This involves accepting the schema's beliefs as true and acting in a manner consistent with them. People who surrender to a negative schema tend to experience and perpetuate the associated painful emotions, as if the schema were inevitable. Example: A person with an abandonment schema might seek relationships with emotionally unstable or distant people, thus confirming their belief that they would always be abandoned.
- **Avoidance:** This involves trying to escape from situations or emotions that trigger the negative schema. This may include avoiding people or contexts that trigger it, or emotionally disconnecting from the related painful feelings. Example: A person with a distrust/abuse pattern might avoid close relationships to avoid exposing themself to possible emotional wounds.
- **Overcompensation:** This involves behaving in extreme ways or in ways that are contrary to what the negative schema suggests, as an attempt to escape the schema's hold. Although it appears to be an effective strategy, it often leads to maladaptive behaviors. Example: A person with an imperfection/shame schema might try to portray themselves as perfect, constantly seeking approval and recognition.

These behavioral responses, if repeated consistently, are established into coping styles, which become stable patterns over time. Coping behaviors, combined with personal temperament, end up perpetuating negative schemas. This occurs because, through surrender, avoidance, and overcompensation, people tend to associate themselves with environments similar to those in which the schemas originated, thus confirming their dysfunctional beliefs. At the same time, these strategies often distance people from healthy environments that could meet their basic emotional needs, making it difficult to satisfy their emotional needs.

1.1.3 The Process of Schema Therapy

The schema therapy process is divided into two major phases: the psychoeducation phase and the schema change phase. Both phases aim to help the client identify, understand, and modify the dysfunctional schemas that affect their lives (Young and Behary, 2019).

1.1.3.1 Psychoeducation Phase

The first phase of the process focuses on psychoeducation about the schema therapy model, with the goal of helping the client understand the model's basic concepts. These concepts include: negative schemas, their activation, coping styles, and their components.

In addition, this stage includes a process of assessing the client's negative schemas. This process is carried out through the application of schema inventories, such as the Young Schema Questionnaire (YSQ); assessment using guided imagery, designed to explore early memories associated with negative schemas; and information gathering through case conceptualization, based on the client's history and current context.

Another key goal of this phase is for clients to develop greater awareness of the activation of their negative schemas and the coping styles they use to address them.

The psychoeducation phase culminates with case conceptualization, which aims to explain the client's problems in terms of the schema model. The conceptualization includes the reason for the consultation, current problems, identified negative schemas, observed coping styles, temperamental factors influencing negative schemas, and the primary goals of therapy.

1.1.3.2 Change Phase

The second phase of schema therapy focuses on modifying negative schemas. This process unfolds in three main stages: cognitive, experiential, and behavioral, with the behavioral stage being the most complex as well as the most important for consolidating change. Furthermore, the therapeutic relationship accompanies the entire process as a model of healthy relationships that the client will use as a guide for relating to himself or herself and others.

The cognitive phase seeks to challenge the logic of negative patterns through strategies such as:

- **Cognitive Debate:** Identifying and questioning maladaptive beliefs.
- **Reality Testing:** Assessing the validity of schemas based on real experiences.

The main objective is for the client to rationally recognize that the negative schema is false and stop relying on it. However, this change is not sufficient, as the emotions associated with negative schemas, recorded in emotional memory, can continue to be activated. For this reason, it is necessary to move on to the experiential and behavioral phases.

The experiential phase focuses on working on emotions associated with negative patterns, using tools such as:

- **Limited Reparenting:** The therapist validates the client's emotions and meets their emotional needs within therapeutic limits, helping to repair unresolved emotional experiences.

- **Imagery Rewriting:** Through guided imagery exercises, the therapist guides the client through the reconstruction of traumatic memories. This involves modifying the emotional narrative of the past, symbolically protecting the client and meeting his or her unmet needs.

The goal of this stage is to reduce the intensity of the emotions associated with the schemas, helping the client regulate their emotional responses. However, if the client does not modify his or her coping behaviors, he or she may continue to live in dysfunctional environments that reinforce the negative schemas.

The behavioral phase involves changing dysfunctional coping styles into healthy behaviors. To achieve this, the therapist encourages the client to:

1. Challenge the logic of negative schemas through concrete actions. This allows the client to empirically verify that the schemas are not as general or valid as they seem.
2. Change the way the client relates to others and choose healthier environments. The client learns to establish relationships that meet their emotional needs and to distance themselves from dysfunctional contexts.

The goal of this stage is for the client to adopt behaviors consistent with positive schemas. Once he or she achieves a healthy response to the activation of negative schemas, the therapeutic process can conclude.

In addition to the three previously mentioned change processes, there is a fourth strategy: the therapeutic relationship, which permeates the entire change process as a central strategy. Within this relationship, the therapist acts as a role model for a healthy adult, showing the client how to manage cognitive, emotional, and behavioral processes in a healthy manner, based on what occurs during therapy sessions and within the therapeutic relationship.

1.1.4 The Work of Negative Schema Modes

Schema modes work arose from the difficulty of working with clients who had several (even 18) negative schemas, and whose cognitive, experiential, and behavioral change work was impractical to address individually. Because of this, modes work was devised, in which the thoughts and feelings of two or more negative schemas, along with their coping behaviors, are grouped into different modes (Young et al., 2015).

Although all modes contain cognitive, emotional, and behavioral elements, some modes are more representative of each of these elements: Inner voice modes are more representative of the cognitions of negative schemas, Child modes are more representative of the emotional memories of negative schemas, and Coping modes are more representative of the negative coping behaviors used to deal with negative schemas (Farrell and Shaw, 2018).

Child modes are divided into three: the vulnerable child, associated with the basic emotions of sadness and fear, as well as different social emotions such as loneliness, guilt, abandonment; the angry child, related to the basic emotions of anger or disgust; and the impulsive and undisciplined child, linked to social emotions such as frustration (Young and Behary, 2019).

The internal voice modes are divided into two: the critical-punitive voice, which reflects the beliefs of negative schemas and denigrates the client through internal attacks, while the demanding voice raises high expectations about the consultant's performance (Farrell and Shaw, 2012).

Coping modes in Schema Therapy are divided into three main categories (Young et al., 2015; Arntz and Jacob, 2013; Arntz and van Genderen, 2009):

- **Surrender Mode:** This mode reflects behaviors congruent with the schema's beliefs, in which the person passively accepts dysfunctional patterns. Surrendering perpetuates the schema, reinforcing the associated painful emotions.
- **Overcompensation Mode:** This mode involves fight-or-flight behaviors to try to escape the schema's hold. Subcategories of this mode include:
  - **Aggressive Attacker:** Responds with dominance or anger to avoid vulnerability.
  - **Perfectionist Controller:** Seeks to control every detail to avoid mistakes or criticism.
  - **Grandiose/Arrogant:** Adopts attitudes of superiority to counteract feelings of inferiority.
  - **Attention/Approval Seeking:** Acts in search of constant validation to feel accepted or worthy.
- **Avoidance Mode:** This mode reflects escape behaviors or emotional disengagement to protect oneself from the pain associated with the schema. Subcategories include:
  - **Isolated Protector:** Disconnects emotionally and avoids interpersonal contact.
  - **Self-consoling Protector:** Turns to self-indulgent activities (such as food, substances, or technology) to escape painful emotions.
  - **Avoidant Protector:** Avoids responsibilities or difficult emotional situations to minimize stress.
  - **Angry Protector:** Responds with anger or irritation to push others away and avoid vulnerability.

Each of these coping modes represents a maladaptive strategy for the activation of schemas and, although initially serving as defense mechanisms, they ultimately perpetuate emotional and relational problems.

This book presents the basic negative schema modes originally proposed in schema therapy; however, many more modes have since been identified. These are not addressed in this book because their explanation is unnecessary, given that, based on this, the Couples Schema Therapy model ultimately simplifies them into two child modes (vulnerable child and angry), three coping modes (overcompensating, avoiding, and surrender), and one inner voice mode, which includes both self-directed and other-directed critical voices.

Some contemporary theorists, such as Arntz and Jacob (2013), Heath and Startup (2020), and Simeone-DiFrancesco et al. (2015), propose that child modes represent basic emotional reactions to the frustration of emotional needs, while coping modes reflect more generalized behavioral patterns to deal with such frustrations. Internal voices, on the other hand, correspond to automatic cognitions or messages directed toward oneself or others, often internalized from parental or authority figures. Although modes are deeply linked to negative schemas, some theorists propose that modes can manifest more flexibly, without being entirely dependent on a specific schema. For example, impulsive behavior is generally interpreted as a surrender to the Low Self-control/Self-discipline schema, since it reflects acceptance of the logic of the schema. However, in certain interpretations, this same behavior can be considered a mode of overcompensation if it involves an active struggle. This approach allows the client to more easily understand the activation of a coping mode, which makes it easier for the client to deal with it more effectively.

Finally, there are the healthy modes, which are the desired therapeutic outcomes in schema therapy (Young et al., 2015; Ceballos and Serrano, 2025):

- **The Healthy Adult:** This is the way in which the beliefs from positive schemas and healthy coping modes are put into practice.
- **The Happy Child:** This is the child's mode that includes beliefs, emotions, and behaviors related to the balanced satisfaction of emotional needs.

1.2 The Contextual Model

Cognitive behavioral therapy has been under evaluation since its roots in behavioral therapy, which began in the 1950s. Rachman (1997) points out that there are three waves in the development of this therapeutic approach, each reflecting an expansion in understanding and therapeutic intervention strategies.

- **First Wave:** Behavior Therapy (1950s–1960s), focused on the principles of behaviorism, with an approach to modifying observable behavior through classical conditioning (Pavlov) and operant conditioning (Skinner). The objective was to modify maladaptive behaviors through techniques such as positive and negative reinforcement, extinction of unwanted behaviors, and systematic desensitization, with an emphasis on observable behavior, largely disregarding thoughts and emotions.

- **Second Wave:** Cognitive-behavioral Therapy (1970s–1980s) integrates the principles of behaviorism with a focus on cognitive processes, emphasizing thoughts, which directly influence emotions and behaviors. The goal is to identify and modify irrational beliefs (Ellis) or cognitive distortions (Beck) to influence emotions and behavior.
- **Third Wave:** Contextual and Acceptance Therapies (1990s–present) expanded the cognitive-behavioral approach by introducing a contextual and experiential framework focused on acceptance, mindfulness, and the value of context in human behavior. This approach does not seek to directly change thoughts or emotions, but rather aims to modify the individual's relationship with them (Bennett-Goleman, 2002).

According to Roediger et al. (2018), the Third Wave includes therapeutic approaches such as Acceptance and Commitment Therapy (ACT); Mindfulness-based Cognitive Therapy (MBCT); Compassion-focused Therapy (CFT); Metacognitive Approaches; Functional Analytic Psychotherapy (FAP); and Relational Frame Theory (RFT). These approaches have in common the ability to help clients detach from automatic thoughts and observe them from a more conscious, reflective perspective.

Relational Frame Theory (RFT), proposed by Hayes et al. (2012), cited in Roediger et al. (2018), is the philosophical basis of Acceptance and Commitment Therapy (ACT). This theory postulates that the human brain has a natural tendency to relate concepts or stimuli that appear simultaneously, creating relational frames. When an element of a relational frame is activated, the entire network of associated relationships becomes active. This allows the generation of rules about how the environment works, which helps anticipate events and, in turn, leads to the generation of attractors or schemas.

Although this process is adaptive, it can lead to cognitive biases that limit flexibility. For example, rigid relational frames can generate dysfunctional thinking patterns that disconnect the person from present reality.

Relational frames can lead to biases that limit an individual's learning potential. Internal experiences ultimately define the subject's perception of the world around them. According to Roediger (2025), from a neuroscientific perspective, most brain processing is oriented toward the internal world. Only approximately 3–5% of neurons are dedicated to processing external stimuli, while the rest focus on internal activities such as memory, emotions, and thoughts. This suggests that, as human beings, we tend to interpret reality based on our own internal experiences.

Relational frames, when linked to internal representations based on past experiences, can generate perceptions of threat that don't reflect what's actually happening in the present. This process, known as cognitive fusion, occurs when a person completely identifies with their thoughts, treating them as absolute truths. Cognitive fusion generates restrictive and dysfunctional thought patterns, trapping the person in their own thoughts and disconnecting them from the external context and present reality.

According to Hayes et al. (2012), cited in Roediger et al. (2018), there are six mental processes that contribute to psychological rigidity, all related to the dominance of relational frames over the perception of the world:

1. **Cognitive Fusion:** Being trapped in one's own thoughts and perceiving them as absolute truths. Example: A person who has the thought "I am a failure" avoids attempting new projects because they believe they will inevitably fail, as if the thought were an immutable fact.
2. **Experiential Avoidance:** Avoiding, repressing, or attempting to escape from unpleasant emotions, thoughts, or sensations. A person experiencing social anxiety avoids going to gatherings or parties, even when they want to socialize, because they don't want to face the discomfort of being around other people.
3. **Inflexible Attention:** Focusing exclusively on negative experiences from the past or fears about the future, without connecting with the present. Example: A person who suffered betrayal in a previous relationship cannot enjoy their new relationship because they constantly fear that their current partner will also betray them.
4. **Attachment to the Conceptualized Self:** Rigidly identifying with a fixed narrative about oneself. Example: "I've always been a shy person, so I'll never be able to speak in public." This belief limits opportunities for personal growth and reinforces avoidance behaviors.
5. **Values Alteration:** Losing sight of personal values due to being caught up in everyday problems. Example: A person who values family, but gets absorbed by his or her work to the point of not spending time with his or her children or clients, which generates dissatisfaction and disconnection.
6. **Inactivity, Impulsivity, or Persistent Avoidance:** Acting on autopilot, avoiding making conscious decisions, or persisting in maladaptive behaviors. Example: A person experiencing chronic sadness spends the day watching television or browsing social media, avoiding addressing the issues that contribute to their distress.

To recover psychological flexibility and escape the negative effects that relational frameworks can bring, Hayes et al. (2012, as cited in Roediger et al., 2018), identified the following six basic processes:

1. **Cognitive Defusion:** Viewing thoughts as mental events, not as absolute truths. Example: A person who thinks "I'm a failure" might tell themselves, "I'm having the thought that I'm a failure, but that doesn't mean I am." This allows them to act against that belief.

2. **Acceptance:** Allowing and making space for difficult emotions or thoughts without fighting them. Example: When feeling anxious before a presentation, a person might say to themselves, "I feel anxious because this is important to me. I can allow this feeling and move forward with the presentation."
3. **Mindfulness/Present-moment Awareness:** Being fully connected to the here and now. Example: A person having dinner with their family practices mindfulness by putting their phone aside and focusing on the conversation, enjoying the moment.
4. **Self-as-context (Me as Context):** Seeing yourself as a flexible observer, not a fixed narrative. Example: Instead of thinking, "I'm a shy person," someone might say, "Sometimes I feel shy, but that doesn't define who I am. I can also be brave when I need to."
5. **Values Clarification:** Identifying what is truly important and meaningful in life. Example: A person who identifies the value of "family care" decides to schedule weekly time to spend with their children, even if they are busy at work.
6. **Committed Action:** Acting in a way that aligns with your values, even in the face of emotional barriers. Example: Someone who values health begins exercising regularly, although at first, they experience resistance and lack motivation.

The evolution of CBT reflects a significant advance in our understanding of psychological processes. The third wave, with approaches such as ACT and MBCT, stands out for its emphasis on acceptance, mindfulness, and connection to personal values, promoting not only symptom relief but also a meaningful and congruent life.

1.3 Integration of Both Approaches in the Dimensional Model

The two models mentioned above, Schema Therapy and Contextual Therapies, are integrated to develop a couple schema therapy model. From the schema model, key concepts are taken, such as unmet basic emotional needs, emotions associated with schemas, coping behaviors (surrender, avoidance, overcompensation), and modes (child modes, coping modes, and inner voices). Contextual therapies, on the other hand, provide tools such as strategies for getting out of autopilot, developing mindfulness, cognitive defusion, and maintaining a focus on the present. These strategies allow couples to become more aware of their automatic patterns of thinking and behavior, connecting more adaptively with their values and the current dynamics of the relationship (McKay et al., 2012; Roediger et al., 2018).

1.3.1 Integration of Schema Therapy

Of the emotional needs presented by schema therapy, two will be used: those related to attachment and those linked to autonomy. In the dimensional model, these will be called the need for attachment-connection and the need for assertiveness-autonomy, respectively (Roediger et al., 2018).

Regarding the emotions associated with negative schemas, Roediger et al. (2018) propose that the dimensional model be focused on basic emotions, grouping them into two large blocks: the first composed of sadness and fear, which will be associated with the Vulnerable Child Mode; the second linked by anger and disgust, which will be related to the angry child mode. Social emotions are those that arise from the influence of culture and language. Therefore, when they appear, they can give an indication of the negative schemas that may be behind them. However, the center of the intervention is based on searching for the basic emotion that lies behind the social emotion. Also, unlike the traditional schema therapy model, in dimensional work, only the vulnerable child and angry child modes are used, excluding the undisciplined and impulsive child mode.

Regarding coping modes, the model proposes three general modes: overcompensation, surrender, and avoidance. However, avoidance is divided into two types: passive avoidance, which is related to the isolated protective avoidance mode, and active avoidance, which is related to the angry protective avoidance and self-consoling avoidance modes (Roediger et al., 2018).

Finally, internal voice modes, whether critical, punitive, or overdemanding, are divided into two types: those directed toward oneself and those directed toward others (Roediger et al., 2018).

Regarding the therapeutic process, Roediger et al. (2018) propose a similar approach. The first phase starts with psychoeducation; however, instead of initially focusing on the assessment of couple schemas, the process begins with the analysis of emotional needs, childhood patterns, and coping strategies. Subsequently, the interaction cycles established in the relationship are evaluated, identifying how these elements influence each partner. As in individual Schema Therapy, it is essential for clients to become aware of how and when these patterns are activated, since ignoring them contributes to perpetuating conflicts in their lives. In the second phase, focused on change, the objective is not only to modify dysfunctional schemas but to achieve a rebalance between the emotional needs, coping patterns, and emotional responses of each individual. Furthermore, it seeks to establish a balance between a satisfying emotional connection, responding to the need for attachment, and the development of autonomy in each partner.

Cognitive, experiential, and behavioral change processes develop throughout the therapy sessions. Cognitive change occurs through the so-called observer mode, in which the couple analyzes and becomes aware of their needs, emotions, and coping modes, as well as the interaction cycle they have established in their relationship. During this phase, the couple reflects on whether this cycle is functional or not for resolving their conflicts. Experiential processes are worked on primarily by activating emotions using chair work. Initially, the therapist reparents the client, then extends this work to the couple, and guides the rewriting of images, which facilitate emotional reconnection and the transformation of dysfunctional patterns. Finally, the behavioral process is stimulated by moving from feeling to action, encouraging the implementation of more flexible and adaptive coping behaviors. Through this approach, the couple achieves emotional rebalance and develops effective strategies for managing conflicts in a healthier way.

1.3.2 The Integration of Contextual Therapies

Throughout the therapeutic process, cognitive defusion is promoted, using metaphors such as the cell phone, which illustrates that there is no single reality. Both partners are encouraged to develop cognitive flexibility, employing techniques such as connected dialogues, which facilitate openness to new perspectives. Acceptance is fostered by helping the couple become aware of their emotions, needs, and coping modes. This process involves validating and accepting current emotional experiences and, subsequently, connecting with those that have been blocked, hidden, or repressed.

Mindfulness and the present moment are fundamental in Couple Schema Therapy and are integrated through two main strategies:

- **Body Mobilization:** The couple is invited to stand, observe, and analyze what is happening in the present, assuming the role of active observers of their interaction.
- **Identifying Emotions Through Bodily Sensations:** Connection with the present is fostered through awareness of the physiological responses linked to emotions.

The therapist plays a key role in constantly reorienting partners, preventing them from straying into past memories or topics unrelated to the therapeutic process, and focusing them on what is happening in the session. Finally, the concept of "I as context" is encouraged by helping each partner to become more flexible and accept their "unseen face," that is, to recognize and connect with needs, blocked emotions, and unused coping modes as a legitimate part of their identity.

2

Theoretical Concepts of the Couple Schema Therapy Model

2.1 Introduction

This chapter reviews the theoretical foundations that explain the approach model for conceptualizing relationship problems and their interventions. To this end, the schema model is reviewed from a contextual perspective, simplifying basic needs, emotions, and coping modes. It then analyzes how some elements of these three concepts are actively displayed while others remain hidden. Finally, the two-legged model is presented, which proposes finding a balance between active and hidden aspects.

2.2 The Three Key Concepts

The three key concepts addressed and explained to the couple in the first part of the treatment, called psychoeducation, are basic needs, basic emotions, and coping modes. These concepts form the basis of the dimensional model that will help the couple understand the problems in their relationship and how to address and resolve them.

2.2.1 Basic Needs

At birth, the first of the two great basic needs, the need for attachment and connection, is activated in humans. From the moment they leave their mother's womb, a baby depends on a parent to provide security, protection, and care, as they are unable to care for themselves. This initial bond encourages them to connect and cooperate with their caregiver, reducing the risk of rejection and ensuring that their needs are met (Collins and Feeney, 2004; Hazan and

Shaver, 1987; Mikulincer and Shaver, 2007; Baumeister and Leary, 1995; Bowlby, 1969; Ainsworth et al., 1978; Roediger et al., 2018).

When this need is met, the body enters a state of calm regulated by the parasympathetic autonomic nervous system. This results in a decreased heart rate, slower breathing, and generalized muscle relaxation, thus promoting energy recovery and rest (Roediger et al., 2018).

For Roediger (2025), in the context of social interaction, the need for attachment and connection fosters active listening, cooperation, and adaptation to the needs of others. This state can predispose people to focus on external demands, manifesting attitudes of submission or complacency as strategies to preserve the emotional bond.

On a psychological level, the activation of the need for attachment and connection leads the individual to introspection: What must I change in myself to be accepted by the other? This reflection promotes behaviors that seek to maintain emotional connection and ensure security in the relationship.

Clinical Case 1 Michelle, 25 years old

Michelle is experiencing difficulties in her relationship with Anthony. In the session, he expressed his perception that she has neglected him emotionally, which generated a dual emotional response in Michelle: fear of losing the relationship and sadness at the perception that Anthony doesn't feel loved by her. As a result of these emotions, Michelle began a process of self-reflection, asking herself the question: What can I do to make Anthony feel more emotionally cared for by me?

Motivated by this question, Michelle asked Anthony, "How long have you felt this way? What do you think I need to change for you to feel better?" Simply hearing these questions made Anthony more approachable during the session. This, in turn, produced a feeling of calm and relaxation in Michelle.

Reflection: What questions could you ask to detect if your client's need for attachment–connection is being activated? What types of comments from your client reflect that their need for attachment–connection is being activated?

Therapist's Advice: If your client is focusing more on figuring out how their partner feels and what they can do for them, what they can do to help them, or understand them more, their need for attachment–connection is active at that moment.

As the baby grows and reaches two years of age, a new basic need arises: the need for assertiveness–autonomy. During this stage, children begin to

(Continued)

Clinical Case 1 (Continued)

express their individual preferences, to say "no," and to develop their own thoughts and desires, different from those of their parents. This is a key moment in development, where we expect others to give in to our demands. If this doesn't happen, an alert system is activated in their body that drives them to fight to get what they want or, failing that, to withdraw (flee) from the environment (Erikson, 1950; Stern, 1985; Winnicott, 1965; Bowlby, 1988; Siegel, 2012; Piaget, 1952).

When the environment doesn't adapt to one's needs, the body enters a state of stress or activation, which leads the individual to assert themselves and even try to impose their point of view. If people don't give in, this activation can intensify, generating a feeling of agitation that culminates in what we know as childhood tantrums (Perry and Szalavitz, 2006; Siegel and Bryson, 2012; Winnicott, 1965; Piaget, 1952; Porges, 2011).

From a physiological perspective, when someone goes against what they want or feel, the sympathetic autonomic nervous system is activated. This system, which prepares for stressful situations, increases heart rate, accelerates breathing, and tenses muscles, preparing the body to fight or flee. This state allows the body to mobilize energy to confront the perceived threat, but also generates specific bodily sensations, such as chest tightness (Cannon, 1932; Porges, 2011; McEwen, 2002; Schore, 2003; Van der Kolk, 2014; Sapolsky, 2004).

Anger is a basic emotion that typically arises when a threat to one's autonomy, desires, or boundaries is perceived. From an evolutionary perspective, anger acts as a defense mechanism that drives the individual to confront or change the environment to resolve the perceived threat. Although it tends to be externalized toward the environment or the people involved, its expression and target can vary depending on the context, personality, and emotional regulation of the individual (Ekman, 1999; Tavris, 1989; Berkowitz, 1989; Lazarus, 1991; Goleman, 1995; Bowlby, 1969).

If others can be made to meet personal demands, the alert system shuts down, and a calm, relaxed state returns. However, if needs are not met, a person may remain in a state of prolonged stress, adopting behaviors such as resentment or passive-aggressive attitudes. In these cases, an attempt is made to show others that they need to adapt to personal demands, emphasizing the importance of doing so to preserve the relationship (Selye, 1976; Lazarus and Folkman, 1984; Van der Kolk, 2014; Goleman, 1995; Porges, 2011; Gottman and Silver, 1999; Bowlby, 1982).

The need for assertiveness and autonomy drives individuals to focus on satisfying their own emotional needs, which can lead them to seek recognition and respect from others. When individuals perceive that their demands are not being met, the sympathetic nervous system is activated, generating a stress response that prepares the body to confront the situation. Conversely, when needs are validated or met, the parasympathetic system helps restore physiological balance, promoting a state of calm (Porges, 2011; Siegel, 2012; Perry and Szalavitz, 2006; Schore, 2003; Erikson, 1950; Bowlby, 1988; Sapolsky, 2004).

Clinical Case 2 Anthony, 26 years old

Anthony experienced feelings of annoyance toward his partner, Michelle, as he perceived that she had emotionally neglected him. This perception triggered a state of emotional alertness characterized by anger and activation of his sympathetic nervous system, which led him to express his needs directly. In therapy, Anthony requested that Michelle show greater interest and attention to his emotions and needs. Thanks to this, Michelle understood Anthony's emotional needs and investigated how she could meet them. This change in the relationship dynamic allowed Anthony to emerge from his state of emotional activation, promoting a response regulated by the parasympathetic nervous system that led him to feel relaxed and emotionally reconnected with Michelle.

Reflection: What could you ask your client to see if their need for assertiveness–autonomy is being activated? What kind of phrases do you think your client uses that might be activating their need for assertiveness–autonomy?

Therapist's Advice: If your client is focused on their partner understanding them, forgiving them, turning over a new leaf, no longer feeling that way, or on what she should do to make them feel better, their active need at that moment is assertiveness–autonomy.

2.2.2 Basic and Social Emotions

Basic emotions are innate, universal, and instinctive affective reactions that all human beings experience when their emotional needs are met or frustrated. When personal needs are threatened or unmet, negative or unpleasant emotions arise, acting as warning signals. These invite the subject to reflect on the situation and act to resolve the problem. Conversely, when needs are met, positive or pleasant emotions are experienced, indicating balance (Goleman, 1995; Sapolsky, 2004; Lazarus, 1991; Van der Kolk, 2014; Bowlby, 1988; Damasio, 1994; Barrett, 2017; Plutchik, 2001; Ekman, 1999).

The brain could be said to function as a regulatory system that responds to two basic needs: attachment–connection and assertiveness–autonomy. When these needs are met, the brain maintains a state of emotional and physiological balance. However, when one of these needs is not met, the emotional system generates warning signals, such as the activation of negative emotions, to indicate that something requires attention (Porges, 2011; Bowlby, 1988; Schore, 2003; Damasio, 1994; Siegel, 2012; Plutchik, 2001; Barrett, 2017; Davidson and Begley, 2012; Goleman, 1995; Sapolsky, 2004).

It is crucial to learn to identify emotions, as these are the signals that allow us to respond appropriately to our own unmet needs.

Roediger et al. (2018), based on Ekman (1999), propose five basic emotions grouped into two dimensions:

- **Positive Emotions:** Happiness.
- **Negative Emotions:** Fear, sadness, disgust, and anger.

These emotions are considered universal and preverbal, meaning they manifest before the development of language, which suggests that they have a more innate than learned origin.

In addition to the universal and innate basic emotions, Roediger et al. (2018) mention that there are also social emotions, which are developed through interactions with significant figures and the cultural environment. These emotions, such as guilt, shame, or pride, are not universal or instinctive but rather emerge from the internalization of norms, beliefs, and values transmitted by caregivers and culture during childhood and adolescence, although they continue to evolve throughout life.

Basic emotions are often expressed through clear bodily responses, such as changes in heart rate, muscle tension, or breathing patterns, as they are closely linked to the autonomic nervous system. On the other hand, social emotions, such as shame or guilt, involve more cognitive processing and are associated with the evaluation of social norms and interpersonal relationships. Although social emotions may be perceived as more mental due to their complexity, both emotion categories involve both bodily and brain responses (Ekman, 1992; McEwen, 2002; Gilbert, 2009; Goleman, 1995; Lewis, 1993; Lazarus, 1991; Barrett, 2017; Damasio, 1994; Panksepp, 1998).

According to the Emotion-focused Therapy presented by Greenberg and Paivio (1997), emotions are universal, automatic, adaptive emotional responses that serve a survival function, being activated by relevant stimuli. These types of emotions can be divided into two:

- **Primary Adaptive:** These are context-congruent emotions that help the person respond effectively (e.g., feeling fear in the face of real danger).

- **Primary Maladaptive:** These are emotional responses learned from past experiences that are no longer useful or appropriate to the context (e.g., feeling intense shame when making a small mistake due to early experiences of humiliation).

In addition to primary (basic) emotions and social emotions, it is useful to distinguish two other types of emotions (Greenberg and Paivio, 1997; Greenberg, 2011):

1. **Secondary Emotions:** These are learned emotional reactions that are triggered by other emotions, such as feeling guilty for being angry or ashamed for crying. They are often influenced by previous experiences or internalized social norms.
2. **Instrumental Emotions:** These do not necessarily reflect the individual's actual feelings but are expressed with the aim of influencing others, such as crying to obtain comfort or showing anger to intimidate.

Primary emotions, then, can become secondary emotions as an attempt to cope with the former. In this way, a primary fear can become secondary anger, and vice versa. Primary anger can become secondary fear (especially in cases where the person is confronted by someone stronger than them). Therefore, secondary emotions are actively and observably the opposite of the primary emotion.

Understanding these types of emotions is key to understanding how people regulate their emotional lives and how this process is influenced by both their personal history and their interpersonal and cultural context.

Clinical Case 3 Henry and Alexandra, 35 years old

Henry and Alexandra argue constantly because they have both discovered that the other has been unfaithful throughout the relationship. Henry displays marked hostility toward Alexandra. At the slightest provocation, he reacts by reminding her of her infidelity, using an accusatory and angry tone. This response seems to have roots in his family history: during his childhood, Henry witnessed how his mother responded with constant criticism and intense reproaches to his father's infidelities. Alexandra, for her part, feels deeply resentful toward Henry because of the betrayal she suffered, but does not communicate this openly. Instead of verbalizing her discomfort, she keeps it silent, accumulating it internally. This pattern also has a correlate in her developmental history: during adolescence, Alexandra observed how her mother contained her emotions in the face of her father's constant criticism, avoiding expressing her anger or pain. This could explain why Alexandra reproduces a

(Continued)

Clinical Case 3 (Continued)

pattern of emotional repression, experiencing anger internally and silently, without directly confronting Henry. In both cases, each partner felt angry with the other. However, Henry's emotion was primary: the betrayal generated anger. Meanwhile, Alexandra's anger was secondary because, instead of anger, she expressed fear in the face of Henry's outbursts.

Reflection: What was the basic emotion in Henry and Alexandra? What was the social emotion that each partner had? Which partner presented a primary emotion and which a secondary emotion?

Therapist's Advice: In therapy, explore the basic emotion underlying the social emotions your clients present. In the previous case, Henry's social emotion was hostility, while Alexandra's was resentment. Both learned these emotions in their respective families of origin. It's also important to identify the underlying emotions underlying the secondary emotions. In both cases, anger was the basic emotion experienced, but Alexandra actively displayed the secondary emotion of anger.

As discussed, emotions lie on a continuum: some (such as anger) have biological correlates and relatively universal expressions, while others (such as hostility and resentment) arise from interaction with cultural norms, the internalization of moral values, and one's history of emotional learning. Therefore, they are not entirely separate categories but rather interrelated experiences (Ekman, 1992; Barrett, 2017; Panksepp, 1998; Lazarus, 1991; Plutchik, 2001; Damasio, 1994; Goleman, 1995; David, 2016; Lewis, 1993).

However, the working model presented in this book focuses primarily on basic emotions. Therefore, throughout the text, the therapist's goal will be to guide the couple from their social emotions to the basic emotions that underlie their experience. Also, the goal is to identify the basic emotion that lies behind the secondary emotion.

To simplify the complexity of the emotional phenomenon, we can distinguish:

1. **Basic Emotions:** Emotions with a more universal and innate basis, associated with fundamental needs and present in similar ways in different cultures.
2. **Social Emotions:** Learned affective responses, linked to the way we have learned to manage and express basic emotions.
3. **Secondary Emotions:** Emotional reactions that are activated in response to other emotions.

2.2.3 Coping Behaviors

According to Cannon's original theory (1915), the response to a threat focused primarily on two reactions: fight or flight. Subsequent research has proposed additional behaviors, such as "freezing" and "submitting," to describe a broader range of responses to danger (Roediger et al., 2018). These four behaviors can be summarized as follows:

- **Fight:** Involves directly confronting the threat, attempting to control or subdue the other.
- **Fleeing:** This involves escaping from the situation, either physically or through distractions and self-comfort.
- **Freezing:** It is a passive response that involves a state of immobility, emotional detachment, dullness, or dissociation.
- **Submitting:** This involves trying to please or accommodate the demands of others to avoid conflict.

Further, each of these coping behaviors is reviewed, exemplified by the presentation of a series of couples' cases, beginning with the coping behavior of fighting.

Clinical Case 4 Francis, 45 years old

Francis seeks couples therapy due to conflicts related to raising his son, David. He notes that his wife, Sofía, adopts an excessively overprotective attitude toward the child, which he considers detrimental to his development. Francis, for his part, tries to counteract this behavior by pressuring David to engage in activities that his mother avoids or considers inappropriate. When parenting differences lead to arguments, Francis tends to approach the situation confrontationally, resorting to yelling and blaming Sofía for the negative behaviors he perceives in their son. Furthermore, Francis has even threatened to end the relationship if Sofía does not change her behavior.

Reflection: How do you think you can detect fighting coping behavior in partners in therapy?

Therapist's Advice: In therapy, you can detect fight coping behavior, when a partner's behavior is aimed at controlling the other person or imposing themselves in interactions with their partner.

The following case exemplifies the coping behavior of flight for this purpose; the case of Sofia is presented.

Clinical Case 5 Sofia, 40 years old

Sofía seeks couples therapy due to her husband, Francis's controlling behavior. She describes how Francis frequently yells and imposes, especially on issues related to raising their son, David. One of the main sources of conflict is Francis's insistence on forcing David to do activities he doesn't want to do, which creates tension in the family relationship. In these situations, Sofía avoids directly confronting Francis. Instead, she chooses to distance herself and often engages with David in activities Francis disapproves of, but she does so in secret to avoid further conflict. This time alone with her son provides her with an emotional refuge, helping her cope with living with Francis and mitigating the impact of arguments.

Reflection: How do you think the therapist can detect in therapy that one of the partners is falling into escape coping behavior?

Therapist's Advice: In session, you can detect escape coping behavior, when the client's behavior is directed toward physically fleeing from their partner and seeking solace in another activity.

The following example shows the coping behavior of freezing; for this, the case of Laura is reviewed next.

Clinical Case 6 Laura, 53 years old

Laura seeks help in couples therapy due to constant conflicts with her husband, Steven, related to his fulfillment of agreements. Steven expresses annoyance because Laura often promises to perform tasks or activities he requests, but subsequently fails to follow through. This has generated frustration and resentment in the relationship. For her part, Laura tends to respond affirmatively to Steven's requests automatically, without considering whether she is willing or whether it is something she truly wants to do. This habit has caused her to sometimes forget about commitments or fail to prioritize them.

Reflection: How do you think the therapist can detect during the session that one of the partners is freezing as a coping behavior?

Therapist's Advice: In session, you can detect the coping behavior of freezing in session, when the client is emotionally disconnected from themselves, their partner, and even from the therapy itself.

To further illustrate coping behaviors, we present the case of Ferdinand, who responds to relationship problems by using the coping behavior of submitting.

Clinical Case 7 Ferdinand, 52 years old

Ferdinand seeks couples therapy due to the constant conflicts he has with his wife, Mariana, related to his jealousy. Every time Ferdinand spends time with someone else, be it friends, coworkers, or family members, Mariana experiences intense jealousy that leads her to reproach him and express her hurt feelings for his apparent "lack of attention." Faced with these reactions, Ferdinand cancels meetings or stops hanging out with the people who make Mariana jealous, in order to calm her down and avoid bigger conflicts. Although this strategy seems to work in the short term, the relief is temporary. As soon as Mariana realizes again that Ferdinand is not focusing exclusively on her, the dynamic reactivates, perpetuating a dysfunctional cycle.

Reflection: How do you think the session shows the submissive behavior of some partners?

Therapist's Advice: The coping behavior of submitting can be detected in the therapeutic consultation when the client tries to please, obey, or submit to the demands of their partner.

To summarize this section, we can say that there are three basic concepts in the couples schema therapy model. The elements of these concepts are organized as follows:

Basic Needs

- **Need for Attachment–Connection:** Involves the establishment of secure emotional bonds, belonging to social groups, and cooperation.
- **Need for Assertiveness and Autonomy:** This refers to the ability to express ideas and emotions, be recognized and respected, develop skills, and maintain control over situations.

Basic Emotions

- **Positive Emotions:** Happiness.
- **Negative Emotions:** Fear, sadness, disgust, and anger.

Coping Behaviors

- **Fight:** Confront, control, or subdue.
- **Flee:** Physically escape or seek self-consolation.
- **Freeze:** Emotionally disconnect or dissociate.
- **Submit:** Please, obey, subjugate.

2.3 The Two-dimensional Model

The three basic concepts (needs, emotions, and behaviors) are interrelated and mutually influence each other. This complex interaction will be simplified in the two-dimensional model. The first is composed of the need for attachment and connection, along with the emotions of fear and sadness, and the coping behaviors of freezing and submitting. The second is composed of the need for assertiveness and autonomy, linked to the emotions of anger and disgust and fight and flight behaviors (Roediger, 2025).

In the case of the need for attachment–connection, some examples of these interrelations are the following: the negative emotions of fear of losing the relationship or the sadness that the person no longer loves them in the same way, drive the individual to ask themselves: "What do I need to change so that my partner connects with me again?" In this way, the individual submits their behavior to please their partner or, in some cases, they emotionally disconnect from themselves so that their own desires do not conflict with those of their partner.

In a very simplified way, we could say that fear and sadness drive the individual to try to preserve the bond through internalization; that is, the individual reflects on how they can understand and support their partner, behaving in ways that allow this action to be carried out. Let's take a closer look at this interrelationship by returning to Ferdinand's case.

Ferdinand, 52 years old
Ferdinand seeks couples therapy due to constant conflicts with his wife, Mariana, related to jealousy and her threats of infidelity. Mariana reacts with reproaches and warnings whenever Ferdinand expresses his desire to socialize with his friends, using phrases like, "I'm going to find another man who values me." These threats generate fear in Ferdinand of possible infidelity, which drives him to frequently cancel his social plans to remain at home with her. When Ferdinand decides not to submit to Mariana's demands and organizes gatherings at his house, her reaction is equally intense. Mariana withdraws from the venue, avoids all interaction with the attendees, and, after the event, stops speaking to him for days. During these episodes, she uses her cell phone to chat with other men. Ferdinand, seeing these interactions between Mariana and other men, feels sad at the thought of losing her love. This situation leads Ferdinand to disconnect from his own needs, apologize to Mariana, and promise that he will never organize meetings again, thus perpetuating the dysfunctional cycle.

In Ferdinand's case, a clear connection is observed between need, emotion, and behavior. The active need was attachment–connection, manifested in his desire for Mariana to be satisfied with him and remain in the relationship. This unmet need generated inward-directed emotions: fear that Mariana might look for someone else and sadness at the possibility that she might stop loving him.

These emotions led Ferdinand to implement submissive behaviors by stopping hanging out with his friends and emotionally disconnecting, prioritizing Mariana's needs, and disconnecting from his own to avoid having problems with her.

Reflection: How do you identify signs that a client is sacrificing their own needs to accommodate their partner's demands? What questions might help you explore how emotions of sadness or fear are motivating this behavior?

Therapist's Advice: Remember that needs, emotions, and behaviors are closely related. If you detect sadness or fear, investigate the underlying need (such as attachment) and observe how the client is responding with behaviors such as submission or withdrawal.

Regarding the need for assertiveness and autonomy, in some cases, negative emotions such as anger at feeling that someone isn't meeting expectations, or displeasure at perceiving unacceptable behavior, can lead individuals to ask themselves, "What can I do to make my partner behave the way I expect?" These types of emotions can generate behaviors aimed at controlling their partner's behavior or, in other cases, emotional withdrawal by seeking in other activities or people what isn't found in the relationship.

One way to understand this dynamic is that anger and disgust act as impulses to assert autonomy or satisfy unmet needs. In this context, the individual attempts to modify their partner's behavior by externalizing, imposing their expectations on their partner (e.g., "You should behave this way to please me") or, in other cases, by emotionally distancing themselves, seeking refuge in other activities or people.

Clinical Case 8 Mariana, 50 years old

Mariana often gets annoyed with her husband, Ferdinand, when she perceives that he doesn't include her in his plans with friends. This feeling of exclusion leads her to react intensely: she accuses Ferdinand of being selfish and even threatens to find another man who will give her the attention she needs.

(Continued)

Clinical Case 8 (Continued)

Mariana expects Ferdinand to change his behavior, cancel his commitments, and spend all his time with her. When Ferdinand organizes get-togethers with his friends at home, Mariana becomes visibly uncomfortable. She avoids spending time with them, retreating to her room to isolate herself. During these times, she seeks distraction by interacting on her cell phone with men who court her romantically.

In Mariana's case, a clear connection was observed between needs, emotions, and behaviors. The active need was assertiveness–autonomy, which required Ferdinand to spend more time with her. This unmet need generated outward-directed emotions: anger toward Ferdinand and disgust toward people she perceived as threatening her undivided attention. The behaviors observed in Mariana were: Fight: Accusations and threats toward Ferdinand, seeking to change his behavior; and Flight: Isolation during meetings and seeking solace in interactions with other men who did provide attention.

Reflection: What signs can you observe in a client when they are experiencing anger, trying to impose their needs, or withdrawing emotionally to seek comfort?

Therapist's Advice: Remember that needs, emotions, and behaviors are interrelated. Identifying one of them can be the key to exploring the others: If you see that the client is angry, it's very likely that their assertiveness–autonomy need is active and that the behavior they are practicing is fighting. Similarly, if the client is trying to assert themselves, the emotion present could be anger or disgust, and the active need is assertiveness–autonomy.

Before concluding the section below, a summary of the needs, emotions, and behaviors of each of the two dimensions of the couple schema therapy model is presented.

Basic Need of Attachment–Connection

Basic Emotion. Fear and sadness

Coping Behaviors

- **Freeze:** To emotionally disconnect or dissociate.
- **Submit:** Please, obey, or subjugate.

Basic Need of Assertiveness–Autonomy

Basic Emotion. Disgust and anger.

Coping Behaviors

- **Fight:** Confront, control, or subdue.
- **Flee:** To physically escape or to comfort oneself.

2.4 The Active and Blocked Sides

The basic needs of attachment–connection and assertiveness–autonomy are not mutually exclusive, but in some cases, the effort to actively meet one need can lead to prioritizing it over the other. Similarly, the emotions and coping behaviors associated with these needs tend to be prioritized (Roediger, 2025).

In this way, although two needs may be active at the same time, one of them is explicitly prioritized in interactions with others.

The same is true of emotions: while one emotion may be evident to others, the other may remain latent within the person. In some cases, what is shown is the secondary emotion, leaving the primary emotion blocked.

In the case of coping behaviors (avoidance, overcompensation, surrender), people will generally tend to actively use one of them, while the others will not be used predominantly in that specific situation.

When people's need for assertiveness and autonomy is activated and they try to satisfy it, they typically experience emotions such as anger or disgust, along with fight or avoidance behaviors. This can cause the focus of attention to be centered on this need, leaving the need for attachment and connection, along with emotions such as sadness or fear, and behaviors such as paralysis or submission, to the background. However, this doesn't mean that these needs, emotions, and behaviors are completely "blocked." Rather, they remain in the background. However, with a conscious effort, they can be activated. To explain this in greater depth, let's look at the following example.

Mariana, 50 years old

Mariana feels upset and has demanded that her husband, Ferdinand, stop spending time with his friends so he can pay more attention to her. However, deeper emotions lie behind this demand: Mariana feels sad because she interprets Ferdinand's desire to socialize with his friends as a sign of emotional distancing, leading her to think he might be losing love for her. This sadness is linked to her need for attachment and connection, as Mariana desires to feel prioritized and loved in the relationship. At the same time, a part of Mariana

(Continued)

(Continued)

also wants Ferdinand to be happy and would be willing to please him, but her fear of being hurt drives her to protect herself. In her past, Mariana experienced situations in which people took advantage of her more vulnerable side, which has generated an emotional defense that makes it difficult for her to openly express her feelings of sadness and her need for attachment and connection. Instead of showing this vulnerability, Mariana tries to control the situation and avoid reliving painful experiences.

Reflection: How can you identify which emotions, needs, or coping styles are active and which are secondary in your client? What strategies can you use to help the client become aware of the underlying emotions, needs, or behaviors and how this is influencing their interactions with others?

Therapist's Advice: Explain to your client that the two needs, the four emotions, and the four coping styles are present simultaneously, but not all of them are visibly expressed at the same time. Use the coin metaphor: just as it has a visible side and an internal side, some emotional or behavioral aspects are perceived by the partner, while others remain concealed or in the background.

As can be seen in Mariana's case, she experiences both the need for attachment–connection and the need for assertiveness–autonomy. On the one hand, she wants to see Ferdinand happy and satisfied (attachment–connection). On the other hand, she would like him to accompany her and spend more time with her (assertiveness–autonomy). However, Mariana prioritizes the latter need, while the former is relegated to the background.

Similarly, her emotions follow the same pattern. Although her primary emotion is sadness at perceiving Ferdinand's distance and fear that he might seek another relationship to replace her, these emotions remain in the background. Instead, what predominates is the secondary emotion of anger toward Ferdinand for not spending more time with her and disgust toward her friends, whom she perceives as a threat that is pushing her out.

As for coping behaviors, freezing or submitting are out of her active repertoire in this situation. Instead, Mariana adopts a fight-back strategy, demanding that Ferdinand spend more time with her. She also tries to manage her discomfort by avoiding the fact that he's happy with his friends and seeks distraction or emotional validation by flirting with other men through text messages.

When a person is focused on satisfying the need for attachment and connection, they may experience emotions such as fear or sadness, accompanied by submissive behaviors or paralysis. These emotions tend to take center stage in a person's emotional experience, which can relegate emotions such as anger or disgust, which are more associated with the need for assertiveness and autonomy and fight-avoidance behaviors, to the background. However, this does not mean that the needs, emotions, or behaviors are completely "blocked." Rather, they are in the background or hidden and can be activated through conscious effort. To clarify this, the following example is presented below.

Ferdinand, 52 years old

Ferdinand feels fear every time his wife threatens to leave him for another man if he doesn't pay enough attention to her. To avoid conflict and potential negative consequences, Ferdinand reacts by submitting: he cancels get-togethers with his friends and disconnects from his need to socialize. Although this strategy seems to momentarily calm the situation, deeper emotions lie behind his submissive behavior. Ferdinand feels annoyed because he considers it unfair that his wife doesn't allow him to spend time with his friends. Furthermore, he deeply dislikes seeing her adopt punitive behaviors, such as flirting with other men, whenever he doesn't give in to her demands. Part of Ferdinand wants to demand respect and set clear boundaries with Mariana, but this is extremely difficult due to his personal history. During his childhood and adolescence, Ferdinand was severely hurt physically and emotionally whenever he tried to confront authority figures or stand up for his needs. This has led to a pattern of submission and emotional disconnection in conflict situations, making it difficult for him to directly express his need for assertiveness and autonomy, as well as his emotions of anger and displeasure. Instead of setting limits, Ferdinand chooses to submit and avoid confrontations to protect himself from potential negative consequences.

Reflection: What strategies can you use when a client thinks they're communicating one thing, but others interpret it differently? How might you help them explore this discrepancy and become aware of the signals they're sending, both verbally and nonverbally?

Therapist's Advice: When a client expresses that what they think they're communicating is different from what others perceive, begin by validating their experience: acknowledge how they feel and what they think they're expressing. Then, invite them to reflect on the signals their body is sending at that moment and how these might be interpreted externally. To facilitate this reflection, use questions focused on the mind-body connection, such

(Continued)

(Continued)

as: How is your breathing right now? How does your stomach feel? How is your chest? This process helps the client connect their internal experience with external perceptions, fostering greater congruence between what they feel, express, and communicate. Explain to your client that: (1) both needs are present in him simultaneously, but he will tend to prioritize the satisfaction of one of them at that moment, (2) the four emotions could be present, but he will tend to show more clearly those associated with the need that is active at that moment while the others will remain blocked or hidden, and (3) of the four coping behaviors, he will focus more on one of them. Use the coin metaphor: "Just as coins have a visible side and an internal side, some emotional or behavioral aspects are perceived by their partner, while others remain hidden or in the background."

In Ferdinand's case, we can observe how he experiences the two primary needs: attachment–connection and assertiveness–autonomy. On the one hand, he feels a strong inclination to modify his behavior to preserve his connection with Mariana. On the other hand, he also wants her to understand and respect his need to socialize with his friends. However, Ferdinand prioritizes meeting his wife's needs, leaving his own desire for Mariana to be more flexible and stop pressuring him to abandon his friendships in the background.

Similarly, Ferdinand experiences a variety of emotions. On the one hand, he feels disgust at Mariana's indirect threats to replace him with another man if he doesn't stop socializing with his friends, as well as anger at her criticisms of his social life. However, these emotions of disgust and anger are relegated to the background. What predominates in Ferdinand is sadness, believing he is losing Mariana's affection, and fear that she will end the relationship and look for someone else.

Regarding coping behaviors, Ferdinand abandons strategies such as fight or flight. Instead, he opts for submission, giving in to Mariana's demands and canceling his get-togethers with friends. He also uses freezing as a mechanism to disconnect from his need for socialization and avoid conflict.

2.5 The Balance Between the Two Needs

As reviewed, there are two basic needs in relationships: attachment–connection and assertiveness–autonomy, which people attend to at different times depending on the circumstances. Sometimes, we prioritize one over the other, which is natural and adaptive. However, the problem arises when people focus exclusively on one need, completely neglecting the other (Roediger, 2025).

For example, if we over-satisfy the need for attachment and connection, we can lose individuality and autonomy. On the other hand, if we focus solely on our need for assertiveness and autonomy, we can neglect emotional connection, becoming controlling, lacking empathy, and very selfish toward our partner's needs.

For this reason, the goal of schema couples therapy is to help partners find a dynamic balance between these two needs. This balance involves learning to move back and forth: from the need for attachment and connection to the need for assertiveness and autonomy, and vice versa, as the situation requires.

To illustrate this concept, Roediger et al. (2018) use the metaphor of "two legs." In this metaphor, they point out that walking and moving forward require using both legs. If you try to walk with only one leg, progress will be limited or even impossible. Similarly, in a relationship, it is necessary to integrate both "legs": the need for attachment and connection and the need for assertiveness and autonomy.

In this metaphor, the "blue leg" represents the need for attachment and connection, along with the emotions of sadness and fear, and the behaviors of freezing and submitting. On the other hand, the "red leg" symbolizes the need for assertiveness and autonomy, along with the emotions of anger and disgust, and the behaviors of fighting and avoiding. Using both legs in a balanced way allows the couple to resolve relational problems and meet each partner's two basic needs, thus strengthening the relationship.

To complement the "two-legged" metaphor, Roediger (2025) introduces the analogy of "dancing" to explain how couples can coordinate and balance their basic needs for attachment–connection and assertiveness–autonomy. This analogy suggests that, to dance as a couple, it is necessary to coordinate the movement of both legs with those of the other person.

For example, when one partner takes a step forward with their "red leg" (assertiveness–autonomy), the other responds by taking a step back with their "blue leg" (attachment–connection). The roles are then reversed: the person who stepped back now advances with their "red leg," and their partner retreats with their "blue leg." This movement is repeated flexibly and synchronously, creating a dynamic balance that allows both partners to move together harmoniously.

However, when this balance is disrupted and there is rigidity in the use of the legs, problems arise in the relationship. For example, both partners only use the "red leg": Both partners move forward at the same time, which generates constant clashes and conflicts. If one partner moves forward with the "red leg" while the other retreats with the "blue leg": This creates a chase dynamic, where one partner pursues the other. Finally, if both partners only retreat with the "blue leg": If both partners focus solely on the need for attachment and connection from a place of fear or submission, they end up drifting apart and becoming emotionally disconnected.

To review more clearly how to help clients balance emotional needs in couples, let's look at the following examples:

Clinical Case 9 Amelia, 62 years old

Amelia is attending therapy with her partner, Thomas, because she feels resentful of him for not helping her enough with household chores. The therapist explained the two-dimensional model using the metaphor of "legs" and the need to balance them.

THERAPIST (T): Amelia, would you like to explore how you might move from your "red leg" to your "blue leg"?

AMELIA (A.): What good is that going to do me?

T: That's a good question. So far, it seems you've relied primarily on your need for assertiveness and autonomy: you've expressed your anger and fought to get Thomas to help out more with the housework. But, Amelia, I wonder, despite relying on your "red leg," have you gotten the results you want?

A.: No, but it's because he doesn't change. If he did, we wouldn't be in this situation.

T: I understand this may seem frustrating. And you're right—if Tom were to move off his leg, that might help solve the problem. However, there's something important here: you can't completely control what he does, but you can decide what approach you want to take. How about trying something different, something that's within your control?

A.: I can try.

T: Excellent. Amelia, what do you think if, instead of telling him what you think, what you feel, and what you expect him to do, you ask him what he thinks, feels, and expects of you?

A: Okay, I can try. Thomas, what do you think about what I'm asking you to do with the housework?

THOMAS (TH.): Well, I think I want to do them, but whenever it suits me best. Sometimes I feel like you want me to do it right away. I also think that when I do it, it's not always how you expect, and that creates tension for me.

A: And how do you feel when I criticize you for the way you did it?

TH: I feel upset because I feel like no matter what I do, I'm not going to please you.

A: And what would you expect from me to make this different?

TH.: I'd like you to give me a little more time to do the housework, to be more tolerant of the way I do it, and to tone down the cleaning standards a bit. For example, I think sweeping the street once a day is enough.

T: Amelia, now that you're hearing this, I want to invite you to connect with the emotion of sadness or fear that may have been left in the background: how does it make you feel to hear that Thomas feels like he can't please you?

A: I feel sad. I don't like knowing that he feels that way.

T: That sadness is important because it connects with your need to maintain a connection with Thomas. What would you like to do now that you've heard his perspective?

A: I would like to tell you that I can accept not sweeping the street twice a day, and I can try to be more patient before criticizing.

T: That sounds like a step toward balance. How do you see it, Thomas?

TH.: It would mean a lot to me. If she can be patient, I promise not to take so long.

T: Amelia, what do you think worked best: continuing to use only your "red leg" or moving to your "blue leg" to balance things out?

A.: Change legs.

Reflection: What other questions could you have asked to help Amelia connect with her blocked emotions and encourage a leg switch? If Amelia had shown resistance or difficulty switching legs, what alternative strategies could you have used to explore the rigidity and facilitate a gradual shift?

Therapist's Advice: Explore additional techniques that allow you to encourage leg switching in your clients, adapting them to their predominant coping styles. For example, you can use the specific exercises for externalizers and internalizers presented later in this book.

As observed in Amelia's case, the shift from her "red leg" to her "blue leg" not only facilitated her connection with the emotions of sadness and empathy toward Thomas, but also motivated her husband to move from his "blue leg" to his "red leg." In practical terms, Amelia's interest in what Thomas was thinking, feeling, and needing, along with her ability to express sadness, allowed Thomas to feel validated and, in turn, to express his need for assertiveness and autonomy. This included sharing how she felt and what he expected of her. This shift broke the rigidity in the couple's dynamic, allowing both to move toward resolving their problems.

(Continued)

Clinical Case 9 (Continued)

It's important to note that leg switching doesn't simply involve switching between emotions or basic needs, but also flexing coping behaviors. For example, instead of Amelia shifting from "dominating" to "submitting," which could perpetuate the dysfunction, the shift was oriented toward cooperating or yielding. This means that rather than giving in completely, Amelia negotiated specific aspects on which she was willing to compromise, such as giving Thomas more time to complete chores and accepting less frequent cleaning than she had initially expected.

The following describes what the session would have been like if the couple's schema therapy therapist, instead of working with Amelia, had worked with Thomas's leg change. The result would have been very similar: balancing the couple's dynamics.

Clinical Case 10 Thomas, 65 years old

Thomas attends therapy with his partner, Amelia, because he's afraid she'll get angry with him whenever he doesn't do household chores the way she expects. During the session, the therapist explains the two-dimensional model and the "legs" metaphor (red and blue) to illustrate how to balance their needs and coping styles.

THERAPIST (T): Thomas, I understand that you feel uncomfortable expressing your needs to Amelia, but would you like to try to move from your "blue leg" (attachment–connection) to your "red leg" (assertiveness–autonomy)?

THOMAS (TH.): Yes, I want to try.

T: Okay, what do you think if, instead of apologizing and promising it won't happen again, you tell Amelia how you feel and what you'd like to see regarding the housework?

TH: Amelia, I want you to know that I'd like us to clean less often. For example, I'd prefer to sweep the street once a day, instead of twice. I'd also like you to allow me to do things on my own time, like washing the dishes by the end of the day at the latest, instead of right after lunch.

AMELIA (A.): Well, I think I could agree to sweeping the street only once a day. Although I don't entirely like it, I suppose I could be more tolerant and wait until the end of the day for you to wash the dishes.

TH: Thank you very much. It's really annoying when you constantly remind me that I haven't washed the dishes.

A: I'm sorry, I didn't know it bothered you so much.

T: Amelia, how do you feel when you hear Thomas express his needs in a firm way?

A: I feel sad. I didn't know so many things I said bothered him. It hurts me to know I made him feel this way.

T: Thomas, what do you think worked best: continuing to use only your "blue leg" or moving to your "red leg" to balance things out?

TH.: Having made the leg change.

Reflection: What strategies could you use if Thomas is unable to move to his "red leg" and assertively express what he needs and wants? How could you help him connect with his anger and his need for assertiveness and autonomy?

Therapist's Advice: There are several techniques that can help partners connect with their need for assertiveness and autonomy, their emotions of anger and disgust, and express assertiveness from their "red leg." These strategies, especially useful for partners with an internalizing style, are explored in detail in the corresponding chapter of this book.

In Thomas's case, the therapist was able to facilitate the shift from his "blue leg" to his "red leg" by helping him become aware of his anger at Amelia's constant demands. Hearing this, Amelia was able to move from her "red leg" to her "blue leg," connecting with her sadness as she realized the impact her criticism had on Thomas and apologizing for any negative effects this may have caused.

In other words, Thomas's assertiveness in expressing what he thought and needed, along with his expression of anger, made it easier for Amelia to truly empathize with him and feel sad, which helped her express her need for attachment and connection. This helped Thomas maintain his assertiveness without falling into a reactive or defensive attitude, promoting a healthier balance between assertiveness and emotional connection in the couple.

It's important to note that shifting legs doesn't simply involve moving from "submitting" to "dominating," which could perpetuate dysfunctional patterns. Instead, the shift focused on assertiveness or initiative. That is, Thomas didn't fight everything Amelia said, but rather clearly expressed his boundaries and needs in a respectful manner. This allowed the couple to move toward a middle ground, where both partners felt heard and validated.

As previously reviewed when analyzing the previous cases, leg switching refers to shifting from a dominant coping behavior to another, previously

(Continued)

Clinical Case 10 (Continued)

inactive response, expressed in a more flexible way. For example, when a person uses freezing or submitting as active strategies (blue leg), it is important to facilitate a shift to a more adaptive behavior, such as initiative-assertiveness. Similarly, when active strategies include fight or flight (red leg), a transition to a more balanced response, such as yielding-cooperating, should be encouraged (Bracha, 2004).

Below is a summary of how leg switching should be performed, showing in a practical way the transitions between coping behaviors and their corresponding adjustments toward more flexible responses.

Blue Leg

It implies a shift from the predominant need for attachment–connection toward the need for assertiveness–autonomy.

The dominant emotions change from sadness or fear to anger or disgust.

At the behavioral level, the tendency to freeze or submit transforms into a firmer and clearer response.

Red Leg

It involves a shift from the predominant need for assertiveness–autonomy toward the need for attachment–connection.

The predominant emotions move from anger or disgust to sadness or fear.

Behaviorally, the fight-or-flight pattern shifts toward a more flexible, cooperative response.

3

The Mode Cycle

3.1 Introduction

Once the basic concepts that influence both one's own behavior and that of one's partner are understood, we analyze how the rigidity of each partner's needs, emotions, and coping behaviors affects their interactions, generating a repetitive cycle in their dynamics.

The Mode Cycle is established from working with modes of schema therapy, simplified to fit the dimensional model described previously. The inner voice, which reflects negative schema beliefs, is divided into two types: one directed toward others and the other toward oneself. These two types of inner voice are linked to coping modes, which are grouped into two main categories. The first is overcompensation-active avoidance, related to fight and avoidance behaviors. The second is surrender-passive avoidance, which includes behaviors such as submission and freezing, reviewed above. In turn, there are two child modes. The first is the angry child, linked to the emotions of anger and disgust, and the second is the vulnerable child, linked to the emotions of sadness and fear (Roediger, 2025).

The following explanation integrates the modes into the dimensional model, clarifying the relationships between needs, internal voices, and child modes described previously. This conceptual integration simplifies the understanding of coping patterns and emotional activations in interpersonal dynamics.

3.1.1 Need for Attachment–Connection

Critical–Punitive or Demanding Internal Voice directed toward oneself.
Coping Mode and Behavior:

- Surrender: Submitting.
- Passive Avoidance: Freezing.

Vulnerable Child Mode, associated with sadness or fear.

3.1.2 Need for Assertiveness–Autonomy

Critical–Punitive or Demanding Internal Voice directed toward others.
Coping Mode and Behavior:

- Overcompensation: Fighting.
- Active Avoidance: Fleeing.

Angry Child Mode, associated with anger or disgust.

Reflection: As a therapist, what strategies can you use to identify your inner voice and determine whether it is directed toward yourself or your partner?

Therapist's Advice: Remember that schemas are perceptions about oneself and others, and that the critical-punitive or demanding inner voice reflects these beliefs. Identifying whether the inner voice implicitly demands rigid changes in one's own behavior or that of one's partner is key to determining its direction. For example, phrases like "I'm never enough" may indicate a voice directed toward oneself, while "He never listens to me" could be directed toward one's partner. Paying attention to these expressions during the session will allow you to detect the direction of the inner voice.

3.2 The Moments of the Mode Cycle

The Mode Cycle begins with an event that triggers memories related to negative schemas in one or both partners. These memories activate an internal voice, which may be demanding or critical-punitive, directed toward oneself or others. In response, each partner initiates a coping mode directed toward their partner, either through passive surrender-avoidance or active overcompensation-avoidance (Roediger, 2025).

This behavior activates the child mode in the other partner, which manifests as a vulnerable emotional state (sadness or fear) or an angry one (anger or disgust). In response, the partner uses their own coping mode, which in turn reactivates the child mode in the other partner. This cycle perpetuates itself, generating repetitive interactions that are difficult to break (Roediger, 2025).

The following graphic illustrates the steps of the Mode Cycle, making it easier to understand how repetitive interactions between partners develop (Figure 3.1).

The figure shows how the Mode Cycle generates a vicious cycle in the interaction between partners. Depending on which "leg" (red or blue) each partner uses, the type of cycle they commonly establish in problematic situations between them will depend. When one partner uses one leg, the other becomes blocked or takes a backseat. It is precisely on this blocked leg that the work will focus to break the cycle and modify the repetitive dynamics.

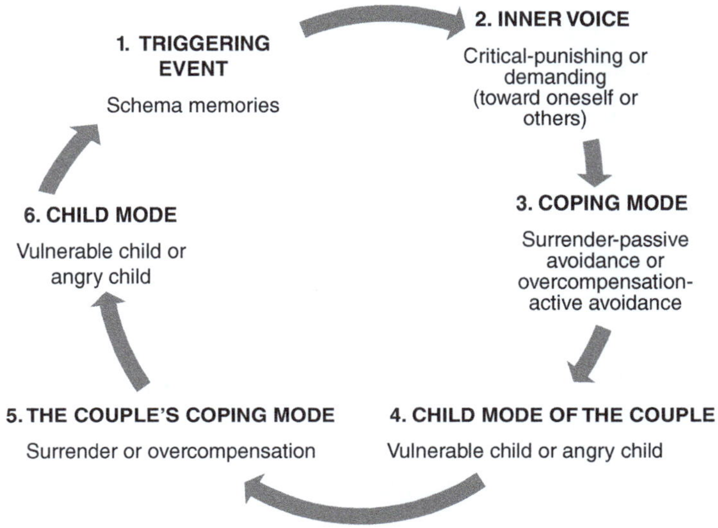

Figure 3.1 Steps in the Mode Cycle. *Source:* Adapted from Roediger (2025).

Partners are not initially fully explained the Mode Cycle. Instead, a simplified version is used that shows how each partner's coping behaviors (overcompensation-active avoidance or surrender-passive avoidance) activate the child mode in the other (either angry or vulnerable). The partner, in turn, responds with their own coping mode, which again triggers the activation of the child mode in the other partner. This process repeats, creating a cyclical interaction pattern (Roediger, 2025) (Figure 3.2).

Reflection: How do you think reducing the schema mode model helps partners better understand the Mode Cycle? What adjustments could you make to your explanation to further facilitate this understanding?

Therapist's Advice: Identifying the Mode Cycle can be a complex process for both therapist and partner. Reflect on whether any of your own schemas, such as unattainable goals, failure, imperfection, etc., are activated while explaining the model to clients. For example, you might notice thoughts like: "You should have done it the first time," "You're useless, you don't do anything right," "You're a failure as a therapist." Discussing these ideas and reparenting your vulnerable child (e.g., by speaking with a compassionate and validating inner voice) can help calm self-criticism. By doing so, you will not only reduce obstacles presented by negative schemas, but it will also be easier to practice analyzing and explaining the Mode Cycle with greater clarity and confidence.

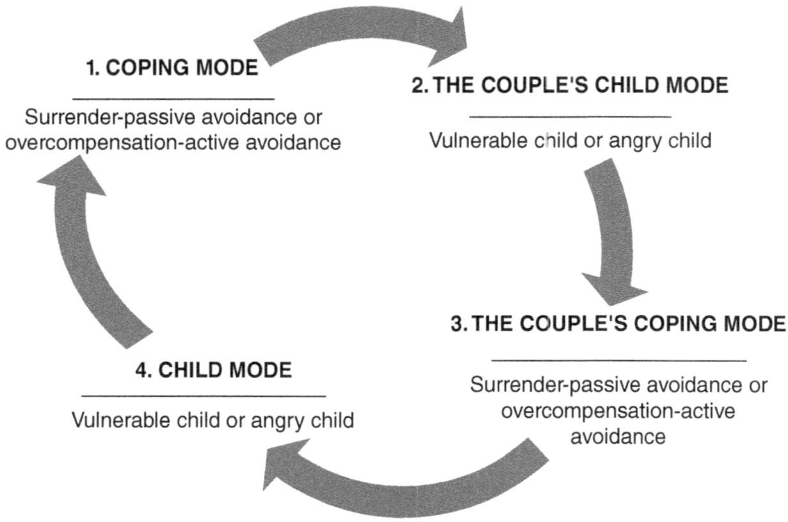

Figure 3.2 Simplified version of the Mode Cycle. *Source:* Adapted from Roediger (2025).

3.3 The Different Mode Cycles

The different Mode Cycles activated in a couple depend on the combination of needs, emotions, and coping behaviors of each partner, represented as the red or blue leg. Roediger (2025) identified four main cycles:

1. **Dominance–Domination:** Both partners try to impose their will.
2. **Dominance–Avoidance:** One person dominates while the other avoids the conflict actively (by isolating themselves and self-consoling) or passively (by disconnecting from their own emotions or needs and those of their partner).
3. **Avoidance–Avoidance:** Both partners evade the problem, either actively or passively, or one actively and the other passively. In all cases, this leads to mutual disconnection.
4. **Dominance–Submission:** One partner dominates while the other passively submits.

The submission–submission cycle that would correspond to the surrender–surrender coping modes is not included among the typical cycles, since these couples rarely seek couples therapy.

In a conflict, when one partner uses the red leg to express their need for assertiveness (what they want or need), the other can respond in various ways:

dominating, avoiding (actively or passively), or submitting. These responses generate the different Mode Cycles, which determine the conflict dynamics in the relationship.

3.3.1 The Dominance–Domination Mode Cycle

In this Mode Cycle, both partners are in overcompensation mode (red leg). This means that both partners are focused on their need for assertiveness–autonomy. Each expects the other to understand their needs and modify their behavior to accommodate them. At the same time, both partners are focused on expressing emotions such as anger and disgust (Roediger, 2025).

In terms of the dance metaphor, this cycle represents both partners advancing with their red leg, symbolizing their insistence on meeting their personal needs. This movement causes a constant clash, as neither is willing to give up space or adjust their position. Although the conflict does not continue indefinitely, it is usually temporarily resolved when one partner chooses to either surrender (passively accepting the other's demands) or actively (physically distancing) or passively (emotional disengagement) avoid the conflict.

However, this resolution is temporary, as the problem can flare up again at any time, reproducing the same dynamic of direct confrontation between the two partners.

To better understand how this dominance-domination cycle works, we will examine the case of Peter and Rose, a 25-year-old couple who have recently faced several problems in their relationship.

Clinical Case 11 Peter and Rose, 25 years old

Peter and Rose are a couple who have faced several conflicts related to household chores. On one occasion, Rose didn't do the laundry as agreed, and Peter didn't clean the yard. This mutual failure to do so led to a conflict.

Rose, upset that Peter hadn't cleaned the yard, considered his attitude unfair, as they had a prior agreement. Frustrated, Rose raised her voice and complained to Peter, seeking to express her need for assertiveness. For his part, Peter, also angry, considered it unfair that Rose criticized him when she herself hadn't fulfilled her commitment to do the laundry. In response, Peter also raised his voice, claiming she was being unfair. Rose interpreted Peter's complaints as a way to divert attention and justify his lack of responsibility. In response, she raised her voice even more, insisting that he not change the subject. Peter, even more annoyed, responded with greater intensity, claiming

(Continued)

Clinical Case 11 (Continued)

that she had no right to get angry over a breach when she herself hadn't fulfilled the agreement.

Reflection: What are the needs, emotions, and coping behaviors that each partner presents in this cycle?

Therapist's Advice: Remember that this cycle is characterized by both partners using their red leg. That is, both partners' assertiveness–autonomy needs, anger-disgust emotions, and overcompensation coping behaviors are active. If at least one partner in this cycle is exhibiting active avoidance, this would not be the cycle the couple is experiencing, but rather part of the dominance-avoidance cycle.

The following section examines how the dominance–dominance cycle developed in the case of Peter and Rose, analyzing the overcompensation responses (red leg) that both partners used during the conflict. This pattern is characterized by an escalation of demands, reproaches, and shouting, reflecting how each partner attempts to assert their need for assertiveness and autonomy without yielding space to the other.

Perpetuation of the Cycle: The more frustrated Peter feels by what he perceives as an injustice, the more intensely he expresses his anger through shouting and accusations directed at Rose. This reaction increases her irritation, leading her to raise her voice and reproach him for trying to justify himself instead of acknowledging his mistake. As the interaction intensifies, Peter responds with greater anger and accuses Rose of focusing solely on his faults while ignoring her own. In this way, both partners enter a cycle of overcompensation in which each attempts to assert their need for assertiveness–autonomy through an escalating pattern of reproaches and demands, ultimately perpetuating the conflict without resolving it.

The previous case illustrates this interaction pattern, showing how the overcompensation behaviors of Peter and Rose reinforced each other. The cycle began with mutual demands and complaints, intensified through shouting and accusations, and culminated in Peter's withdrawal, as he opted for an active avoidance strategy. This graphical representation helps visualize how both partners contributed to perpetuating the conflict by remaining in the overcompensation mode.

When the red leg predominates in both partners, the blue leg becomes blocked, which means that the need for attachment and connection, emotions of fear and sadness, and flexible cooperative coping behaviors are relegated to the background. Activating these elements in both partners will be the therapeutic objective in this Mode Cycle.

3.3.2 The Dominance–Avoidance Mode Cycle

This Mode Cycle is characterized by the interaction between one partner in overcompensation mode (red leg) and the other in avoidance mode, which can be active (red leg) or passive (blue leg). This gives rise to two possibilities (Roediger, 2025):

1. **Active Dominance–Avoidance:** Both partners are on their red leg, displaying anger or displeasure. However, one partner uses overcompensation, demanding that their needs be met, while the other actively avoids conflict by withdrawing or seeking self-soothing activities.
2. **Dominance–Passive Avoidance:** In this case, one partner demands that the other adapt to their needs, acting from the red leg with emotions of anger and disgust. Meanwhile, the other partner, dominated by sadness or fear, attempts to adapt to the demands by submitting and emotionally disconnecting from both themselves and their partner. For example, they may accept the demands without fully understanding them, simply to avoid conflict, which perpetuates the disconnection.

In the dance metaphor, this cycle can be represented as one partner taking a step forward while the other retreats (passive avoidance), or taking a step forward, but in a different direction from the partner (active avoidance). This creates a dynamic in which one partner pursues the other while the other actively or emotionally distances themselves.

3.3.2.1 The Dominance–Passive Avoidance Mode Cycle

To explain in greater detail how the dominance–passive avoidance cycle works, we present the case of Charlie and Joseph, a couple aged 30 and 35, respectively, who are seeking therapy for sexual problems.

Clinical Case 12 Charlie, 30 years old and Joseph, 35 years old

Charlie and Joseph are a couple facing relationship problems due to Joseph's erection difficulties, which Charlie interprets as a loss of sexual connection. Although Joseph committed to seeing a specialist, he has postponed or forgotten his appointments with the urologist. These situations generate

(Continued)

Clinical Case 12 (Continued)

annoyance in Charlie, and he complains about Joseph, accusing him of being the one responsible for his feelings of rejection due to the loss of his erection (red leg). In response, Joseph feels sad, thinking he is affecting Charlie's needs and fearing that Charlie will stop loving him. Therefore, Joseph, disconnecting from his own emotions and needs, automatically apologizes and promises that he will not fail again (blue leg). If Joseph were to connect with his red leg and his need for assertiveness and autonomy, he could identify that his erection problems are related to an emotional disconnection generated by his failure to express his needs. He could also directly tell Charlie that he does not want to see a doctor and explain his reasons. However, being disconnected from this need, he answers yes and ends up forgetting this commitment, perpetuating the cycle.

Reflection: What needs and emotions predominate in each partner during this cycle? How do the coping behaviors of Charlie (overcompensation, red leg) and Joseph (passive avoidance, blue leg) contribute to maintaining this pattern?

Therapist's Advice: This cycle combines overcompensation by one partner, who seeks to impose their needs directly, with passive avoidance by the other partner, who disconnects from themselves and their partner. If the latter partner didn't avoid disconnecting but instead responded by submitting, the cycle would shift to one of dominance–submission.

As can be seen, the dominance–passive avoidance Mode Cycle was present in the case of Charlie and Joseph, showing how the overcompensation of the former (red leg) and the passive avoidance of the latter (blue leg) contributed to maintaining this interaction pattern.

Perpetuation of the Cycle: The angrier Charlie gets with Joseph and accuses him of being selfish and irresponsible, the sadder and more afraid Joseph feels at the thought that Charlie might stop loving him. In response, Joseph apologizes and promises to change, but he does so automatically, without reflecting on what is really happening inside him. This disconnection leads him to not fulfill his commitment, perpetuating the problem. This intensifies Charlie's frustration, and he reacts again with anger, accusing Joseph of being irresponsible and reinforcing the dynamic. This cycle reflects the interaction between Charlie's overcompensation (red leg), who tries to impose his needs through demands, and Joseph's passive avoidance (blue leg), who disconnects from his own emotions and needs to avoid conflict.

In therapy, the goal for the overcompensating partner (red leg) is to unblock these areas, helping them reconnect with their attachment and connection needs, process their emotions of fear and sadness, and develop the flexible coping behavior of cooperation. On the other hand, for the passively avoidant partner (blue leg), therapeutic work will focus on connecting with their need for assertiveness and autonomy, fostering emotions such as anger and disgust, and strengthening their flexible coping behavior of acting assertively. These goals aim to restore balance in the couple's dynamics by helping each partner meet their previously unmet or backgrounded needs.

3.3.2.2 The Active Dominance–Avoidance Mode Cycle

To describe the active dominance–avoidance cycle, let's review the case of Isabella and Caroline, two 34-year-old women who are seeking therapy for problems related to the freedom with which Isabella can make her relationship public.

Clinical Case 13 Isabella and Caroline, 34 years old

Caroline and Isabella face a conflict in their relationship related to the public acceptance of their sexual orientation. Caroline feels upset because Isabella doesn't openly accept her sexual orientation, which means she hasn't introduced her to her parents, they don't share photos as a couple on social media, and they can't express romantic affection in public places. For Caroline, these restrictions represent an invalidation of their identity as a couple. On the other hand, Isabella perceives Caroline's demands as constant pressure and feels that her own personal process of acceptance and coming out is not being respected. This generates discomfort and reinforces her resistance to making her sexual orientation public. Both partners of the couple are trying to satisfy their need for autonomy and assertiveness, but they perceive the other's behaviors as a frustration of their own desires. The coping strategies they use are different and contribute to perpetuating the conflict. Isabella engages in overcompensatory behaviors, trying to control aspects such as the photos Caroline posts on social media, her clothing style, or public expressions of affection. Caroline interprets these actions as invasive and controlling, which increases her discomfort. These behaviors make Caroline feel disgusted with Isabella; however, instead of expressing it directly, she practices an active avoidance coping behavior, in which, although she does not post photos with her, she does post photos with other women, directly expressing her sexual orientation. Also, when Caroline perceives Isabella as controlling, she prefers

(Continued)

Clinical Case 13 (Continued)

to cancel meetings with her using pretexts and go out with other friends with whom she can express her sexual orientation without difficulty (red leg). Isabella, realizing that she cancels outings with her under pretexts and that she uploads photos openly showing her sexual orientation, gets angry with Caroline and begins to complain, demanding explanations (red leg). This cycle is perpetuated when Isabella, noticing Caroline's evasiveness, confronts her, demanding explanations. Caroline responds with refusals and justifications, leaving both partners trapped in a cycle of mutual frustration.

Reflection: What needs and emotions predominate in each partner during this cycle? How do Isabella's (overcompensation, red leg) and Caroline's (active avoidance, red leg) coping behaviors contribute to maintaining this pattern?

Therapist's Advice: This cycle combines overcompensation by one partner, who seeks to impose their needs directly, with active avoidance by the other partner, who physically withdraws and seeks self-soothing activities. If the latter partner were to avoid disconnecting from themselves and their partner, the cycle would be one of dominance–passive avoidance.

The dominance–active avoidance Mode Cycle emerged in the case of Isabella and Caroline through the interaction between Isabella's overcompensation and Caroline's active avoidance. Both responses are grounded in the activation of the red leg (assertiveness–autonomy), although they are expressed differently: one through direct control and demands, and the other through distancing and the reaffirmation of autonomy outside the relationship.

Perpetuation of the Cycle: Isabella, by getting angry with Caroline and trying to control the expression of her sexual orientation to prevent others from finding out they are a couple (red leg), provokes a negative reaction in Caroline. In response, Caroline becomes upset, distances herself from Isabella, and reasserts her autonomy by expressing her sexual orientation with others (red leg). This generates a greater sense of threat in Isabella, as she fears being publicly associated with someone of a homosexual sexual orientation. As a result, Isabella intensifies her attempts to control Caroline (red leg), which leads Caroline to further distance herself and more determinedly reinforce her sexual orientation (red leg). Thus, the negative cycle is perpetuated.

When the red leg dominates in both partners, and the blue leg becomes blocked or remains in the background, this means it's necessary to activate the need for attachment and connection, the emotions of fear and sadness, and the flexible coping behavior of cooperation. Enabling both partners to foreground these elements is the goal of couples therapy in addressing this type of cycle in a couple.

3.3.3 Dominance–Submission Mode Cycle

This Mode Cycle describes how, within a couple, one partner tends to express their needs, while the other adopts a submissive role. Although this dynamic can be functional for a time, its rigidity can lead to dysfunction. In this scenario, one partner may appear selfish, focusing exclusively on their shortcomings, while the other adopts self-sacrificing behavior, constantly neglecting their own needs to meet those of their partner (Roediger, 2025).

Furthermore, this Mode Cycle is not static, as it can evolve into other dysfunctional patterns. For example, if the submissive partner decides to emotionally disconnect from the dominant partner, the passive-avoidant dominance cycle could emerge. On the other hand, if the submissive partner tires of their role and begins to overcompensate, this could lead to a dominance–domination cycle. Finally, if the dominant partner grows bored with a relationship with such a passive partner, they will likely seek to start a new relationship, which would end the current relationship (Roediger, 2025).

Similar to the passive dominance–avoidance cycle, this pattern can be represented through the metaphor of a dance. In this dynamic, one partner constantly advances while the other retreats. This "dance" reflects the dysfunctional relationship, where one partner seems to constantly pursue the other.

Over time, this dynamic tends to break down: the active partner may grow tired of advancing without response and decide to withdraw, while the passive partner may tire of continually retreating. In the latter case, the submissive partner may change their behavior, advancing abruptly and generating direct conflict, or disengage completely, perpetuating the cycle of avoidance.

To illustrate the dominance-submission cycle, we present the case of Richard and Christine, a 45-year-old couple who have recently faced various conflicts in their relationship. These problems arise primarily from power struggles related to financial management in the home.

Clinical Case 14 Richard and Christine, 45 years old

Christine and Richard are a couple who have recently faced conflicts triggered by Richard's retirement, after he stopped working due to an accident that left him disabled. This change impacted the family dynamics, especially in terms

(Continued)

Clinical Case 14 (Continued)

of finances and daily routines, since Richard now spends all his time at home. Faced with the decrease in pension income, Richard began imposing new rules related to savings, such as reducing water consumption, avoiding the purchase of certain products, or limiting the amount used on household chores (red leg). For her part, Christine tries to understand Richard's frustration with the new economic situation and his perception that his expenses are excessive. In response, she prioritizes being empathetic and adjusts her behavior: she saves water, uses less soap when washing clothes, and stops buying fabric softener, among other changes (blue leg). However, although there were apparently no open conflicts between them, Christine began to accumulate tension due to the constant criticism and restrictions. Eventually, Christine becomes overwhelmed and expresses her frustration explosively, demanding that Richard respect her way of doing household chores. This reaction temporarily leads the couple into a dominance–domination cycle, where direct confrontations arise. However, after this episode, Christine feels guilty about her reaction and returns to submissive behavior, once again responding to Richard's demands with empathy. This pattern, in which tension builds and eventually erupts, only to return to the original dynamic, perpetuates the dysfunctional cycle in their relationship.

Reflection: What needs and emotions predominate in each partner during this cycle? How do Richard's (overcompensation, red leg) and Christine's (submissive, blue leg) coping behaviors contribute to perpetuating this pattern?

Therapist's Advice: This cycle reflects a combination of overcompensation on the part of one partner, who seeks to impose their needs directly, and submission on the part of the other, who gives in. However, when the submissive partner tires of this role and begins to overcompensate, attempting to control or impose their position, the couple can transition into a dominance–domination cycle.

Perpetuation of the Cycle: Richard, angered by the perception that Christine is not using household resources efficiently, constantly demands changes (red leg). In response, Christine, feeling saddened by Richard's frustration, voluntarily and consciously acquiesces to his demands (blue leg). However, by not setting clear limits on Richard's demands, she ends up validating his attitude, which reinforces his perception that it is always possible to save more. This causes Richard to continue feeling dissatisfied and angry when identifying new ways in which Christine could reduce her resource use. Thus, despite Christine's efforts, her complacency does not calm Richard's frustration, but rather validates his demanding attitude, perpetuating the cycle. Richard demands changes again, and the dysfunctional dynamic repeats itself.

In this type of cycle, the first partner (Richard) is excessively anchored in his red leg, which blocks or neglects his blue leg. For this reason, the therapeutic goal for this partner focuses on helping him reconnect with his attachment–connection needs, his fear-sadness emotions, and fostering flexible, cooperative coping behaviors.

On the other hand, the second partner (Christine) is fixated on her blue leg, displaying submissive behavior that perpetuates the dynamic. The therapeutic goal for this partner is to strengthen her ability to activate her red leg, that is, to develop her need for assertiveness and autonomy. This involves connecting with emotions such as anger or disgust in a functional way and promoting flexible coping behavior based on assertiveness.

3.3.4 Avoidance–Avoidance Mode Cycle

The avoidance–avoidance Mode Cycle describes a couple's interaction where both partners use an avoidance-based coping mode, either active (red leg) or passive (blue leg). This cycle can occur in three distinct configurations (Roediger, 2025):

1. **Passive Avoidance–Passive Avoidance:** Both partners are in their blue leg, focused on their need for attachment and connection, dominated by emotions of fear or sadness. In this cycle, each partner opts for passive avoidance coping, in which both partners give in, but disconnect from themselves, their partner, and their environment.
2. **Active Avoidance–Active Avoidance:** In this case, both partners are in the red leg, prioritizing their need for assertiveness and autonomy, accompanied by emotions of anger or disgust. This coping mode is characterized by fleeing from the conflict, seeking compensatory activities (e.g., distractions or hobbies) that provide self-comfort but reinforce mutual disconnection.
3. **Active Avoidance–Passive Avoidance:** One partner is in their red leg, focused on their need for assertiveness and autonomy, and experiencing emotions such as anger or disgust. This partner physically distances themselves from their partner, seeking refuge in compensatory activities. Meanwhile, the other partner is in their blue leg, prioritizing their need for attachment and connection, experiencing emotions of fear or sadness, and adopting a passive avoidance mode that disconnects them from both themselves and their partner.

The avoidance–avoidance cycle can be represented through the metaphor of a dance, with three possible dynamics: Both partners take steps back, increasingly distancing themselves emotionally. Both move forward, but in opposite directions, which creates a physical disconnect. One partner takes a step back, distancing themselves emotionally, while the other moves forward in a different direction from their partner. In any of these scenarios, the result is the same: the partners distance themselves emotionally and/or physically, perpetuating the cycle of disconnection.

3.3.4.1 Passive Avoidance–Passive Avoidance Mode Cycle

The passive avoidance–passive avoidance Mode Cycle, in which both partners are in their blue leg, as a way to satisfy their need for attachment–connection and cope with emotions of fear or sadness, both partners freeze, disconnecting from their own emotions and those of their partner. To illustrate this Mode Cycle in couples, let's look at the case of Emmanuel and Valeria.

Clinical Case 15 Emmanuel, 56 years old and Valerie, 54 years old

Emmanuel and Valerie seek therapy due to a mutual feeling of emotional distance in their relationship. Both report that, although they don't have open conflicts or frequent arguments, they feel a growing dissatisfaction and loneliness that has begun to chill their bond as a couple. Valerie perceives Emmanuel as constantly sad in the relationship, which generates fear of losing him. However, instead of directly addressing this concern and asking Emmanuel what he needs to feel better, Valerie chooses to emotionally disconnect from her fear and his sadness. This passive avoidance mechanism (blue leg) allows her to avoid a potential conflict, but at the same time contributes to deepening the distance between them. On the other hand, Emmanuel interprets Valerie's attitude as a sign of disconnection or lack of interest in the relationship. This generates sadness in him, but like Valerie, he chooses not to express this emotion. Instead, Emmanuel avoids confronting what might be happening between them and emotionally disconnects from the relationship, also repeating a pattern of passive avoidance (blue leg). If Emmanuel could connect with his anger and his need for assertiveness and autonomy, he could directly express his desires and ask Valerie to be more affectionate and attentive in her dealings with him (red leg). For her part, if Valerie could recognize her own need for assertiveness and autonomy and manage her fear of conflict, she could communicate to Emmanuel her desire for him to take more initiative in areas such as sexual intimacy (red leg).

Reflection: What needs and emotions predominate in each partner during this cycle? How do Emmanuel's (passive avoidance, blue leg) and Valerie's (passive avoidance, blue leg) coping behaviors contribute to perpetuating this pattern?

Therapist's Advice: In this cycle, both partners disconnect from their need for assertiveness–autonomy, their emotions of anger or disgust. If one partner withdraws from the other, but does so physically, trying to satisfy their need for assertiveness–autonomy with compensatory activities, the cycle would be active avoidance–passive avoidance. If, for some reason, one partner adopts a stance of direct confrontation with their needs and the expression of anger or disgust, the cycle would shift to dominance–passive avoidance. The submission–passive avoidance cycle is uncommon and is more difficult to establish because if one partner is actively seeking to satisfy their need for attachment–connection (submission), it is more difficult for the other partner to remain emotionally disconnected.

Perpetuation of the Cycle: Valerie, perceiving that Emmanuel is distant, avoids directly asking about his emotions and needs, despite her need for attachment–connection, prompting her to do so. Instead, she emotionally disconnects, driven by the fear that such a conversation will generate conflict between them (blue leg). Emmanuel, for his part, also responds similarly. Noticing that Valerie seems sad and emotionally distant, he chooses not to address the situation for fear of confronting her. Instead, he disconnects from his own emotions and avoids exploring what is really happening between them (blue leg). This passive avoidance–passive avoidance cycle leaves both partners trapped in a pattern of emotional disconnection, where the blue leg predominates. In their attempt to escape fear and sadness, both partners relegate their red leg to the background, preventing them from accessing their need for assertiveness–autonomy, and the emotions of anger or disgust that could help them break the cycle.

The main objective in therapy will be for both partners to reconnect with their need for assertiveness and autonomy, allowing them to access their emotions of anger and disgust as a resource for expressing their needs in a healthy way. Through the development of flexible coping behaviors based on initiative and assertiveness, both partners will be able to assertively confront difficulties in the relationship, breaking the pattern of disconnection and preventing the cycle from continuing.

3.3.4.2 Active Avoidance–Active Avoidance Mode Cycle

In this Mode Cycle, characterized by mutual active avoidance, both partners resort to their "red leg" to cope with the anger or displeasure generated by the frustration of their need for assertiveness and autonomy. Instead of facing the conflict directly, both partners emotionally detach from their partner and seek to satisfy their needs individually through self-soothing activities. This pattern not only perpetuates disconnection but also intensifies the emotional distance in the relationship.

To illustrate this cycle, we present the case of Alfredo and Alice. Both have developed active avoidance behaviors that, far from resolving the problems in their relationship, have contributed to a progressive distancing between them, affecting the stability and emotional connection they shared.

Clinical Case 16 Alfred and Alice, 55 years old

Alfred and Alice are facing a relationship crisis due to infidelity, a situation that comes as a surprise to both of them, as they believed their relationship was in good shape. However, this perception of stability was based on a disconnection and avoidance patterns that both adopted to deal with their dissatisfaction. Alfred feels annoyed when he perceives Alice becoming distracted while he tries to share personal situations. Instead of expressing his displeasure directly, he chooses to stop telling her his problems and resorts to gambling and alcohol consumption as a form of active evasion to satisfy his need for autonomy and assertiveness (red leg). For her part, Alice also experiences disgust when she notices Alfred's disconnection when he turns to gambling and alcohol. However, instead of addressing the problem directly, she seeks attention through provocative posts on social media and responding to the comments generated by those posts. In this way, both avoid confronting the problem directly, perpetuating a dynamic of emotional distancing. Although these avoidance behaviors initially seemed to satisfy their individual assertiveness and autonomy needs, over the long term, they eroded the connection in the relationship. This emotional void intensified until Alfred, seeking comfort and connection from his friend Catalina, ended up committing an act of infidelity by kissing her.

Reflection: What needs and emotions predominate in each partner during this cycle? How do Alfred's (active avoidance, red leg) and Alice's (active avoidance, red leg) coping behaviors contribute to maintaining this pattern?

Therapist Advice: This cycle is a clear example of an active avoidance–active avoidance pattern, in which both partners attempt to satisfy their need for assertiveness–autonomy outside of the relationship, avoiding directly confronting their emotions and needs with the other. If one partner were to adopt a passive avoidance stance, completely disconnecting from their needs instead of seeking satisfaction through other means, the cycle would shift to active avoidance–passive avoidance. On the other hand, if one partner were to attempt to express their needs directly, but from a controlling or domineering perspective, the cycle would transform into dominance–active avoidance, generating a direct conflict with one partner seeking to impose their perspective.

The previous case illustrates how the active avoidance of both partners (red leg) reinforces the Mode Cycle, showing that these coping strategies, although aimed at protecting their respective needs, ultimately deepen the disconnection and emotional distancing within the relationship.

Perpetuation of the Cycle: The more Alfred avoids confronting his anger with Alice by turning to alcohol and gambling (red leg), the more frustrated and annoyed Alice becomes. Alice, in turn, responds by avoiding Alfred and seeking refuge in social media (red leg). This dynamic of active avoidance on both sides perpetuates the emotional distancing. As Alice ignores Alfred, he feels increasingly ignored, leading him to intensify his retreat into alcohol and gambling (red leg). Thus, the cycle of active avoidance perpetuates, reinforcing the disconnect between them and making it difficult to directly address their needs and emotions.

The goal in this Mode Cycle is for both partners to connect more with their blue leg, actively seeking to connect with the needs of the other partner, actively seeking to understand them and their needs. Similarly, both partners could connect with the sadness or fear of seeing their partner disconnected physically and emotionally from them and exhibit the flexible coping behavior of giving in and cooperating to change the situation.

3.3.4.3 Active Avoidance–Passive Avoidance Mode Cycle

The active avoidance–passive avoidance cycle is composed of one partner who is focused on their red leg, their need for assertiveness–autonomy, their anger or disgust, and who uses an active avoidance coping mode, in which they physically withdraw from their partner and seek self-soothing activities outside the relationship. The other partner is fixated on their blue leg, their need for attachment–connection, and their fear or sadness, in addition to using a passive avoidance coping mode, in which they dissociate from their emotions and from their partner. This active avoidance–passive avoidance pattern intensifies the disconnection between partners in the relationship.

To explain the cycle, we present the case of Steven and Claire. Steven has developed active avoidance behaviors, which lead to physical distance from his partner and the need to seek satisfaction outside of them. Claire has developed passive avoidance behaviors, which cause her to disconnect from the situation and increase the emotional disconnection between them.

Clinical Case 17 Steven, 53 years old and Claire, 42 years old

Steven and Claire have decided to attend couples therapy due to the growing physical and emotional distance they both perceive in their relationship. Steven, focused on his need for autonomy and assertiveness, has adopted an active avoidance stance. After long workdays, he prefers to spend his free time on activities like going to the gym instead of spending time with Claire. Furthermore, he has expressed frustration regarding Claire's weight, indicating that he has grown tired of insisting that she lose weight and has decided not to address the topic further (red leg). Claire, focused on her need for attachment and connection, has developed a passive avoidance strategy. Although her doctor explained that her thyroid problem makes weight loss difficult and that, due to a back condition, she can only exercise in water, Claire decides not to share this information with Steven. Instead of explaining her medical situation, she chooses to apologize to him to avoid conflict. This attitude leads her to disconnect from reality and not face Steven's frustration regarding his inability to lose weight (blue leg). The lack of open communication about these issues has led Steven to assume that Claire isn't making any effort to improve her physical condition, which leads her to distance herself further. Consequently, Steven seeks to satisfy his need for interaction and attraction at the gym by striking up conversations with people he finds attractive (red leg). This behavior generates feelings of fear and insecurity in Claire; however, she chooses to emotionally disconnect to avoid confronting the reality that her physique won't change anytime soon (blue leg).

This pattern of behavior has trapped both of them in a cycle where their coping strategies, based on active avoidance on Steven's part and passive avoidance on Claire's part, perpetuate the disconnection rather than fostering a solution.

Reflection: What needs and emotions predominate in each partner during this cycle? How do Steven's (active avoidance, red leg) and Claire's (passive avoidance, blue leg) coping behaviors contribute to maintaining this pattern?

Therapist's Advice: This pattern is a clear example of an active avoidance–passive avoidance cycle, where both partners attempt to protect their respective needs through strategies that, rather than resolving conflicts, reinforce emotional distancing. In this cycle, one partner (Steven) has the need for assertiveness–autonomy activated, along with the emotions of anger or disgust. To deal with this situation, this partner uses active avoidance as a coping mode, physically distancing themselves and seeking to satisfy their needs with other people. The other partner (Claire) is fixated on her need for attachment–connection, her need for sadness or fear, and her passive avoidance coping mode, which protects her from confrontations with her partner by dissociating herself from reality. If Claire were to decide to seek satisfaction of her emotional needs outside the relationship, the cycle would shift to an active avoidance–active avoidance pattern, resulting in more evident mutual distancing. On the other hand, if Steven were to become more concerned about Claire's feelings but avoid expressing them so as not to cause conflict, the cycle would transform into passive avoidance–passive avoidance, with both partners emotionally disconnected and inactive when faced with problems. In a different scenario, if Steven were to decide to be more direct and control Claire so she loses weight, the cycle would become one of dominance-passive avoidance.

The previous case showed how the coping strategies of both partners—the active avoidance of Steven (red leg) and the passive avoidance of Claire (blue leg)—reinforce this cycle. Although these behaviors seek to protect their respective needs, they ultimately increase the disconnection and emotional distancing in the relationship, leaving the underlying conflict unresolved.

Perpetuation of the Cycle: In this active avoidance–passive avoidance cycle, when Steven seeks to spend time with women he finds attractive or to exercise alone, he does so motivated by the perception that Claire doesn't care about her weight (red leg). This behavior increases Claire's fear that Steven will abandon her because of her excess weight. To cope with this insecurity, Claire chooses to disconnect from reality and avoid confronting her situation. Although she knows that her health problems make it difficult to change her appearance in the short term (blue leg), she dissociates from her emotions to momentarily reduce her fear. However, this emotional disconnection doesn't solve the problem. In the medium term, Steven becomes frustrated when he sees no changes in Claire's physique, which fuels his anger and reinforces his decision to continue exercising without her (red leg). In this way, the cycle of disconnection between them is perpetuated, where each partner's coping strategies contribute to maintaining emotional distance and hinder the resolution of the underlying conflict.

The main objective for transforming this Mode Cycle is for the partner using the active avoidance mode to foreground their blue leg, that is, to focus on their need for attachment–connection, allowing themselves to recognize and express emotions such as fear or sadness, and adopting a flexible coping behavior of yielding and cooperating. On the other hand, the partner

Clinical Case 17 (Continued)

using the passive avoidance mode must redirect their attention to their red leg, activating their need for assertiveness–autonomy, connecting with emotions such as anger or disgust, and practicing a flexible coping behavior of initiative-assertiveness.

After identifying the coping cycles that generate conflicts in a couple, the next step is to expose the cycle in a way that can generate balance in the relationship. This cycle, by allowing for a more functional interaction between both partners, not only facilitates problem-solving but also prevents the emergence of long-term conflicts, which often arise when one of the basic needs (either the red or the blue leg) is abused. This new cycle is called assertiveness/cooperation-cooperation/assertiveness, and represents a model in which both partners find a healthy balance between their needs for assertiveness–autonomy and attachment–connection.

3.3.5 Assertiveness/Cooperation–Cooperation/Assertiveness Mode Cycle

Establishing this Mode Cycle is a proposal designed to help partners address problems in their relationship. Its main objective is to achieve a balance between the basic needs of both partners, promoting the harmonious use of the two legs (assertiveness–autonomy and attachment–connection). It is emphasized that, although it is not possible to completely control whether the other partner tends more toward being dominant or submissive, it is within their control to work on their own balance of needs, emotions, and coping behaviors. This approach not only allows for better personal management but can also positively influence the couple and the relational dynamics, helping to meet the emotional needs of both partners.

To illustrate the assertiveness/cooperation–cooperation/assertiveness cycle, we present the case of Andrés and Emilia, a 38-year-old couple who, thanks to the help of Couple Schema Therapy, have learned to balance their basic needs and significantly improve the quality of their relationship.

Clinical Case 18 Andrew and Emily, 28 years old

Andrew and Emily have recently faced financial difficulties, as Emily lost her job, forcing them to adjust their household expenses. One afternoon, upon returning from work, Andrew felt angry because Emily began listing all the pending expenses as soon as she got home (red leg). Andrew reacted assertively by expressing his need for autonomy and connection: "I feel a little overwhelmed because I've been worried a lot about money. Also, today was a tough day for me, and I feel annoyed because when I get home, all I hear is how much I still need to buy" (red leg). "I understand that you also worry about what's missing and that you want to solve it quickly" (blue leg), "that's why I would like us to talk about other things when I get home so I can take my mind off the stress of work" (red leg). "In return, I commit to being more available to listen to financial problems and address pending expenses" (blue leg). Initially, Emily reacted angrily, feeling attacked, as she interpreted Andrew as implying that she was selfish for not considering his tiredness. However, she remembered what they've worked on in couples therapy and responded with vulnerability, balancing her needs: "I understand you're tired from work, and you're right that I should wait a little longer before discussing these issues with you; I don't mean to overwhelm you" (blue leg). "But I also feel worried. During my childhood, we went through several economic crises, in which, at times, basic services like gas, water, or electricity were cut off. That's why it bothers me to see overdue bills" (red leg). "I'm willing to give you your space when you arrive before reminding you of outstanding bills" (blue leg). "However, I would ask that you make an effort to prioritize paying bills before the due date" (red leg).

Reflection: What needs and emotions predominate in each member during this cycle? How do Andrew's (assertiveness/cooperation, red-blue legs) and Emily's (cooperation/assertiveness, blue-red legs) coping behaviors contribute to maintaining this pattern?

Therapist's Advice: This pattern represents an example of a healthy Mode Cycle, in which both partners manage to balance their two legs (red leg and blue leg). In this cycle, each partner is able to assertively express the need for the other to modify their behavior. This includes an assertive and regulated expression of emotions such as anger or disgust, associated with the need for assertiveness and autonomy (red leg). Subsequently, each partner can also connect with their need for attachment and connection, expressing emotions of fear or sadness in a regulated manner and adopting cooperative coping behavior (blue leg). This balance between assertiveness and cooperation allows for a more constructive interaction, promoting both personal well-being and strengthening the relational bond. A key aspect of this healthy cycle is that both partners are able to identify which "leg" is activated in themselves and in the other during an argument. This allows them to adapt to the situation, using the opposite leg to the one their partner is using. This perspective favors reciprocity: once one "leg" is activated, space opens up for the other to come into play, promoting mutual balance. This dynamic process can be understood as a kind of relational "dance," where each partner follows the other's lead until a harmonious interaction is achieved.

(Continued)

Clinical Case 18 (Continued)

The following chart shows how assertiveness/cooperation coping strategies (red and blue legs) reinforce the cycle. Balancing needs, emotions, and flexible coping behaviors ultimately creates a balance between both partners and resolves problems as they arise (Figure 3.3).

Perpetuation of the Cycle: Andrew's initial balance between his needs allowed him to assertively express his request to Emily, asking her not to mention the expenses immediately upon arriving home (red leg). At the same time, Andrew was receptive to her concern, committing to paying the outstanding bills (blue leg). In many cases, this type of balanced response can resolve the problem from this first step. However, in this case, Emily activated her need for assertiveness (red leg), feeling angry that Andrew was suggesting that she was selfish, which prolonged the cycle. Emily's response demonstrated a balance between her needs, as she agreed to Andrew's request not to address financial issues immediately upon arriving home (blue leg). At the same time, she expressed her need for assertiveness, asking him to prioritize paying the bills before the due date (red leg). In this case, the cycle

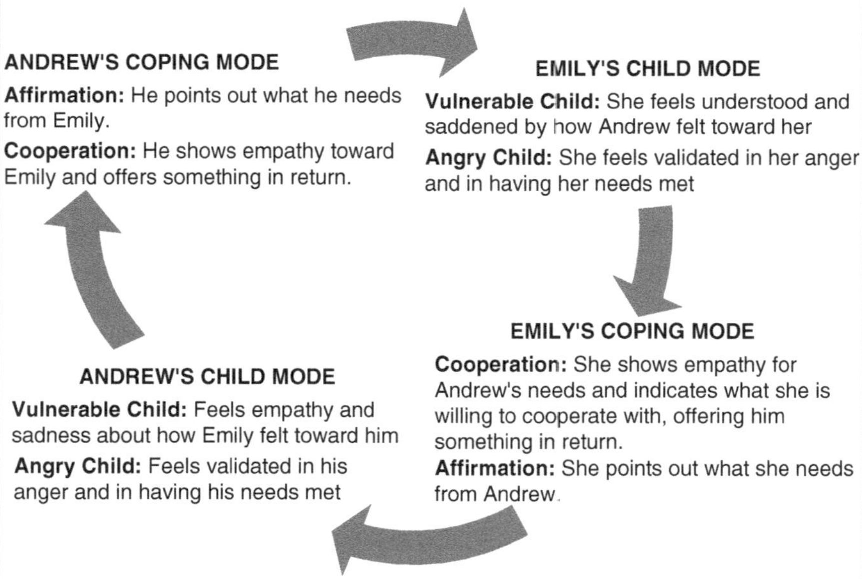

Figure 3.3 Assertiveness/cooperation–cooperation/assertiveness Mode Cycle, reflected in Andrew and Emily.

ended here, resolving the problem. Both partners of the couple managed to assert themselves while connecting with each other's needs.

It is important to clarify that, although all the Mode Cycles are described in this chapter, in the following chapters, the cases will be more oriented to describing the dynamics between the dominance–avoidance cycles (passive and active), avoidance–avoidance, and dominance–domination, since these cases represent the majority of couple interactions that reach therapy (Roediger and Frank, 2021). However, these types of dynamics, as mentioned above, can change throughout the interaction between couples.

3.4 Identifying Child and Coping Modes in Therapy Using Chairs

During the session, the therapist uses chairs to help partners identify the active coping mode (behaviors) and the active child mode (emotions). To facilitate this process, the therapist introduces the analogy of a stage. At the front of the stage are the coping modes, representing the observable behaviors that others can see (chairs 2A and 2B in Figure 3.4). At the back of the stage are the child modes, which represent the emotions experienced internally and are often less visible to others (chairs 4A and 4B in Figure 3.4).

To illustrate this arrangement, the therapist places one chair at the front to represent the active coping mode displayed by one partner of the couple. Behind it, symbolizing the backstage, two chairs are placed to represent the child modes: one for the vulnerable child and one for the angry child.

To analyze what is occurring in the different coping and child modes, the therapist asks the couple to stand up, thereby forming an observer team. From this position, the active and blocked modes that emerged during the interaction can be identified (with the therapist in position 1B and the partners in positions 5A and 5B in Figure 3.4).

Once this framework has been explained, the therapeutic work across sessions involves placing the active coping mode in the front chair and the child modes behind it. Typically, the person first sits in the chair representing the active child mode and, as therapy progresses, moves to the chair representing the blocked or background child mode. During the cognitive work, the partners and the therapist stand and adopt a metacognitive perspective from which they analyze what occurred in the couple's interaction during the session.

As the therapy process progresses and the therapeutic model has been internalized, the therapist may choose a simplified chair-work model, in which one chair

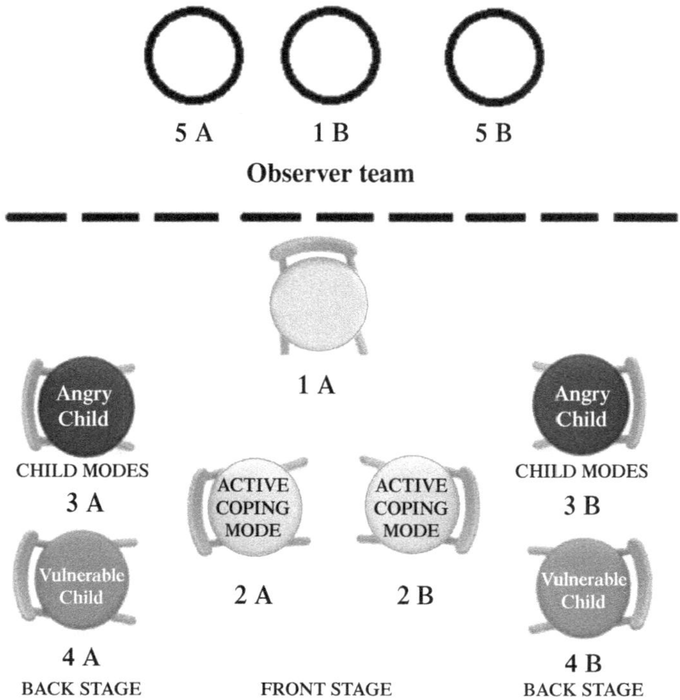

Figure 3.4 Chair arrangement to represent coping modes, child modes, and the observer team in therapy.

is used to represent both the coping mode and the child mode for each partner (Figure 3.5).

This arrangement will be used throughout the book to describe the different chair configurations employed during therapeutic interventions. To facilitate understanding, Figure 3.5 shows and numbers the chairs representing each mode, as well as the possible positions that both the therapist and each partner of the couple may occupy. In addition, to provide a visual reference for chair work, readers are invited throughout the book to consult Figure 3.5, which illustrates the placement of the chairs and the spaces used during the intervention.

In some cases, once the couple has understood the two-leg model, the therapist may choose to use a brief version of the chair work. In this modality, a single chair is used to work with both the active coping modes and their healthy counterparts, as well as the active child modes and those that are blocked or pushed into the background. In these cases, chairs 2A and 2B in Figure 3.5 are used to place the different modes as they are identified and addressed during the intervention: chair 2A is used for one partner of the couple, and chair 2B for the other.

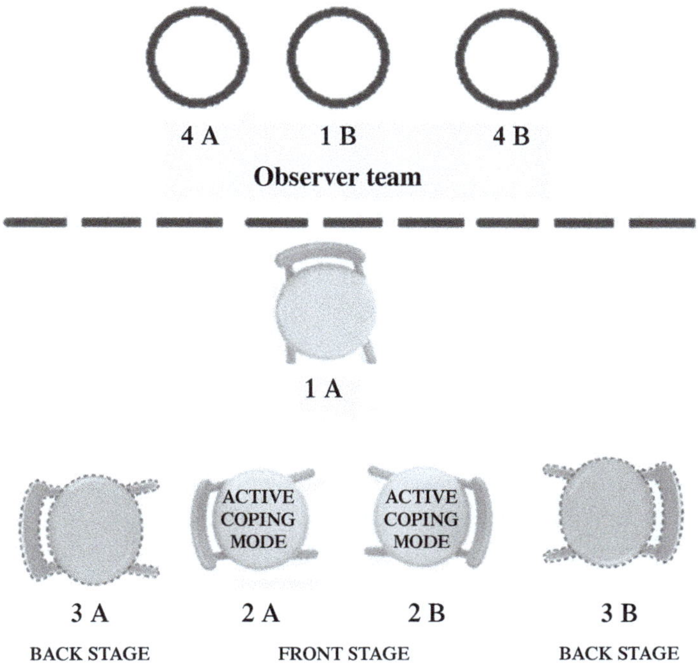

Figure 3.5 Simplified chair work to represent coping modes and active child modes in therapy.

Before continuing, it is important to clarify that the chair arrangement described earlier is intended to help the reader understand the different positions that therapy participants may adopt during the therapist's interventions, both cognitive and experiential, particularly when the couple is invited to speak directly to each other. The numbering of the chairs used in this description corresponds to that shown in Figure 3.5, which serves as a reference for identifying the position of each participant during the therapeutic work. However, at the beginning of the session, before any intervention takes place, the seating arrangement is different. In this initial position, the therapist sits in chair 1A, while each partner of the couple sits in chairs 2A and 2B, respectively. These chairs are positioned rotated approximately 90°, so that both partners of the couple are facing the therapist directly.

4

Neurological and Cerebral Bases of Therapeutic Interventions

4.1 Introduction

Therapeutic work not only involves teaching, guiding, and training the couple to develop new skills that improve their relationship with themselves and their partner, but also encompasses a deep process of interaction with the neural circuits that support their thoughts, emotions, and behaviors (Johnson, 2004; Siegel, 2010; Van der Kolk, 2014; Schore, 2003; Fisher, 2004; Gottman and Gottman, 2015; Damasio, 1994; Perry and Szalavitz, 2006; Davidson and Begley, 2012; Hebb, 1949).

From a neuroscientific perspective, clients' beliefs and behavioral patterns are sustained by neural networks that have been formed and consolidated throughout life through repeated experiences. These networks also determine how the client processes the past. In this process, episodic and working memory play a crucial role, helping to economize brain resources by automating responses or the so-called "autopilot" (Damasio, 1994; Hebb, 1949; Siegel, 2012; Perry and Szalavitz, 2006; Van der Kolk, 2014; Barrett, 2017; Davidson and Begley, 2012; Pascual-Leone, 2001).

Promoting therapeutic change requires clients to develop neuroplasticity, which is the brain's ability to form new connections and reorganize existing ones. However, this process is neither immediate nor simple; it requires a conscious effort to unlearn established patterns and build new neural networks that support a different way of interpreting the past, perceiving current relationships, and responding in the present (Hebb, 1949; Doidge, 2007; Pascual-Leone, 2001; Van der Kolk, 2014; Siegel, 2012; Schwartz and Begley, 2002; Merzenich, 2013; Damasio, 1994; Davidson and Begley, 2012; Dweck, 2006).

- This "relearning" involves a high consumption of brain resources, which can generate resistance to change, since the brain tends to avoid significant efforts to preserve energy and maintain homeostatic balance (Kahneman, 2011; Damasio, 1994; Doidge, 2007; Hebb, 1949; Davidson and Begley, 2012; Siegel, 2012; Merzenich, 2013; Perry and Szalavitz, 2006; Barrett, 2017; Sweller, 1988).

The energetic cost of this process is challenging since the brain consumes approximately 20% of the body's energy at rest, and this consumption will increase during the reconfiguration process due to the effort needed to carry out the following brain processes (Raichle and Gusnard, 2002):

- **Forming New Synaptic Connections:** Neurons generate new connections to represent the new narrative by strengthening synapses through long-term potentiation (Bliss and Lømo, 1973).
- **Modifying Existing Memories:** This requires simultaneous activation of the hippocampus (memory), the dorsolateral prefrontal cortex (conscious reasoning), and the amygdala (emotional processing) for the brain to integrate the new perception of reality (Nader and Einarsson, 2010; Ochsner and Gross, 2005).
- **Network Competition:** Old and new networks compete for activation, requiring greater effort by the brain to reorganize (McClelland et al., 1995).
- **Modifying Associated Emotions:** Changing neural networks not only reorganizes memories, but also the associated emotions. This process is mediated by the limbic system, particularly the amygdala, which manages emotional responses to change (Phelps and LeDoux, 2005).
- **Increased Conscious Activity:** Getting out of "autopilot" and entering a state of conscious observation involves greater activity in the dorsolateral prefrontal cortex (Miller and Cohen, 2001).
- **Impact on Identity:** On the one hand, adjusting one's sense of identity involves activating regions such as the medial prefrontal cortex, which is responsible for integrating one's personal narrative (Northoff et al., 2006). On the other hand, facing cognitive dissonance (Festinger, 1957) implies that during the transition, old and new networks coexist, and a dissonance arises that generates a state of internal conflict, in which the brain must reconcile previous beliefs with new information, generating emotional and cognitive stress.

In some cases, therapeutic interventions can lead to profound cognitive reorganization, challenging core beliefs that clients have held for years (or their entire lives). This process can temporarily destabilize their sense of identity or security, creating a sense of uncertainty while new connections are rebuilt. This phenomenon is especially relevant in situations where the client experiences a dissonance between what they previously believed to be true and the new insights that emerge in therapy (Festinger, 1957; Damasio, 1994; Van der Kolk, 2014; Schwartz and Begley, 2002; Johnson, 2004; Siegel, 2012; Barrett, 2017; Pascual-Leone, 2001; Davidson and Begley, 2012; Dweck, 2006).

Given this context, it's understandable that change can be slow and challenging. Motivation, both intrinsic and extrinsic, plays a fundamental role in facilitating the brain's willingness to engage in this process of change. Therefore, in therapy, we not only work on cognitive, emotional, and behavioral levels, but also create an environment that facilitates neurobrain processes to foster this transformative process. This approach allows new neural connections to strengthen over time, fostering lasting changes in the couple's relationship and self-perception (Deci and Ryan, 1985; Doidge, 2007; Pascual-Leone, 2001; Siegel, 2012; Schwartz and Begley, 2002; Johnson, 2004; Dweck, 2006; Davidson and Begley, 2012; Perry and Szalavitz, 2006; Damasio, 1994).

To examine this in greater detail, let's look at the case of Roger, who is seeking couples therapy due to the problems between his mother and his wife, Monica. She is unwilling to continue unless he changes the dynamics between the two families.

Clinical Case 19 Roger and Monica, 35 years old

Roger and Monica came to therapy due to an ultimatum posed by Monica: if Roger didn't set clear boundaries with his mother, their relationship would end. During the first sessions, the therapist introduced the possibility that Roger's mother might have narcissistic traits. Initially, Roger was reluctant to accept this idea, as he had grown up perceiving his mother as a woman who had suffered greatly and sacrificed for him. For Roger, his mother was a symbol of selflessness and sacrifice. However, as the sessions progressed, a different reality began to emerge. With the therapist's support, Roger began to observe patterns in his mother's behavior that displayed selfish and manipulative attitudes. His mother used victimization to generate sympathy and manipulate others, making him feel indebted and guilty for the "sacrifices" she had supposedly made for him. This new perspective revealed that what he had interpreted as acts of sacrifice were, in fact, basic responsibilities inherent to motherhood. This discovery represented a significant internal conflict for Roger, who found himself confronted with two opposing realities: was his mother a victim or a narcissist? After one of the most intense sessions, Roger emerged emotionally exhausted and confused. These emotions accompanied him for the following weeks as he tried to reinterpret numerous memories from his life from this new perspective. Little by little, Roger began to modify his way of living with his mother. Instead of reacting automatically, he adopted a more observant stance, analyzing the dynamics between them and contrasting them with the theories proposed by the therapist. This change marked a process of transformation both in his perception of his mother and in his way of relating to her, although the path proved challenging and emotionally demanding.

In Roger's case, the process of changing his perception of his mother involves a profound neuronal reconfiguration, as his brain must modify the established neural networks that support his old reality and form new connections that represent the current information.

During the first therapy sessions, Roger operated from the old neural networks that sustained the belief that his mother was a self-sacrificing woman, a victim of difficult circumstances. These networks were deeply consolidated by years of family experiences, emotional memories, and social narratives that reinforced this view. Whenever Roger thought of his mother as a figure who suffered for him, these neural connections were automatically activated, providing a sense of stability in his perception.

The therapist's suggestion that Roger's mother might have narcissistic traits and manipulate through victimization generated an internal conflict. This new information simultaneously activated old neural networks (which supported the image of his mother as a victim) and brain areas responsible for processing discrepancies, such as the dorsolateral prefrontal cortex, which analyzes the logic of new information, and the amygdala, which managed the emotional threat posed by this change.

As Roger explored episodes from his past, he began to recognize patterns of behavior in his mother that fit the description presented by the therapist. This marked the beginning of the formation of new neural connections, which represented his mother as selfish and manipulative, rather than a victim. These memories, which previously seemed isolated, began to integrate into a new narrative framework. However, these new connections were weak at first and required repetition and reflection to consolidate.

Roger's brain experienced a conflict between old and new neural networks. While the old ones continued to fire automatically, reinforced by years of experience, the new ones began to compete for space and relevance. This clash caused mental exhaustion, as the brain tried to reconcile two contradictory realities. For example, every time he recalled moments in which his mother appeared self-sacrificing, he had to reinterpret them as manipulative strategies, which required considerable cognitive effort.

One of the most profound changes occurred in Roger's memories. Situations he previously viewed as examples of his mother's sacrifice were now reinterpreted as manipulative acts designed to generate guilt. This memory reconsolidation process involved the hippocampus, which works to update memories, and the anterior cingulate cortex, which helps integrate new interpretations into his personal narrative. For example, moments when his mother claimed to have given up her dreams for him were no longer seen as genuine sacrifices, but rather as attempts to emotionally control him.

Roger began to move out of autopilot, where he reacted automatically to his mother's demands, and into a state of conscious observation. This meant that, instead of immediately feeling guilty or responsible, he could observe the dynamics between them and contrast them with the theory put forward by the therapist. This shift required increased activity in his prefrontal cortex, which regulates reflection and conscious decision-making, which was mentally exhausting but essential for establishing new forms of interaction.

Over time and with repetition, Roger began to consolidate the new neural connections that represented this new perception of his mother. These connections strengthened as he reflected on his current and past interactions and contrasted his experiences with the new narrative. At the same time, the old neural networks that supported his initial belief began to weaken due to a lack of reinforcement.

This change not only transformed the way Roger viewed his mother, but also how he interacted with her. By becoming more aware of manipulative dynamics, Roger was able to set clearer boundaries, breaking automatic behavior patterns, and responding in healthier ways, which was what Monica was asking of him in the relationship.

As can be seen in the previous case, therapy involves a change at the neuronal level in which the brain must reorganize and form new neural connections in response to the learning or experience being had in the therapeutic process. For this neuronal reconfiguration to occur, it takes weeks to months, depending on the emotional intensity, constant practice, and repetition (Kandel, 2001; Doidge, 2007). That is, they require conscious effort to be activated, since in the first weeks the new connections are weak (Kleim and Jones, 2008). For these new neural networks to compete with the old ones and achieve greater stability, they must be repeated and practiced (Hebb, 1949). Only after months of consistent practice do the new networks become strengthened, and the old ones are eliminated through synaptic pruning (Chechik et al., 1999).

It is important to note that, although not all cases are as extreme as the one described above, the neuronal and emotional reconfiguration processes described tend to occur to a greater or lesser extent in most cases. Therefore, it is essential for the therapist to have well-founded strategies to effectively address these situations, considering the brain processes involved. These strategies should be designed to facilitate the integration of new perceptions, manage resistance to change, and promote an emotionally safe transition toward a more adaptive understanding of relational dynamics.

4.2 Stimulate Executive Function to Get Out of Autopilot and Intense Emotional States

As reviewed in the previous section, the process of change or learning involves the establishment of new neural connections, which can be strengthened through awareness and repetition. These new neural connections, or "new pathways," eventually replace the "old pathways" associated with previous learning. This change requires the activation of the dorsolateral prefrontal cortex, a key region for executive control, which allows the client to move from the "autopilot" state to a more conscious and deliberate approach.

An effective strategy for fostering this shift is "mode awareness," a state in which the person adopts a metacognitive or observant stance. This approach helps interrupt "autopilot" and allows for analyzing what is happening from a more objective perspective. Mode awareness is especially useful when the client faces a situation that generates intense emotions associated with emotional memories. In such cases, the emotional memory activates the amygdala, which can lead to a reactive response. Adopting a mindful stance allows the client to distance themselves from that emotional state and analyze it from an external, reflective position (Valente in Roediger and Valente, 2025).

Below are some techniques that can be used to help the client manage intense emotional arousal and develop greater conscious control over their responses (Roediger and Valente, 2025).

- **Awareness of the Negative Implications of Coping:** This strategy encourages clients to reflect on whether their emotional and behavioral responses are facilitating or hindering the satisfaction of their emotional needs. This analysis promotes greater self-understanding and encourages change in maladaptive patterns.
- **Awareness of the Positive Implications of Flexible Coping:** This strategy helps to avoid polarizing behaviors by understanding that taking initiative and firmness, as well as yielding and cooperating, are behaviors that, when balanced, facilitate the establishment of a healthy dynamic in the couple's relationship.
- **Speaking in the Third Person:** Using third-person language allows the client to distance themselves from their immediate experience and assume a metacognitive stance. By speaking about themselves and their partner in this

way, it is possible to observe personal and relational dynamics from a more objective and analytical perspective.

- **Changing Posture or Moving:** Making a physical change, such as standing or walking, helps interrupt "autopilot mode" and reduce the emotional activation of emotional memories, facilitating the transition to a reflective state. In therapy, this may include taking the couple out of a direct face-to-face interaction and placing them in a standing position, which symbolizes observing the situation "from above." This change in posture facilitates emotional distancing by generating a broader view of what is happening in the moment, both internally and in the interaction with the other partner.
- **Bodywork:** Adopting an upright posture, with your head up and your shoulders relaxed, can facilitate access to internal resources that promote self-reflection and the shift from a reactive emotional state to a more conscious one.
- **Extension Technique:** In this strategy, the partner faces a problematic situation by adopting the perspective of another, trusted, and kind person who provides advice. This technique broadens the client's perspective, reduces the emotional burden, and allows you to access blocked internal resources, promoting more effective solutions.

These strategies can be illustrated with the elevator metaphor (Valente in Roediger and Valente, 2025). If the client is overly emotionally aroused (on the "lower floor"), the therapist uses these cognitive techniques to "take the elevator up" to a more reflective level. These techniques are aimed at activating the dorsolateral prefrontal cortex and the brain's executive control system, promoting conscious analysis and emotional regulation.

Conversely, when a client is disconnected, ruminating, or rationalizing excessively (on the "top floor"), the therapist seeks to bring them "downstairs" through more experiential strategies. These techniques are designed to activate the amygdala and the brain's emotional system, facilitating access to emotions and promoting connection with deeper internal experiences. Strategies for this purpose are described in the following section.

4.3 Stimulate the Emotional System to Overcome Avoidance or Rational Blockage

As noted at the beginning of the chapter, the process of change requires a significant amount of brain energy, which can lead people, in some cases, to avoid being aware of certain emotions. This occurs especially when these emotions reveal that their previous interpretation of reality is no longer valid, which can generate cognitive dissonance and resistance to change. Likewise, reactions learned in the past, such as rationalizing or emotionally disconnecting, have been strategies that allowed them to cope adaptively with pain at the time. However, to promote significant change, it is necessary to activate the emotional system and connect with emotions, since these provide the energy and motivation necessary to induce transformation (Kahneman, 2011; Festinger, 1957; Van der Kolk, 2014; Siegel, 2012; LeDoux, 1996; Phelps and LeDoux, 2005; Schwartz and Begley, 2002; Davidson and Begley, 2012; Damasio, 1994; Deci and Ryan, 1985).

This process takes place at an emotional level, allowing people to access what they are feeling in the moment. This involves activating their emotional memory through the amygdala and other brain areas related to emotion regulation, such as the cingulate cortex and the hippocampus. These regions are key to integrating emotions and memories into a coherent narrative (LeDoux, 1996; Phelps and LeDoux, 2005; Damasio, 1994; Siegel, 2012; Van der Kolk, 2014; Ochsner and Gross, 2005).

An effective way to facilitate this emotional access is through "forward mode," which promotes connection with present or past emotions through bodily sensations (Valente in Roediger and Valente, 2025). This allows emotions and memories stored in the emotional system, particularly in the amygdala, to be activated and consciously processed. Some strategies for activating this mode include techniques that connect the body and mind, helping to bring associated emotions into the present and promoting emotional integration.

Below are some strategies designed to activate this mode and work with the emotions and memories stored in the emotional system (Roediger and Valente, 2025).

- **Use of Chairs:** The therapist uses chairs to represent the client's activated and blocked child modes, allowing them to express their emotions and work with core emotions more directly.
- **Use of First-person Language:** Clients are encouraged to use first-person language when expressing their emotions, for example, "I feel..." to foster a deeper connection with their emotional experience.
- **Tone of Voice and Personal Closeness:** The therapist adopts a close posture, speaking with a warm and gentle tone of voice, which facilitates an atmosphere of trust and emotional security.
- **Standing Behind the Partner:** This strategy makes it easier to connect with the partner's emotions. The other partner usually also connects with their partner's emotions through observation or imagination.
- **Closing Your Eyes:** Asking the client to close their eyes helps them disconnect from external stimuli, promoting a deeper connection with their internal emotional world.

- **Seated Exercise:** Performing the exercise in a seated position facilitates emotional activation, promoting a greater connection with basic emotions.
- **Focusing on Bodily Sensations:** The therapist guides the client to focus on specific physical sensations, such as those in the chest and stomach, which are directly related to basic emotions. Emotional language is also connected to these sensations.
- **Using Simple Words:** The therapist addresses the client in a simple and direct manner, using language similar to that which he or she would use to speak to a child, which facilitates the connection with the client's child state.
- **Adopting an Open Posture:** The client is encouraged to adopt an open body posture (without crossing arms or legs) and lean forward, which promotes greater emotional receptivity.
- **Imagery Exercises:** The client is invited to imagine a painful situation while paying attention to their bodily sensations, especially in the chest and stomach area.
- **Movement Amplification:** The therapist asks the client to amplify the small body movements they make unconsciously, helping to intensify and explore the associated emotions.
- **Activation of Negative Schemas:** The client is guided to focus their attention on dysfunctional thoughts, connecting them with their bodily sensations and child modes, facilitating emotional integration.
- **Limited Reparenting:** During emotional activation, the therapist supports the client through a limited reparenting experience, providing a corrective emotional experience and helping them overcome experiential avoidance.
- **Image Rewriting:** This involves working with the emotional memories that the negative schema is bringing from the past to the present. This is done through an imagination exercise in which both the therapist and the reparenting client's partner intervene to stop the traumatic event that occurred in childhood and/or adolescence and help the client satisfy the emotional need that was frustrated at that time in their life.
- **Substitution Technique:** Before reparenting their own vulnerable child, the client symbolically reparents a child in a similar situation, which facilitates practice and reduces resistance.
- **Mentalization:** This technique helps connect feelings with words, promoting reflection on the emotional experience. The therapist may use questions such as: "What did you feel in your body?" "What thoughts were you having at that moment?" "What did you really need?" and "How do you think the other person felt?" These questions foster a deeper understanding of the emotional and behavioral impact (Fonagy et al., 2002).

- **Using Cards to Represent the Vulnerable Child:** Providing a card that represents the Vulnerable Child Mode helps the client stay in touch with that emotion and work with it more effectively.

The above techniques lead the partner to go "upward" when they feel very emotionally activated or "downward" when they are emotionally blocked. In the first case, contextualization and metacognitive processing are used: The observer stance and explicit approach allow the client to reflect on their experience in a conscious and analytical manner. In the second case, implicit emotional processing is applied: Through reparenting and mentalization, the client connects with their deepest emotional world and associated memories, promoting a more complete emotional integration (Roediger and Valente, 2025).

Finally, there is a third approach called "choice mode," whose main objective is to activate behavioral responses in the client (Valente in Roediger and Valente, 2025). This mode is used as a complement to transform the state of emotional arousal into concrete actions. In other words, after becoming aware of the underlying emotions and needs, this mode allows the client to identify and verbalize what they need to do or request to satisfy those needs. The choice mode approach focuses on promoting action, directing communication directly toward their partner or the environment.

4.4 Moving from a Sympathetic State to a Parasympathetic State

One of the goals of couple schema therapy is to reestablish emotional connection between each partner. To achieve this, it is essential that both partners move from a fight-or-flight state (activation of the sympathetic nervous system) to a state of safety and connection (regulated by the parasympathetic system, especially the ventral vagus nerve) (Porges, 2011).

One way to facilitate this process is to encourage the authentic expression of vulnerability, as this allows partners to respond with empathy and compassion, fostering an environment of emotional safety (Gilbert, 2009; Johnson, 2004). This type of interaction can facilitate a transition from a defensive state to a state of emotional regulation, where partners feel protected and able to respond flexibly and adaptively (Coan and Sbarra, 2015; Roediger et al., 2018).

Each module in Couples Schema Therapy includes strategies to regulate the autonomic nervous system, facilitating the transition from a fight-or-flight state (sympathetic system) to a state of safety and connection (ventral parasympathetic system).

- **Psychoeducation Modules:** In this phase, the couple is helped to identify dysfunctional coping patterns and how these influence their interaction. Interrupting the cycle of patterns and analyzing needs, emotions, and response patterns allows partners to move beyond emotional reactivity, decreasing sympathetic activation (Porges, 2011; Siegel, 2012). As the couple begins to request and offer support, the perception of safety increases, which favors the activation of the ventral vagus nerve, associated with social connection (Porges, 2011).
- **Rebalance Modules:** Expressing attachment and connection needs clearly and nonreactively makes it easier for both partners to respond with empathy. This process helps to leave a state of sympathetic hyperactivation and enter a state of joint emotional regulation, promoting co-regulation through secure attachment (Coan and Sbarra, 2015; Johnson, 2004).
- **Reconnection Modules:** During this phase, each partner is encouraged to experience the other as a secure attachment figure. Expressing emotional vulnerability and engaging in empathic dialogue helps restore trust, facilitating the activation of the ventral parasympathetic system, which promotes relaxation and a sense of security in the relationship (Roediger et al., 2018; Siegel, 2012).
- **Additional Module** (Facing Critical Voices): Harsh self-criticism is associated with activation of the threat system, which can keep the person in a state of sympathetic hyperarousal (Gilbert, 2009). Developing self-compassion and receiving support from one's partner allows the person to perceive emotional security, promoting activation of the attachment system and the ventral parasympathetic system (Porges, 2011; Gilbert, 2009).

Part II

Education

This second part of the book focuses on explaining the initial modules that couple schema therapy proposes to work with partners. These modules are focused on educating partners about the dimensional model of mode cycles so that the couple can stop them on their own and subsequently actively seek rebalancing.

The first three modules address the emotions that drive behavior and help partners become aware of the unperceived need or lack. Module four focuses on reflecting on the need left in the background as a starting point for fulfilling it through asking for and offering something in return.

In this sense, it is essential for partners to understand that, in the initial phases of therapy, the goal is not to resolve specific problems but rather to identify and stop dysfunctional behavioral response patterns and coping modes. Therefore, during the first sessions, the primary focus will be on interrupting the dysfunctional interaction pattern, rather than on an in-depth analysis of the specific content of the couple's conflicts.

The purpose of this stage is for partners to become aware of their interaction patterns and learn to interrupt them before developing new ways of relating based on the flexible coping behaviors of cooperating-giving in or firmness-initiating. To achieve this, the therapist must be attentive to the emergence of these dysfunctional cycles during the session and stop them as soon as they arise.

The basic structure of the sessions in this first phase of couple schema therapy (which will be reflected primarily in the first three modules) follows these steps:

1. **Identification of the issue to be worked on:** The couple is asked to identify the conflict they are bringing to therapy.
2. **Beginning of the mode cycle:** When the couple manages to agree on a conflict to be worked on, the therapist asks them to try to resolve it by communicating directly with each other.
3. **Mode cycle interruption:** Once a dysfunctional cycle is detected, the therapist intervenes immediately to stop it as soon as it begins.

4. **Observer team work:** The therapist and both partners stand and perform a cognitive observation exercise. This exercise aims to help the couple exit a state of emotional dysregulation, in which the amygdala dominates brain function, and facilitate the activation of the prefrontal cortex, promoting better integration between emotional regulation and executive function (LeDoux, 1996; Siegel, 2012). Through this process, the couple can adopt a more flexible perspective, reducing emotional reactivity and promoting greater integration between their emotions and their responsiveness (Ochsner & Gross, 2005; Coan & Sbarra, 2015). The use of movement and postural change can also facilitate this process, as it allows for changes in the activation of the autonomic nervous system, favoring the transition from a state of fight or flight to a state of safety and social connection (Porges, 2011; Van der Kolk, 2014).

This basic structure of the first three modules can be maintained and extended to the following modules if necessary to strengthen the process, especially when the couple has not yet fully internalized it.

In those cases in which, during the first three modules, the couple demonstrates the ability to identify the mode cycle and recognize the active (and, ideally, blocked) components in each partner and are able to stop the mode cycle on their own, the therapist can move on to a reconnection intervention. During the reconnection phase, a formal and detailed analysis of active and left in the background needs, child and coping modes, and the mode cycle will no longer be required at the beginning of the sessions. This is because the couple has developed sufficient awareness and autonomy in identifying these patterns.

In this second part, we analyze in depth a specific case that exemplifies the dominance-domination interaction pattern. The objective is to allow the reader to observe the complete development of this first phase of treatment with a specific couple. However, it is important to emphasize that the principles addressed in this section, such as education about the dimensional model, interrupting the mode cycle, and relational rebalancing, are applicable to other types of dysfunctional cycles, such as dominance-avoidance, avoidance-avoidance, and dominance-submission. In other words, the therapeutic process follows the same structure of steps, regardless of the type of interaction cycle the couple presents.

It is important to clarify that the different mode cycles described in Chapter 6 are not permanent or constant in the interaction between partners. That is, couples do not present only one type of mode cycle; rather, these can vary according to the context and adapt to specific situations within the couple's dynamic. However, for practical reasons in therapy, we prioritize working with those mode cycles that represent a recurring pattern in the relationship and are clearly displayed during the session, as this approach facilitates the process of emotional change and regulation.

5

Explanation of the Simplified "Two-leg" Model (Module I)

5.1 Introduction

This chapter addresses the theoretical concepts explained in depth in the first part of the book. Therefore, to avoid redundancy, it places more emphasis on how these concepts can be explained to partners rather than describing them in depth theoretically.

5.1.1 General Objective of the Module

Familiarize the couple with the basic concepts of couple schema therapy so that they can refer to them during the different phases of therapeutic treatment.

5.1.2 Specific Objectives

- Focus on the pattern of interaction and the active and blocked basic needs that comprise it rather than trying to resolve the disagreement between the couple.
- The couple should become aware of their active and blocked basic needs for attachment–connection and assertiveness–autonomy, as well as the importance of balancing them to establish good interaction in the relationship.
- Both partners should be able to recognize their active and blocked basic emotions, identifying how these arise from the frustration of their basic needs.
- Ensure that both partners identify which of the three major categories of coping behaviors (surrender, avoidance, and overcompensation) are active, as well as distinguish them from flexible, balanced, or healthy coping behaviors that facilitate meeting emotional needs.
- That both partners can understand the two-legged model, along with the needs, emotions, and behaviors associated with each leg.

- That both partners can distinguish between their active needs and emotions and those that are blocked.
- That each partner can identify the active coping mode and the unused flexible behavior that could replace it.
- Guide them to work on a specific problem and stop the Mode Cycle in a firm but cordial and kind manner.

5.2 Starting the Session

5.2.1 Identify the Problem to Work On

In the first session, after taking a general clinical history, the couple is asked to identify one of the recent problems that represents the typical difficulties that led them to seek therapy. If the couple begins to generalize or present multiple relationship problems, the therapist gently interrupts, validating the importance of all the issues raised but pointing out that, for the moment, it is necessary to focus on a single problem represented by a specific situation. The therapist recommends applying this advice to their daily lives: when they want to discuss something as a couple, talk about a specific topic, as this will help them avoid generalizing and find relevant solutions applicable to that specific issue.

To demonstrate how the therapist can provide information in a directive yet gentle manner, without appearing overly rigid, a sample script is presented below that demonstrates how to carry out this intervention effectively.

Example 5.1 Script for Empathic Confrontation to Focus the Problem in Session

Forgive me for interrupting you. I understand that all these issues you're sharing with me are important to work through in couples therapy and to understand what's happening in your relationship in general. However, to avoid opening too many emotional fronts that can later be difficult to resolve and to avoid emotional overload for both of us, at this time I'd like us to focus on a single problem. I want you to know that therapy attempts to model what you expect each other to do in everyday life. That's why, just as we're doing right now, I recommend that when you talk about a problem, you focus on a specific situation rather than generalizing. That's why I'd like you to tell me about a specific and concrete situation that happened between you and that we can analyze together.

To illustrate the identification of the problem, the following case is presented: Sarah and William, a 35-year-old couple who face difficulties arising from the relationship between William and Sarah's family of origin.

Clinical Case 20 Sarah and William, 35 years old

Sarah and William come to couples therapy because William believes Sarah is more focused on her family of origin than on her relationship with him and their children. This situation generates recurring arguments, especially when a family reunion approaches, as William perceives that Sarah prioritizes her family of origin over her relationship and children. After gathering clinical information, the therapist invites the couple to discuss one of their specific issues.

THERAPIST (T): I would like you to share with me some of the most recent discussions that you think represent the types of common issues that bring you to therapy.

WILLIAM (G): Sarah always prioritizes her family. They're very rude to me, and she doesn't do anything about it. Also, when it comes to helping them, she doesn't mind giving them money, but when it comes to our children, she always makes excuses. I'm also fed up with Sarah's parents coming home unannounced because ...

T: Excuse me for interrupting you, William. I understand that all of these issues are important to you, and we'll work on each one. However, I think I can help you most effectively if we start with just one. Would you like to start with the rejection you feel from Sarah's family?

G: Yes.

T: Does that sound okay to you, Sarah?

SARAH (S): Yes.

T: Perfect. William, tell me about a specific situation where you felt that rejection. Talking about a specific situation helps you avoid generalizing and focus your energy on solving a specific problem. That's why I advise you to adopt this approach whenever you want to talk about something you don't like about the other person. Does it make sense to you?

G: Yes.

S.: YES.

T: Who wants to start?

G: Last weekend, we went to my sister-in-law's birthday party, and when I said hi to Sarah's mom, she ignored me and didn't say anything.

T: Okay, so now we've identified a specific situation. I'd like you to talk among yourselves about what happened that day.

5.2.2 Starting the Mode Cycle

Once the event or situation has been identified, they are asked to resume the conversation, looking each other directly in the eye as they speak, while the therapist observes what needs, emotions, and coping behaviors are present in each partner (chairs 2A and 2B in Figure 3.4). During this interaction, the therapist pays special attention to the Mode Cycles described in the previous chapter and how these generate recurring patterns in the relationship. If one partner stops talking to their partner and begins addressing the therapist, a discreet signal is given to indicate that communication should continue with their partner. Also, if either partner gets sidetracked by talking about other problems or other situations in which their partner has behaved in a certain way, the therapist gently stops them and points out that it is necessary to address only one problem at a time. Similarly, the therapist advises both partners to discuss only one problem at a time in their daily lives when they argue, explaining that if they don't respect this rule, they are likely to become saturated, overwhelmed, or emotionally exhausted, and ultimately fail to satisfactorily resolve any of the many difficulties addressed.

To describe how the therapist facilitates the initiation of the modes cycle in the session, the following continues with the case description of Sarah and William.

Sarah and William, 35 years old

T: I'd like you to face each other, looking into each other's eyes. My goal is to observe how you interact so I can better understand the dynamics between you. Is that okay with you?

G AND S (IN UNISON): Yes.

G: It bothers me that you want to go to those meetings without caring how I feel. You don't care that I'm treated badly ...

T: Sorry, William. Maybe I didn't explain myself well. I'd like you to talk only about the specific situation that happened that day, when your mother-in-law didn't greet you.

G: Okay. I felt really upset because your mom was rude to me by not saying hi, and you didn't do anything. You didn't set any boundaries.

S: You're really exaggerating. My mom doesn't say hi to anyone; you shouldn't take it so personally. I hate that you're so sensitive and that you complain about things I can't control ...

5.2.3 Stopping the Mode Cycle

When the therapist identifies the Mode Cycle, they interrupt the couple's interaction, making it clear that an agreement is not necessary at that time. The main goal of this exercise is to closely observe the couple's characteristic interaction cycle. It usually only takes a few minutes to detect whether each partner is excessively focused on a single need, emotion, or coping behavior. After the interruption, the therapist asks if this form of interaction is a typical pattern in their relationship.

By interrupting the Mode Cycle in a couple, the therapist confronts a common belief among some partners: the idea that emotional arousal should not be interrupted, but should continue until it is completely released. As a result, the therapist's intervention may generate frustration, a sense of disconnection, or even be perceived as disrespectful. However, in the context of Couples Schema Therapy, it is recognized that pausing emotional arousal can be a key intervention to prevent conflict escalation and promote regulation. Therefore, below is a sample script showing how the therapist can pause the emotional process in a gentle and contact-based manner, without invalidating the couple's emotional experience.

Example 5.2 Script for Stopping a Couple's Argument Once the Therapist Has Detected the Couple's Mode Cycle

Excuse me for interrupting you at this moment. While listening to you, I realized something that I believe may be valuable in understanding what is happening between you as a couple. If it is okay with you, I propose pausing the discussion for a moment so we can analyze together some important concepts that could help us better understand the situation. I would like to tell you that in this type of therapy, we focus first on the process, not the content. That is, we will not focus on resolving specific situations or problems, but rather on understanding the patterns of behavior in both of you that are preventing you from solving your problems. That is why, before continuing, I would like to ask you: Is this type of interaction that we are observing now something that occurs frequently between you?

Reflection: How difficult is it for you to interrupt partners? How do you feel about not focusing on the couple's specific problems in the early stages of treatment and instead placing more emphasis on stopping negative interaction patterns?

Therapist's Advice: Remember that you're working with the couple's interaction pattern, not the specific content itself.

If the answer is negative, the reasons why this behavior is unusual are explored. In these cases, we investigate whether one or both partners are behaving differently due to the therapist's presence. If so, we ask them how they typically react to gain a clearer idea of the typical interaction cycle. If the problem presented is not representative of their usual dynamics, we seek to identify another situation that is.

If the answer is affirmative, and they confirm that this is a recurring pattern, the therapist proceeds to analyze the structure of the problem. At this stage, the goal is not to solve the problem, but rather to analyze its structure and dynamics. Once a typical pattern of interaction between the partners has been identified, the next stage can be moved on to.

To illustrate how the therapist interrupts the discussion when the couple's Mode Cycle begins, the following continues with the description of the therapy session between Sarah and William.

Sarah and William, 35 years old

T: I'm going to stop the discussion here. I think I have an idea of what's going on between you. Is that okay with you?

G.: Ok.

S.: Yes.

T: I understand. I know it may seem strange that I'm stopping the discussion without resolving it, but I want to explain why. My intention is for us to focus on the process of the discussion, rather than the content. That is, before trying to solve problems, it's essential to break the patterns that repeat themselves over and over again in your discussions. That way, instead of addressing conflicts one by one, we can work on changing the structure that originates and maintains them. Is that clear?

G.: Yes.

S.: Yes.

T: Okay. On that note, I'd like to ask: Is this way of interacting a typical pattern in your discussions?

G.: Yes.

S.: Yes.

5.3 Cognitive Work

5.3.1 Observer Team Work

After interrupting the Mode Cycle, the therapist asks both partners to stand up, pointing out that the goal of this is to get out of autopilot, which is how their brains are already accustomed to reacting to certain stimuli (with the therapist in position 1B and the partners in positions 5A and 5B in Figure 3.4). While standing, the therapist invites the partners to look "from above" at the chairs "below" where they were sitting and points out that they will now form a team of observers who will describe what happened in the argument between the couple sitting in the chair. It is later specified that, to facilitate this task, third-person language will be used when describing what happened with the couple "below." For example, "he told her that" or "she showed herself to him," etc.

Once the therapist explains the observer team's work, he or she introduces the key concepts of the dimensional model: basic needs, basic emotions, coping modes, and the two-legged metaphor. Understanding these concepts is essential for the couple to later understand the concept of the Mode Cycle.

To psychoeducate the dimensional model, the therapist can use various teaching resources, depending on the needs and preferences of the couple:

- **Videos:** For example, you can show a short video like the "still face experiment."
- **Work Cards:** Use the Mode cards as a visual tool.
- **Whiteboard:** Write relevant information on a whiteboard for a more dynamic explanation.
- **Printed Material:** Provide brochures or other pre-prepared materials.
- **Bibliographic References:** Recommend books such as How to Improve Your Relationship (Ceballos and Serrano, 2025) or (Stevens and Roediger, 2016).
- **Verbal Explanation:** Explain the model directly verbally, without the support of materials.

5.3.1.1 Identify Basic Needs

The therapist begins the explanation of the two-legged model by explaining its association with the two basic needs: the need for attachment–connection and the need for assertiveness–autonomy. A script is then presented that can be used in the therapy session to facilitate understanding of the explanation.

Example 5.3 Script to Explain the Dimensional Model and the Two Basic Needs

I would like to share with you the model I use in couples therapy. It's a simplified version of the evidence-based method known as schema therapy. This theory posits that we all have two basic needs. The first is the need for attachment–connection, which leads us to ask ourselves: What does my partner need me to change about me? What can I ask them to make them feel better? What can I do to adapt to their needs? The second is the need for assertiveness–autonomy, which leads us to ask ourselves: What do I need my partner to understand? What do I want them to change? What can they do to adapt to my needs? To maintain a healthy relationship, it is essential to balance these two needs. Using the analogy of "two legs," it posits that to walk in a balanced way and move forward in a relationship, it is necessary to use both legs in a coordinated manner. In this model, the need for attachment–connection is called the "blue leg," while the need for assertiveness–autonomy is called the "red leg." If a person focuses solely on the blue leg, that is, the need for attachment and connection, they run the risk of forgetting themselves and losing their identity in the relationship. Conversely, if the focus is exclusively on the red leg, the need for assertiveness and autonomy, this can lead to excessive individualism, leading to self-centered attitudes. It's important to note that, although both needs are always present, at certain times one of them tends to be activated while the other becomes blocked or relegated to the background. This means that, in certain situations, a person may rely solely on one "leg," which hinders progress in the relationship, generating conflicts or imbalances. In that sense, I'd like to ask you: What do you think about this two-needs theory? Could you describe these two needs in your own words? In the recent conflict, which do you think is the active need you are showing your partner, and which is the need that remains in the background? Which need do you think is active in your partner during this argument, and which is blocked?

It also begins by explaining how, when one of these needs is active, the other takes a backseat, and it emphasizes that an imbalance between the two brings negative consequences to the relationship.

One way to explain this concept is through the coin metaphor, based on the central idea that all people have two fundamental needs: attachment–connection and assertiveness–autonomy. However, just like a coin, when we see one side, the other is hidden. To see it, we need to turn it over. The same is true of emotions: when one is active, the other often remains blocked in the background. To illustrate how to present this metaphor to partners, below is a sample script that can serve as a reference in the therapy session.

Example 5.4 Script to Explain the Coin Metaphor

A coin is never resting on its edge: it's either more on the red side or the blue side. It's always going to be more on the active side or the responsive side. If I'm talking, I'm more on the red side, and if I'm listening while the other person is talking, I'm on the blue side. You can't be neutral; you're always a little bit on one side or the other. Neutral means learning to be flexible.

Once the explanation is complete, the therapist verifies that the concept of the two needs, the balance between them, and the difference between active and blocked needs have been fully understood, asking both partners any questions or asking them to explain these concepts in their own words. Each partner then identifies, from the perspective of an observer, how they presented themselves to both partners during the discussion of the problem.

To further clarify how the two-legged model and its associated needs can be explained to partners during the session, we continue with a description of Sarah and William's case.

Sarah and William, 35 years old

T: I want to share with you a model I use in couples therapy called Schema Therapy. Simply put, this model is based on three fundamental elements: needs, emotions, and coping styles. Let's start with needs. All human beings have two essential needs: attachment–connection, which drives us to care for and worry about our partner, and assertiveness–autonomy, which drives us to defend our desires and care for ourselves. For a relationship to function healthily, these needs must be balanced. If we focus only on the need for attachment, we risk forgetting about ourselves. On the other hand, if we focus solely on our autonomy, we could become too selfish. To illustrate, I like to use the metaphor of two legs: we need to balance the blue leg (attachment–connection) and the red leg (assertiveness–autonomy) in order to move forward as a couple. Does this make sense to you?

G.: Yes, it makes sense.

S.: Yes, I understand it better now.

T: Perfect. Now, I'd like us to stand and observe from an outside perspective what happened between Sarah and William. Imagine we're watching two characters in the scene, and our role is to be a team of observers. If we focus on William, when he said to Sarah a moment ago, "It bothers me that you want to go to those meetings without caring about how I feel." What need do you think was activated in him? Connection or autonomy?

G.: The autonomy one. I think William wanted Sarah to recognize how rude her mother was and to care about how she felt about it.

T: Do you agree, Sarah?

SARAH: Yes, William was thinking about him without considering what Sarah feels or thinks.

T: Okay. And what need was blocked at that moment?

G.: The connecting one, that is, the blue leg.

(Continued)

(Continued)

T: Do you agree, Sarah?

S.: Yes.

T: Now, when Sarah responded to William, saying, "You're exaggerating." What need was active at that moment?

S.: I don't know.

T: Let's imagine Sarah's thoughts at that moment. When William told her, "It bothers me that you want to go to those meetings without caring about how I feel." Do you think her first reaction was to think about how to help William feel better, or rather to consider that he was exaggerating and should change his perspective?

S.: I think he thought more about the second, about his need for autonomy, which means that the need for attachment was blocked, right?

T: Exactly. Do you agree, William?

G.: Yes, Sarah definitely thought about herself and not how William was feeling.

T: Exactly! You've perfectly identified what's happening in this couple. Congratulations!

5.3.1.2 Identify Coping Modes

The therapist explains to the couple the three coping modes used when trying to manage unmet needs:

1. The first mode is overcompensation, which involves fighting or dominating in order to satisfy one's own needs; in this case, the person actively confronts the situation, imposing their demands.
2. The second mode is avoidance, which is related to two behaviors:
   a. **Fleeing the Situation by Physically Moving Away:** This type of behavior is called active avoidance
   b. **Freezing by Emotionally Disconnecting from Oneself, Others, or Reality:** This type of behavior is called passive avoidance.
3. Finally, there is the surrender mode, which involves submitting or obeying the other person's wishes, putting aside one's own needs in an attempt to defuse the situation or avoid confrontation.

These coping modes are linked to the two legs of the dimensional model: Overcompensation and active avoidance are related to the red leg, which represents the need for assertiveness–autonomy and the emotions of anger or disgust.

On the other hand, surrender and passive avoidance are associated with the blue leg, which reflects the need for attachment-connection, along with the emotions of fear or sadness. In this way, it becomes evident how coping modes are directly connected to needs and how an imbalance between them can generate problematic cycles in the relationship.

Similarly, the therapist explains that when one of the coping modes is active, the other is relegated to the background. The goal with coping modes is to make them more flexible. In the case of overcompensation or active avoidance, the flexible alternative would be taking the initiative and being firm, while in surrender, the balanced behavior would be yielding and cooperating. In this sense, when discussing coping modes, balance is established when the person manages to move toward the flexible coping behavior that represents the counterpart of that active coping mode.

After psychoeducating the couple on the concept of coping modes, the therapist verifies that each client has correctly understood it, and then the team of observers analyzes the active coping behaviors displayed by each partner. To do this, the therapist places two chairs facing each other and then explains to the partners that each chair will represent the coping mode displayed on the front stage during the discussion they had when directly addressing the problem in the therapy session (chairs 2A and 2B in Figure 3.4).

The therapist, pointing to the chair representing one partner's coping mode, asks that person which coping response they believe was active, saying something like: "Do you think the visible behavior was overcompensation, avoidance, or surrender?" Once the partner responds, the therapist asks for the other partner's perspective. If necessary, the therapist provides feedback to help accurately identify the coping mode.

Special attention is required in the case of avoidance, as the therapist must support the couple in distinguishing between active and passive avoidance. Finally, the coping mode is linked to one of the two legs in the model, with overcompensation and active avoidance corresponding to the red leg and surrender and passive avoidance to the blue leg.

Once the coping mode represented in one partner's chair has been identified, the therapist proceeds to explore the active mode of the other partner. To do this, the therapist asks directly which coping mode they believe was predominant, validates their response with their partner's perception, and, if necessary, offers feedback.

If appropriate, the therapist may invite each partner to identify the flexible behavior that would allow them to shift to the other leg.

To illustrate how to explain the animal model to partners, below is a sample script that can be used in a session.

Example 5.5 Script to Explain the Animal Model

When two dogs meet on the street, there are three possibilities: "three dogs" as top-dog, under-dog, and no-dog. The top-dog (fight): It may choose to confront the threat directly. This is manifested through growling, barking, or even an attack. It is an active coping response aimed at resolving the conflict through confrontation. The under-dog (submit): In some cases, one of the dogs chooses to lower its head, showing its belly, or avoiding eye contact. This is a submissive response, intended to deactivate the threat without the need for direct confrontation or flight. No-dog (flight): The other dog, instead of confronting, may choose to retreat quickly from the encounter. This is an avoidance response, in which the individual chooses to escape to ensure their safety.

To facilitate the explanation of the coping modes, below is a script that can serve as a guide for the therapist to adapt and use in session.

Example 5.6 Script to Explain the Coping Modes

Coping modes are the behaviors we use to confront our emotions and try to meet our needs. Simply put, there are three main modes: the first is overcompensation, which arises when we feel anger or frustration because we perceive that our need for assertiveness and autonomy is being blocked. In this behavior, we seek to impose ourselves, dominate, or fight to have our needs met. This mode is associated with what we call red leg, and the goal in therapy will be to help flex this response and transform it into initiative-assertiveness, that is, a more balanced and assertive way of expressing what we need. The second mode is surrender, which appears when we face emotions like sadness or fear and feel that our need for attachment and connection is at risk. In this case, the behavior leads us to submit, obey, or adapt to make our partner feel comfortable, even if this means ignoring our own needs. This behavior is associated with what we call the "blue leg," and the goal in therapy is to help flex this response and transform it into yielding-cooperating, that is, clearly expressing what we can offer our partner without jeopardizing the satisfaction of our own needs. The third coping mode is avoidance, where we tend to physically or emotionally distance ourselves from problems with our partner. Depending on the cause, this behavior can be associated with either the red leg or the blue leg. If we avoid because we are angry or upset and seek to satisfy our needs with someone else or through another activity, this avoidance falls under the red leg. The goal of therapy is to transform this type of avoidance into the flexible coping behavior of assertiveness and initiative. However, if we avoid things to avoid sadness, fear confrontation, or fear of losing attachment to our partner, we end up disconnecting from our emotions. This avoidance belongs to the blue leg. In this case, the goal is to modify this form of avoidance with the flexible coping behavior of giving in and cooperating. In therapy, we will work on identifying these coping modes and making them more flexible. The goal will be to help you face your emotions and needs in a more balanced and healthy way, thus strengthening your relationship and your individual emotional well-being. In this regard, I would like to ask you: What do you think about the relationship between these behaviors, needs, and emotions? Does this theory seem logical to you? Now, I'm going to place two chairs, each one representing the coping mode that each of you showed during the recent discussion. Let's start with the first chair: What coping mode do you think this person expressed when talking with their partner? Would you say it was overcompensation, avoidance, or surrender? Also, what do you think was the flexible coping mode that could have been used? Alright, now let's move on to explore the coping mode of the other person.

Reflection: If a couple does not react favorably to the three coping styles model, what do you think would be a second alternative?

Therapist's Advice: Some couples respond well to the animal model, while others don't. The therapist must decide whether to work more from the dimensional model or the animal model. The examples in this book are more oriented toward the former, but this doesn't mean they can't be worked from the latter.

To illustrate how to explain to the couple their active coping modes and their flexible counterparts, their relationship to the two-legged model, and the awareness of these during the session, the development of the therapy with Sarah and William is described below.

Sarah and William, 35 years old

T: There are three main coping modes: overcompensation, where we try to impose our needs, which corresponds to the red leg; surrender, where we adapt to what our partner wants, using our blue leg; and avoidance, where we distance ourselves emotionally or physically. We'll call physical distance active avoidance, which corresponds to the red leg, while emotional disconnection, we'll call passive avoidance, will be linked to the blue leg. Regarding coping modes, the goal is to make them more flexible to achieve a balanced behavior. Surrender and passive avoidance modes can be made more flexible by adopting a yielding-cooperating behavior. On the other hand, overcompensation and active avoidance modes must be transformed into a flexible coping behavior of taking the initiative-assertiveness. Do you have any doubts about these three ways of reacting?

(Continued)

(Continued)

S AND G: No, everything is fine.
T: Okay, now I'm going to place two chairs, one facing the other. This chair will represent William's coping style, and this other one will represent Sarah's. Remember, these are the behaviors that others can see, what's "in front of the stage." Let's start by analyzing the first one. When William tells Sarah that she doesn't care how he feels, what coping behavior do you think he had?
G: Overcompensation, because he wanted to impose his need.
T: Correct. What would have been the flexible behavior you could have used?
G: Give in a little and cooperate.
T: Very well. Do you agree, Sarah?
S.: Yes.
T: And in Sarah's case, when she said to William, "I don't like that you're so sensitive," what kind of coping did she show?
S: Overcompensation.
T: And what would be the flexible behavior not shown?
S: To give in or to cooperate.
T: Excellent. Do you agree, William?
G.: Yes.
T.: We could conclude that, in terms of coping modes, both are leaning on the red leg. Does that make sense to you?
G.: Yes.
S.: Yes.

5.3.1.3 Identify Basic Emotions

The therapist explains to both partners the relationship between basic emotions and needs within the "two-legged" model. It is proposed that the negative emotions of fear and sadness arise when the need for attachment and connection, represented by the blue leg, is frustrated. On the other hand, the emotions of anger and disgust are linked to the need for assertiveness and autonomy, represented by the red leg. The positive emotion of happiness appears when these needs are met in a balanced way. It is also pointed out that, as with needs, when one emotion is active, it is displayed in an observable way, while the other emotion, corresponding to the counterpart of the unused leg, remains blocked; that is, nonverbal language does not communicate it clearly and evidently.

Once the basic emotions have been psychoeducated, the therapist verifies that the couple has effectively understood this concept. Next, the therapist places two chairs behind each of the chairs representing the coping mode of each partner. The therapist explains that, in each case, one chair represents one of the two emotions: the "red chair," associated with anger and disgust (red leg), and the "blue chair," associated with sadness and fear (blue leg). This pair of chairs symbolizes the back of the stage—that is, the internal emotions each partner experienced during the discussion of the problem at the beginning of the session (chairs 3A and 4A for one partner and chairs 3B and 4B for the other, in Figure 3.4).

Once the chairs have been placed, the therapist, from the observer's position, invites each partner to identify which emotion was present during the conflict. The process begins with one partner, asking them to name both the active and the blocked emotion. Once identified, the therapist confirms this perception with the other partner and, if necessary, provides feedback.

If there is difficulty identifying the emotions, the therapist can guide the process by exploring bodily sensations in the chest and stomach. For example, fluid breathing and an expanded chest and abdomen are often linked to emotions like anger and disgust. In contrast, a contracted chest and abdomen and labored breathing are usually associated with sadness and fear.

After completing the analysis of the active and blocked emotions in the first partner, the therapist proceeds to explore the emotions of the second partner, again confirming them with the other partner and offering feedback when needed.

Once the active emotions of both partners have been identified, the therapist places the chair representing the active emotion behind the coping mode chair and sets aside the chair representing the blocked emotion (chairs 3A and 3B in Figure 3.5). Once the setup is complete, the therapist links the identified need, coping mode, and active emotion to the corresponding leg: the red leg represents the need for assertiveness–autonomy, the coping mode of overcompensation or active avoidance, and the emotion of anger or disgust; while the blue leg represents the need for attachment–connection, the coping mode of surrender or passive avoidance, and the emotions of sadness or fear.

To make it easier to explain this concept to partners, below is a sample script that can be used in a session.

Example 5.7 Script to Explain the Relationship Between Emotions and Basic Needs

Emotions are signals that help us identify which need is active and which is blocked. For example, if we feel anger or disgust, it's very likely that the active need is assertiveness–autonomy, meaning we're using the red leg. This implies that the blocked emotions, which remain in the background, are fear or sadness, and with them, the need for attachment–connection linked to the blue leg. Similarly, if the predominant emotions are fear or sadness, it means that the need we're trying to satisfy is attachment–connection using the blue leg. In this case, the emotions of anger or disgust would be blocked along with the need for assertiveness–autonomy using the red leg. In this sense, I'd like to ask you: What do you think about the association between needs and emotions? Does this theory make sense to you? While you were discussing this a moment ago, what emotion were you feeling when talking about the matter with your partner? Was it fear, sadness, anger, or disgust? And what were the emotions that were blocked or remained in the background?

To explain to partners the basic emotions that are active and blocked within the two-legged dimensional model, as well as their manifestation during the therapeutic session, the case of Sarah and William is reviewed.

Sarah and William, 35 years old

T: Now, let's reflect on emotions. Typically, when we feel anger or disgust, the active need is assertiveness–autonomy, and when we experience sadness or fear, the active need is usually attachment–connection. Furthermore, when we experience anger or disgust, fear and sadness are often blocked, and vice versa. Do I make myself clear?

G.: Yes.

S.: Yes.

T.: So, we can say that in front of the stage is the active coping mode, the behavior that everyone can see. However, behind the stage are the internal emotions that each person is experiencing, which may not be as evident to others. To represent these emotions, I'm going to place two chairs behind the one that represents your coping mode. One of these chairs, which we'll call the "red chair," will represent the emotions of anger or disgust, and the other, which we'll call the "blue chair," will represent the emotions of sadness or fear. The work we're going to do next is to identify which of these emotions were active during the discussion and which were blocked or hidden. Does that sound good to you?

G.: Yes.

S.: Yes.

T: In that sense, when William told Sarah that he didn't care, what emotion predominated, and which one was blocked?

S.: I think he showed anger, and the fear or sadness was blocked.

T: Exactly. And that anger, what need and which leg do you think it's associated with?

S.: To the need for assertiveness–autonomy, which is the red leg.

T: And which leg were you not using?
S.: The blue leg, the one of attachment–connection.
T: Do you agree, William?
G.: Yes, William looked upset and not sad or scared.
T.: So, we remove the "blue" chair, which represents the emotions of sadness or fear, and we leave the "red" chair, associated with anger, behind the overcompensating coping mode. This completes the picture: William's active red leg is made up of his need for assertiveness–autonomy, the overcompensating coping mode, and the emotion of anger. Does that make sense to you both?
G.: Yes.
S.: Yes.
T: And in Sarah's case, when she answers William, "I don't like that you're so delicate and that you complain about things I can't control," what emotion was active and which one was blocked in her?
G.: Sarah sounded upset, not sad or scared.
T: Which leg did she use?
G.: I was using the red leg, and the blue leg was blocked.
T: Very well! Do you agree, Sarah?
S.: Yes.
T: Exactly.
T.: Let's remove the "blue" chair, which represents the blocked emotion of sadness or fear, and keep the "red" chair, which represents the active emotion of anger or disgust. This way, the picture is complete. In Sarah's case, the active leg is the red one, composed of the need for assertiveness–autonomy, the overcompensation coping mode, and the emotion of anger. Does that sound right to you?
G.: Agreed.
S.: Yes.

Reflection: What happens when clients believe they are expressing an emotion, need, or behavior, but what is actually manifested is its opposite?

Therapist's Advice: An effective way to clarify needs, emotions, and coping behaviors is through role-playing. In this exercise, the initial discussion is recreated, and the therapist models how they would react to the blocked emotion. This contrast allows the partner to compare their habitual response with the modeled reaction, helping them identify the differences between what they actively expressed in session and what might actually be underlying. This facilitates a deeper understanding of their active and underlying emotional and coping needs.

To carry out this exercise (Figure 3.5), the therapist sits in chair 2A, and one partner sits in chair 2B, while the other remains standing in position 4B. Afterward, in order to work with the other partner, this person sits in chair 2A, the therapist moves to chair 2B, and the first partner who participated in the exercise stands in position 4A.

To demonstrate this process in difficult cases, where partners have difficulty distinguishing between the use of the red leg and the blue leg, believing they are using one when in fact they are expressing the other, the case of Sarah and William is reviewed.

Sarah and William, 35 years old

T: Perfect. Now, I'd like us to stand and observe from an outside perspective what happened between Sarah and William. Imagine we're watching two characters in the scene, and our role is to be a team of observers. If we focus on William, when he said to Sarah a moment ago, "It bothers me that you want to go to those meetings without caring about how I feel." What need do you think was activated in him? Connection or autonomy?

G.: The attachment–connection one. I think what William really wants is for Sarah to connect with him.

T: I understand your point, and I agree that you're seeking connection. However, I get the impression that what you're expressing externally is different. To clarify this further, I'd like to do an exercise. Would that be okay with you?

G.: Yes.

T: Okay, so standing up, we're going to recreate the scene between William and Sarah. But this time, I'll take the role of William, and you'll play Sarah, reacting just as she would. Is that clear what we'll do? William: Yes.

T: So, let's begin. Remember, at this point you'll be describing what Sarah would say, and you're impersonating her.

--------------------------Start Roleplaying-------------------------

G.: Sarah would say, "I hate that you're so sensitive."

T: William could say to her, "What bothers you about my attitude?"

G.: She would say, "You're exaggerating my mother's reaction."

T: William, on his blue leg, would ask him: "And how do you feel when you perceive that I am exaggerating?"

G.: She would answer: "As if you were inconsiderate. You know my mother is very important to me."

T: William, leaning on empathy and connection, would answer: "I'm sorry, I don't mean to make you feel like I'm being inconsiderate. I know how important your mother is to you."

G.: Sarah would answer: "It doesn't seem like it."

T: William from the blue leg would respond something like: "I want you to feel good about me, but sometimes I wish I were as important to you as your mother is. When I realize I'm not, I feel sad. I'm willing to take your actions less personally, but I also wish you would express more directly that you matter to me. It makes me feel good when you ask me how I feel."

--------------------------End Roleplaying-------------------------

T: I'd like to end the exercise here. Did you notice any differences between the emotions, needs, and behaviors you expressed compared to the ones I displayed during the roleplay?

G.: Yes.

S.: Yes, it was very different.

T: What I showed in the exercise is an example of using the blue leg. Does this practice make it clearer how this need manifests?

G.: Yes, I understand better now. That's not what I did in our discussion.

S.: Yes, it is clearer to me, too.

T: Now, this doesn't mean that using the red leg (assertiveness–autonomy) is bad or less important than the blue leg. Both are essential. However, it's key to find a balance and learn to identify how we use both. In particular, it's important to recognize the leg we block most frequently, as that's the one that needs the most attention in our growth as a couple.

5.4 Closing the Session: Therapeutic Task: Awareness of Needs, Emotions, and Coping Modes

The therapist concludes the session by giving the couple homework to identify the needs, emotions, and coping modes that arise in their arguments as a couple. This will allow them to observe which of these are active and which may be blocked, pushed into the background, or unused—both in themselves and in the other partner.

To support this task, the therapist may choose to use the following diary to identify active and background needs, emotions, and coping modes (Table 5.1).

To illustrate how the therapeutic task is assigned, the following is how the therapist concludes the session with Sarah and William.

Table 5.1 Diary of needs, emotions, and coping modes that were active, as well as those that were pushed into the background, blocked, or not used.

Instructions: Over the next few days, keep a journal to record important interactions or arguments with your partner. To complete this activity, complete the following table, keeping the following in mind:

1. **Date:** Note the date the interaction occurred.
2. **Problem:** Briefly describe the situation or conflict you had with your partner.
3. **In yourself:** Identify which needs, emotions, and coping modes were active in you during the discussion. It also includes identifying the neglected need, the hidden or blocked emotion, and the flexible coping behavior that you could have used
4. **In your partner:** Reflect on the needs, emotions, and coping modes you noticed as being active in your partner. It also includes identifying the neglected need, the hidden or blocked emotion, and the flexible coping behavior your partner might have used.

You can then use the following table as a guide:

Date: ______________

Problem: ___________

	Needs	
	Active	Left in the background
In oneself		
In the partner		

	Emotion	
	Active	Blocked or hidden
In oneself		
In the partner		

	Behaviors	
	Active	Flexible behavior to use
In oneself		
In the partner		

Source: Adapted from Roediger (2025).

Sarah and William, 35 years old

T: Finally, as homework, I ask you to observe your interactions throughout the week and note down the active needs, emotions, and coping styles. I also ask you to identify the needs that were left in the background, their blocked or hidden emotions, and the flexible coping behaviors they could have used in themselves (and, if possible, in their partner). This will help you become more aware of your patterns and find a balance between your two legs. Do you agree?

S.: Yes.

G.: Yes.

As a summary, the steps to follow in the session when applying Module I of Psychoeducation are presented:

Starting the Session

- **Identify the Problem to Work On:** The couple is asked to identify the conflict to be worked on in the therapy session.
- **Beginning of the Mode Cycle:** Both partners are asked to try to resolve the problem by talking it over directly with each other.
- **Stop the Mode Cycle:** Once detected, the therapist stops the Mode Cycle as soon as it starts.

Cognitive Work

- **Observer Team Work:** The therapist and the partners stand up (or in difficult cases also use role playing) and psychoeducate them so that both partners become aware of the relationship of the two-dimensional model (two legs) and its:
- **Basic Needs:** Attachment–connection and assertiveness–autonomy needs, both active and blocked.
- **Coping Behaviors:** Active coping behaviors (overcompensation, surrender, or avoidance), and their flexible counterparts, coping behaviors.
- **Basic Emotions:** The basic emotions of sadness, fear, anger, or disgust, active and blocked.

Closing the Session

- **Therapeutic Task:** The therapist allows each partner to become aware of the needs, emotions, and coping modes active (and left in the background, blocked, or unused) that arise during arguments or conflicts with their partner.

6

Presentation of the Mode Cycle (Module II)

6.1 Introduction

After explaining the dimensional model, which uses the metaphor of two legs along with the three basic concepts (needs, emotions, and coping styles), the next step is to introduce how the interaction of these three elements between both partners generates a cycle of interaction. This cycle is key to understanding how problems persist within the relationship.

6.1.1 General Objective of the Module

The couple learns to recognize their active coping and child modes and how these, in interaction with those of the other partner, generate a pattern of interaction that is repeated.

6.1.2 Specific Objectives

- The couple understands the relationship between child modes and basic emotions.
- Both partners identify the relationship between coping modes and coping behaviors.
- Both partners understand how one partner's coping mode activates the other's child mode, reacting from their own coping mode, thus triggering the first partner's child mode, to which they react from a specific coping mode, thus causing a self-perpetuating cycle that affects the relationship.

- Continue reinforcing both partners' ability to identify active needs, emotions, and coping behaviors. In addition to reinforcing the identification of the need that was left in the background, the blocked or hidden emotion, and the flexible coping behavior to activate.
- Firmly but gently stop the cycle of behavior in your relationship as soon as it starts, pointing out the importance of doing so.

6.2 Beginning of the Session

6.2.1 Identify the Problem to Be Worked on

The session begins, like all sessions, by asking what they "bring to therapy," asking them to discuss it directly (you could also choose to return to what was identified in the previous session).

To illustrate the identification of the problem, we return to the case of Sarah and William, who continue to face conflicts because both are strongly positioned in their red leg.

Sarah and William, 35 years old

T: I'd like to begin the session by strengthening our ability to identify the dynamics that are activated in each of you when you face difficulties. To do this, I would ask you to share a specific situation you've had since our last session. Who would like to start?

G.: Me. Last weekend we went to a restaurant with Sarah's family, and she ended up paying her parents' bill, and well, I think ...

T: Sorry, William. I think this is a very good example, but instead of explaining it to me, I'd like you to discuss it directly with Sarah.

A variation on the previous exercise involves videotaping the couple's discussion using one of their cell phone. The recording is then reviewed to observe the emotions and coping modes present in the interaction. This analysis allows for the identification of the coping behaviors used by each partner, as well as the predominant negative emotions (associated with the red or blue leg). Below is a script that can serve as a reference for this task.

Example 6.1 Script for Proposing to the Couple That They Videotape the Discussion of the Problem as a Way to Analyze the Active and Blocked Leg in Each Partner

Now that we've identified the problem, what do you think about using one of your cell phones to record a video of the discussion? This will allow us to analyze together, later on, the needs, emotions, and behaviors each of you expresses, as well as identify the needs that were left in the background, the blocked or hidden emotions, and the flexible coping behaviors that could be activated.

6.2.2 Starting the Mode Cycle

Once the problem to be addressed during the session has been identified, the therapist invites both partners to discuss it directly, so that each partner's needs, emotions, and coping behaviors can be observed (chairs 2A and 2B in Figure 3.5). To illustrate this step, we continue with a review of Sarah and William's case.

Sarah and William, 35 years old

T: I would ask you to stand face-to-face and start talking it over with each other.
G.: Why is it that you are always so wonderful when it comes to your family of origin, but you don't behave the same way when it comes to your children or me?
S.: You're exaggerating. I only help my parents once a month. They don't have many resources, and we're financially stable. Why does it bother you so much that I support them?
G.: (Turning to the therapist) It infuriates me that she justifies herself...
T: William, tell Sarah. This is a dialogue between you.
G.: It really bothers me that, instead of listening to me, you justify yourself. What I want is for you not to mind contributing money for your children, or at least to do it with the same enthusiasm with which you pay your parents' bills.
S.: It's never enough for you. It makes me angry that you don't appreciate the times I've done it. You're very unfair to me.

6.2.3 Stopping the Mode Cycle

By observing the interaction, the therapist can clearly identify the active needs, emotions, and coping modes of each partner. At this point, it is important to stop the cycle and reflect on what happened.

Continuing with the previous example, below is how the therapist stops the couple's Mode Cycle, whose dominance–domination Mode Cycle has already been identified by the therapist.

Sarah and William, 35 years old
T: I'm going to interrupt you for a moment because I think we've just entered a Mode Cycle again. Both of you need to be aware of when this happens to prevent it from escalating. Once the Mode Cycle is stopped in the second session, psychoeducation and awareness-raising are provided regarding how it perpetuates the problem in the couple. This involves explaining to the couple how each partner's coping modes trigger emotions and responses in the other, which, in turn, generate new emotions and behaviors that contribute to the formation of a vicious cycle in the relationship.

6.3 Cognitive Work

6.3.1 Observer Team Work

Once the therapist stops the Mode Cycle, he or she asks both partners to stand up to begin the observer team's work (therapist in position 1B and partners in positions 4A and 4B in Figure 3.5). From this position, the therapist psychoeducates the couple so they can understand the Mode Cycle in their relationship.

At this point in therapy, the couple has already acquired a basic understanding of the two needs, the four emotions, the six coping behaviors, the three coping modes, and the red leg and blue leg metaphor.

To explain the Mode Cycle in the couple, the therapist returns to the concept of coping modes (behaviors) and introduces a new concept in therapy, child modes (emotions).

Afterward, the therapist provides psychoeducation to the couple regarding the child modes, explaining that they will be organized as follows: the Vulnerable Child Mode, which includes the emotions of fear and sadness, will be associated with the blue chair and leg; while the angry child mode, which encompasses the emotions of anger and disgust, will be linked to the red chair and leg.

To conclude the explanation of the Mode Cycle, the relationship is established as to how the coping behavior of one partner first activates the child mode, and in response, the coping mode of the other partner is activated. This, in turn, activates the child mode and the coping mode of the original partner, thus establishing a vicious cycle.

To facilitate the explanation of these child and coping modes, a script is presented below that can serve as a reference in the therapeutic session.

Example 6.2 Script to Explain Coping Modes and Child Modes

Now that we understand what happens in each of you during an argument—that is, which leg you tend to use—I would like to explain how the inflexible use of this leg not only creates problems but also maintains them. To do this, let's focus on coping modes and what we'll call child modes, which are related to the emotions of each leg. When we talk about the emotions of fear or sadness of the blue leg, we group them under the Vulnerable Child Mode. On the other hand, the emotions of anger or disgust of the red leg make up the angry child mode. In an argument, the coping modes each of you uses tend to activate the child mode in the other person. This provokes a coping reaction in your partner, which in turn activates another child mode in you. Thus, a cycle is formed that reinforces emotions and behaviors, maintaining conflict in the relationship.

Once the concepts of the Mode Cycle have been explained, including the coping modes and child modes represented by the red or blue leg, this idea can be reinforced using the metaphor of a dance. In this metaphor, the flexible coping behavior of assertiveness or initiative is represented by taking a step forward (red leg), while the partner responds with a step back, representing the behavior of cooperation or yielding (blue leg). The partner then takes a step forward (assertiveness–initiative, red leg), and the other person follows with a step back (cooperation–yielding, blue leg). This pattern is repeated successively, creating a harmonious dance in which both partners move in a balanced manner.

Below is a way to explain this "dance" metaphor, which can serve as a guide for the therapist to adapt and explain it more easily during the session.

Example 6.3 Script to Explain the Mode Cycle in Couples Using the Metaphor of Dance

This Mode Cycle can be explained through the metaphor of dancing. If both partners take steps forward using the red leg, they will inevitably collide. If, on the other hand, both partners step back with the blue leg, they will end up moving away from each other. If one partner constantly advances with the red leg, while the other retreats with the blue leg, the former will chase the latter, creating an imbalance in the relationship. The goal of therapy is to achieve balance in the couple's movement. This means that one partner takes a step forward, taking the initiative by asserting their stance, while their partner gives way by taking a step back, cooperating. The couple then reverses roles: the one who gave way now takes a step forward, while the other accompanies the movement with a step back. This continuous exchange allows the couple to move systematically and harmoniously, resulting in a balanced and fluid dance, rather than constant clashing or emotional disconnection.

6.3.1.1 Identify Coping Modes

Once the couple has been psychoeducated about the coping modes involved in the Mode Cycle, the next step is to identify which of them was activated in each partner during the discussion of the problem they just addressed in the session (chairs 2A and 2B in Figure 3.5). To facilitate this analysis, the therapist again emphasizes the importance of getting out of "autopilot" and adopting a metacognitive perspective on the situation. He emphasizes the importance of changing physical position by standing up, as well as speaking in the third person when describing what happened in the interaction, in order to be able to observe the problem from the outside.

When identifying coping modes, the therapist needs to ensure that each partner's impression matches their observable behavior. When this is not the case, the therapist provides feedback and establishes a dialogue until an agreement is reached between both partners and the therapist on the behaviors actively displayed in the discussion. To illustrate this process, let's continue by reviewing the case of Sarah and William.

Sarah and William, 35 years old

T: One way to help us shift out of autopilot and into a state of reflection is through physical movement. So, I'm going to ask you to stand up. In front of you, I'll place two chairs facing each other. These will represent Sarah and William's coping modes. Behind them, I'll place two more chairs: the red chair will represent the emotions of anger or disgust, and the blue chair will symbolize the emotions of sadness or fear. Have I been clear so far?

S.: Yes.

G.: Yes.

T: Perfect. Now that we're standing, let's take a look at Sarah's coping chair. Behind that chair, let's reflect: What coping mode did Sarah display with William? Was she overcompensating, actively avoiding (red leg), giving in, or passively avoiding (blue leg)? Sarah, what coping mode do you think was active, and what flexible coping mode could have been used?

S.: The red leg's overcompensation mode was active, and it could have used the blue leg's flexible cooperate-or-yield behavior.

(Continued)

(Continued)

T: William, do you agree with this observation?
G.: Yes, I agree.
T: Ok. Now, let's look at the chair that represents William's coping mode. Let's think: What behavior were you displaying at that moment? William, do you think your active coping mode was overcompensation or active avoidance of the red leg, or surrender or passive avoidance of the blue leg?
G.: Overcompensation of the red leg.
T: And what flexible coping behavior could you have used?
G.: The cooperation or giving in of the blue leg.
T: Sarah, do you agree with this reflection?
S.: Yes.
T: Excellent. Now that you've both identified your active coping modes, I'm going to give you a mode cycle card. On it, you'll need to locate the corresponding section to record both your own coping mode and your partner's. Please complete that section by writing down the coping modes we just identified together. Now, let's explore how these modes activated emotions, or what we call the child modes, in the other partner.

While identifying coping modes, there are several options for the couple to clearly and graphically visualize the Mode Cycle. These options include:

- **Whiteboard or Poster Board:** The therapist can use a whiteboard or poster board to complete the cycle in real time, while explaining and detailing it with the couple.
- **Printed Physical Format:** A printed paper format can be used for partners to complete with the therapist during the session, allowing them to actively participate in the process.
- **Mode Cards:** These cards help you identify and understand active coping modes and their flexible counterparts.
- **Online Work:** If the session is conducted virtually, the therapist can use a word processor to fill out the form as the session progresses. This file can then be sent as an electronic document to the couple for review and reflection.
- **Use of Chairs:** One chair is used to represent the active coping mode, and two additional chairs are used for the child modes: one for the active child mode and another for the blocked or hidden child mode. These chairs are placed for each partner. Alternatively, the shorter version can be used: one chair placed behind the coping mode to represent only the

active child mode (or the one to be worked on), as shown in most of the examples starting from Module III of the book.

- **Use of Photos:** Photos of the couple or other images representing child and coping modes can also be used

The therapist can help the couple identify their Mode Cycle by providing a basic template that serves as a guide for organizing the information. As the partners complete this format, they gradually recognize the interaction cycle that develops between coping modes and child modes (Figure 3.2).

6.3.1.2 Identify Child Modes

Once the couple has identified their active coping modes, the next step is to recognize the child modes associated with them (chairs 3A, 3B, 4A, and 4B in Figure 3.4). This involves identifying the emotions that drove the coping behaviors displayed by each partner. For example, overcompensation or active avoidance are often linked to anger or disgust (angry child mode), which corresponds to the red leg. On the other hand, surrender or passive avoidance are often associated with sadness or fear (Vulnerable Child Mode), which belongs to the blue leg.

In some cases, all four emotions (anger, disgust, sadness, and fear) may be implicated in the situation. Therefore, it is important to distinguish between the active or displayed emotion toward the other partner and the blocked emotion. For example, if one partner reports feeling sad while overcompensating, the therapist validates that emotion but may also question whether that sadness was clearly displayed toward their partner. To clarify this distinction, the therapist may invite the other partner to share the emotion they perceived in the situation, while the therapist also offers their observation. In case of discrepancies between what was perceived and what was actively displayed while the couple discussed the problem in session, the therapist provides feedback.

To further explore the identification of child modes and the completion of the pattern cycle reminder card, the case of William and Sarah is used as a practical example.

Sarah and William, 35 years old

T: Let's continue standing and reflect on the child modes that were behind the coping modes that William and Sarah displayed. To do this, I will place two chairs behind each of the chairs representing Sarah and William's coping modes. One will be the "red" chair, symbolizing the emotions of anger or disgust associated with the Angry Child mode. The other will be the

(Continued)

(Continued)

"blue" chair, representing the emotions of sadness or fear corresponding to the Vulnerable Child Mode. Let's start with Sarah. Behind her overcompensating behavior—that is, when she accused William of being too exaggerated—which child mode do you think was present? The angry child with the red leg or the vulnerable child with the blue leg? That is, were you experiencing anger or disgust, or fear and sadness?

S.: Sadness.

T: I definitely think that emotion was present, but I think it was in the background. What I perceived from Sarah at that moment was anger, because I noticed her breathing was labored, her facial muscles, like her jaw, were tense, and her voice was high and firm. William, what active emotion did you perceive in Sarah?

G.: Anger.

T: So, although Sarah probably felt sad, what she clearly displayed was anger. Remember, some emotions are more visible, while others are hidden. Sarah, what do you think about this perception?

S.: Yes, I think the active emotion was anger, which means the activated child mode was the angry child with the red leg. However, she also felt sadness, although she didn't show it.

T: Exactly. Let's record this on our Mode Cycle card. So, let's remove the vulnerable child's chair and leave the angry child's chair. Now, let's move on to William. Behind his overcompensatory behavior, which child mode do you think was activated? The angry child or the vulnerable child?

G.: The angry child.

T: Sarah, do you agree with this perception?

S.: Yes.

T: Perfect. Let's also remove the vulnerable child's chair from William and leave him with the angry child's chair. Now, let's write this information down, and with that, we've completed the Mode Cycle card by highlighting the child modes displayed both in ourselves and in our partner. If it's okay, let's review it together so we can better understand how these dynamics were activated in our interaction.

As seen in the previous example, the therapist validates the emotion expressed by Sarah, but at the same time invites her to reflect on whether that was really the emotion she actively displayed during the discussion. This approach allows us to distinguish between emotions felt and the emotions displayed, which enriches the understanding of the dynamics of the active child mode.

6.3.1.3 Display the Mode Cycle

Finally, the couple is explained how one partner's coping style activates the other partner's child mode. This activation leads the second partner to initiate a coping mode to deal with the perceived child mode. In turn, this coping mode generates a reaction in the first partner, activating their own child mode, which leads them to respond with another coping mode.

In this way, a cycle of interaction develops in which the coping behaviors of both partners feed into each other, maintaining the problematic dynamic and perpetuating the conflict in the relationship. Identifying and understanding this cycle is the first step toward breaking it and building a healthier and more balanced pattern.

This dynamic holds regardless of which partner we begin with, as either can initiate the interaction cycle. To illustrate, the Mode Cycle is described below from the perspectives of both partners, starting with a different one in each case:

- **Mode Cycle Starting with William:** William accuses Sarah (William's overcompensation mode, red leg) of prioritizing her family of origin over her own children. This makes Sarah feel upset (William's angry child mode, red leg). In response, Sarah points out that William is exaggerating (William's overcompensation mode, red leg), which leads William to feel disqualified and also get angry at her (William's angry child mode, red leg).
- **Mode Cycle Starting with Sarah:** Sarah accuses William of being exaggerated (Sarah's overcompensation mode, red leg) due to the accusation that she prioritizes her family of origin over her children. William feels upset (William's angry child mode, red leg). Consequently, William accuses Sarah of being unfair and not accepting that she treats her children differently (overcompensation mode).

At the end of the explanation, the couple is asked if the illustrated cycle represents a typical pattern in their relationship. To facilitate this reflection and analyze it more clearly, the case of William and Sarah is used as a practical example.

Sarah and William, 35 years old
T: Let's now look at how this Mode Cycle works and how each person's coping mode reinforces the other's. For example, Sarah, your overcompensation mode activates William's angry child mode. To cope with this child mode, William responds with his own overcompensation mode, which in turn activates your angry child mode, causing you to react again with overcompensation toward him. This creates a cycle that repeats itself over and over again. Can you identify it?

(Continued)

(Continued)

S.: Yes, when he claims that I have preferential treatment with my family of origin, I get angry.
G.: And when she gets angry, she accuses me of being exaggerated, which in turn makes me angry.
S.: And then he confronts his anger by accusing me of being unfair and not accepting my mistakes.
G.: That makes me angrier, and the cycle continues.
T: Exactly. Now, what do you think you can do when you realize you've entered this circle?
S.: Stop before it grows any further.
T: And who can stop it?
G.: Either one. If you stop it, the cycle stops.
T: Exactly!

To identify the different modal cycles that exist between couples, you can consult Figure 3.1.

6.4 Closing the Session: Therapeutic Task: Try to Identify and Stop the Mode Cycle

Finally, as a therapeutic task, partners are asked to identify when a Mode Cycle begins between them, attempt to stop it, analyze which leg they are standing on, and, if possible, complete the Mode Cycle card (Figure 3.2). Practicing how to stop the Mode Cycle represents a first step before the next session (Module III), in which we will explore this process in greater depth.

To illustrate this last step, the following is how the therapist concluded the session in the case of Sarah and William.

Sarah and William, 35 years old

G.: Either one. If you stop it, the cycle stops.
T: This is why I'd like to leave you with a task: from now until our next session, try to notice when, every time you have a conflict and notice yourself entering a Mode Cycle, pause, stop it, analyze the leg you're leaning on, and, if possible, fill out the Mode Cycle card. What do you think?
S. AND G.: Yes.

Summarizing what has been presented in Module II, the following steps are recommended to be carried out during the session:

Beginning of the Session

- **Identification of the Problem to be Worked On:** The couple is asked to identify the conflict to be worked on in the therapy session:
- **Beginning of the Mode Cycle:** Both partners are asked to try to resolve the problem by discussing it directly with each other.
- **Stop the Mode Cycle:** Once detected, the therapist stops the Mode Cycle as soon as it starts.

Cognitive Work

- **Observer Team Work:** The therapist and partners stand and are psychoeducated to become aware of the following.
  - **Coping Modes:** Your active coping behaviors (overcompensating, surrendering, or avoiding).
  - **Child Modes:** Your Angry Child Mode (represented by the emotions of anger or disgust) or Vulnerable Child Mode (represented by the emotions of sadness or fear) is active.
  - **The Mode Cycle:** How the interaction between each partner's child and active coping modes perpetuates a Mode Cycle that maintains their problems as a couple.

Closing the Session

- **Therapeutic Task:** The therapist encourages each partner to stop the Mode Cycle (if possible, using the Mode Cycle card) when it occurs and identify which leg they are standing on.

7

Stopping the Mode Cycle (Module III)

7.1 Introduction

Once the couple is able to identify their needs and emotions, both active and blocked, as well as the coping modes that were active and the flexible coping behaviors that could have been used—and once they understand how one partner's coping mode activates the other partner's, creating a vicious cycle that maintains the problem—the next step is to help the couple identify and stop these modes themselves.

7.1.1 General Objective

Helping the couple stop the Mode Cycle by themselves using the "time out" technique.

7.1.2 Specific Objectives

- The couple should agree on a signal to stop the Mode Cycle each time it occurs and set a time to resume living together.
- Both partners identify the importance of stopping the Mode Cycle themselves as an indispensable requirement for improving their relationship.
- Both partners identify the process to follow after interrupting the Mode Cycle: make the agreed-upon signal, separate into two rooms, reflect on their child mode and active coping mode (and, if possible, identify the Mode Cycle that was triggered, the blocked emotions, and the flexible coping behaviors that could be used), and then resume coexistence without discussing the issue until the next session.

- Model in the session the process to follow to stop the Mode Cycle by themselves.

7.2 Beginning of the Session: Identify the Problem to Be Worked on and Start and Stop the Cycle

As in previous sessions, the therapist begins the session by asking the couple what they would like to work on during the session. Once the topic is identified, he asks them to address it directly among themselves (chairs 2A and 2B in Figure 3.5). The therapist stops the Mode Cycle as it begins.

To see how work begins in this module, we review the case of William and Sarah. The session begins by asking them to try to resolve a conflict directly by talking to each other.

Sarah and William, 35 years old

T: What would you like to work on today in our session?
G.: I'm not sure.
S.: I would like to talk about a discussion we had recently.
T: Sure, go ahead.
S.: William didn't want to come with us to visit my parents this weekend.
T: William, do you think it's okay if we talk about this topic here?
G.: Yes, it's fine.
T: Perfect. Would you like to place the chairs facing each other and talk directly, as we've practiced in previous sessions?
G.: Okay.
S.: Yes, that seems fine to me.
T: Okay then, let's get started.
S.: I'm very upset. You had no valid excuse for not joining us.
G.: You could have stayed, too. Why do we always have to spend Sundays with your mom?
S.: You know that my mother is already old, and your children want to live with their grandparents.
G.: But they also want to spend more time with us as a family. It seems like you care more about seeing your mom than being with me.
S.: You're selfish! You only think about yourself and what you need.
G.: Me, selfish?
T: Sorry to interrupt, but I notice the Mode Cycle has already begun.

7.3 Cognitive Work

7.3.1 Observer Team Work

Once the therapist interrupts the interaction and asks the partners to stand up, the following steps are carried out:

1. **Disadvantages of the Mode Cycle:** The therapist motivates partners to stop their Mode Cycle by pointing out the disadvantages and negative consequences that allowing the cycle to develop and run its course has on the relationship.
2. **Stopping the Mode Cycle Themselves:** The therapist points out to the couple that without "excuses" or "buts," it is essential, no matter who, that when either of them identifies that a Mode Cycle is developing, they stop it.
3. **Establishing a Cue:** The therapist asks the couple to choose a nonverbal cue that will allow them to signal to the other that they have noticed the Mode Cycle has been activated. The following suggestion can be made: "One cue that might work effectively for you is to signal for time-out by making the letter T with both hands. What do you think of this idea?" If the couple agrees with the cue, they agree that once one partner shows it to the other, both partners must stop.
4. **Establish a Time to Reconnect:** The therapist clarifies that the partner who signals the need for a time-out will be responsible for setting its duration. During this period, both partners should physically distance themselves from each other, for example, by retreating to their respective bedrooms.
5. **Separate into Different Rooms:** The therapist asks participants to turn their chairs in opposite directions, simulating a living separately but together. At home, when one of the two gives the signal, they will go to different rooms (chairs 2A and 2B, positioned so that they are back to back in Figure 3.5).

Reflection: If one of your clients asks you how long it is reasonable to establish the separation necessary to try to rebalance emotionally, what would you answer?

Therapist's Advice: The time required for a person to emotionally regulate after intense arousal may vary from person to person. However, research has established certain general parameters. Mennin and Fresco (2014) explain that prolonged emotional arousal can influence the interpretation and processing of the experience, skewing thoughts and hindering emotional regulation. In this sense, maintaining intense emotional arousal for more than 30–45 minutes can reinforce dysfunctional response patterns rather than promoting recovery. Based on this, a 30-minute period is a good starting point to facilitate emotional regulation before resuming discussions or making important decisions.

To illustrate how the therapist guides partners through the process of stopping the Mode Cycle on their own, the case of Sarah and William is continued as an example.

Sarah and William, 35 years old

T: Remember that when the Mode Cycle starts, it's important to stop it. I think with the work we've done, you're better equipped to identify when a cycle starts and stop it on your own. What do you think?

S.: Yes, I think so.

G.: Me too.

T: Perfect. I want to emphasize that if we don't stop the cycle in time, problems tend to escalate. Therefore, I suggest that when either of you notices the cycle starting, you stop it without excuses. To facilitate this, I suggest using a nonverbal signal, such as a "T" with your hands, indicating that you need a "time-out." What do you think of this idea?

S.: Sounds good to me.

G.: Me too.

T: Okay, then let's establish the commitment. Starting today, when either of us gives the signal, both of us will stop at that moment. Is that okay?

S.: Yes.

G.: Yes.

T: Once one of you signals "time-out," you must separate into separate rooms and cannot return until the time established by the person who signaled the time-out. Try to come up with a reasonable amount of time that will allow you to balance yourselves during the time-out before returning to your own company. Do you agree?

S.: Yes.

G.: Yes.

T: Okay, now let's move the chairs so they're facing opposite directions. This will represent, in the session, that they both went to separate rooms.

Reflection: What would you do if one of the participants does not agree with implementing time-out?

Therapist's Advice: It is important to work on the cognitive aspect so that both partners understand the importance of time-out as a tool for regulating emotions and avoiding conflict escalation. It is suggested that potential resistances be explored and the disadvantages of not using this technique be highlighted. Likewise, the reluctant partner can reflect with the partner on whether current strategies are meeting their needs and how time-out

(Continued)

(Continued)

could be a more effective alternative. In some cases, one partner's negative schemas are so intense that they trigger strong emotions during time-out. This causes resistance to implementing the time-out exercise. In these cases, it is recommended that the client work on their negative schemas in individual therapy.

7.3.2 In-session Work to Support Rebalancing

The therapist explains to the couple that, once in separate rooms, each partner will work on rebalancing themselves by standing up and, as practiced in therapy, first reflecting on the currently active need. Then, they will place an empty chair in front of them to represent the coping mode that was active during the conflict, and another chair behind it to symbolize the activated Child mode. This setup will help them become aware of which "leg" they are standing on, opening the possibility to shift to the other leg.

In Figure 3.5, chairs 2A and 2B represent each partner's coping modes and are positioned back-to-back to symbolize the separation. From these positions, each partner stands up and moves to positions 4A and 4B, while the therapist stands in position 1B.

To do this, they will need to identify: The unmet or background need; the blocked or hidden emotion (Child mode); and the flexible coping behavior that could have been used instead.

Reflection: What happens if the partners don't have chairs in their rooms?

Therapist's Advice: This book offers basic working principles and a structured approach to applying them. As a therapist, it's important to use your creativity when implementing the model, as long as the structural logic is respected. For example, if partners are in separate rooms and don't have chairs available, each partner can simply imagine the chairs in front of them—provided they stand up to do the work from the observer's stance.

In the session, the therapist conducts a guided rehearsal to help each partner practice this task. First, the therapist works with one partner to identify which "leg" is active and which is blocked during the discussion shown in the session. Then, the therapist repeats the same exercise with the other partner, facilitating the partner's identification of their own active and blocked "legs."

A useful tool to help couples identify their current needs and emotions during a conflict is to provide them with the following guiding questions. These questions are divided into three main categories: needs, emotions, and coping modes, and are organized according to the perspectives of the blue and red "legs" (Table 7.1).

Subsequently, the therapist invites the couple to reflect on the needs, emotions, and coping modes that were present during the interaction. To do this, the same questionnaire is used, but this time it is completed from the perspective of the other partner in order to identify the "leg" from which each person was reacting during the conflict.

Table 7.1 Reflection questions to identify one's own needs, emotions, and active coping modes during time-out.

Leg	Blue	Red
Need	Right now, my mind is going toward:	
	• What to ask my partner to understand them better.	• Let him understand what I'm saying.
	• What I have to change so that my partner feels better.	• What my partner needs to change for me to feel better.
	• My share of responsibility in the problem.	• My partner's share of responsibility in the problem.
	• Finding what my partner needs from me right now.	• See what I need from my partner at this moment.
	• Identify how my partner is feeling about what happened.	• Think about how I feel about what happened.
	• Apologize for my mistakes.	• That my partner recognizes his mistakes and apologizes for them.
Emotions	At this moment, I feel that:	
	• My chest tightens.	• My chest is expanding.
	• My stomach is in knots.	• My stomach expands.
	• My breathing is difficult.	• My breathing is easy.
Coping modes	At this moment, I feel the impulse to:	
	• Submit: obey so that he feels better.	• Fight: complain, accuse, or impose my point of view.
	• Saying yes: accepting to prevent the conflict from continuing.	• Withdrawing: Moving away from my partner and seeking an activity that comforts me for the bad time I went through.
	• Disconnect: distract myself from what is happening right now.	• Getting revenge indirectly: expressing sarcasm or responding rudely.

Source: Adapted from Roediger (2025).

Once the active leg and the blocked leg have been identified, and in order to facilitate a shift toward the blocked one, each partner is invited to answer the following questionnaire while remaining in separate rooms, focusing on the leg that was blocked (Table 7.2).

To illustrate how the therapist guides the couple through the process of emotional rebalancing while they are in separate rooms, the case of Sarah and William is further developed as an example.

Table 7.2 Reflective questions to identify, during the time-out, your own neglected needs, hidden or blocked emotions, and the flexible coping behaviors that could be used.

Blocked leg	Blue	Red
Need	Reflection questions to connect with the blocked need:	
	• How does my partner feel about this situation? • What do you need from me right now? • In this situation, what is my share of responsibility for the problem? • Based on her life history, what is triggered in her from her past by my behavior? • What has my partner given up on in the past to make me feel better?	• How do I feel about this situation? • What do I need from my partner right now? • In this situation, what is my share of responsibility for the problem? • Based on my own life, what is triggered in me from my past when she behaves that way? • What have I given up on in the past and need to stop doing so in order to achieve a more reciprocal and balanced relationship?
Emotions	Complete the sentence:	
	• It makes me sad that my partner____________ • I'm afraid that my partner____________	• It makes me angry that my partner_________ • I feel disgusted that my partner_________
Coping modes	Reflection questions to connect with more flexible coping behavior:	
	• What aspects of the situation could I be willing to give in to without sacrificing my essential needs? • How could I cooperate with my partner while still respecting my own needs?	• What do I need to express or suggest so that my needs can also be understood and considered? • In what aspects do I need to stand firm in order to protect my most important needs?

Source: Adapted from Roediger (2025).

Sarah and William, 35 years old

T: When each of you is in separate rooms, the first thing I ask you is to stand and, from an observer's stance, reflect on what needs, emotions, and coping modes you were experiencing during the conflict. As we've practiced in therapy, I suggest using a chair in front of you as a symbolic resource to analyze the situation "from above." I'd like us to work through this exercise together here in session to exemplify how you can do it at home. Would you mind if we started with you, Sarah?

S.: Yes.

T: Do you agree, William?

G.: Yes.

T: Okay, Sarah. Let's imagine we're in your room after the conflict. You've separated from William, you're standing, and you've placed this chair in front of you. Now ask yourself: What need was active in Sarah during the argument with William?

S.: Her need for assertiveness. She wanted William to understand how much it hurt her that he did not support her.

T: What emotion were you experiencing?

S.: Anger.

T: And what coping mode did you adopt?

S.: Fighting. She tried to impose her point of view on him.

T: Very well. Now, William, when you're in your room, you'll also analyze both your needs and Sarah's. Do you agree with the assessments Sarah just shared?

G.: Yes.

T: Perfect. Remember to do this analysis separately when you're home. William, during the conflict, what need was active in him?

G.: His need for assertiveness. He wanted Sarah to understand and support him in not going with his mother on Sunday.

T: Regarding emotions, do you think he was more angry, upset, sad, or afraid?

G.: I think I was more angry.

T: I agree. And what about coping?

G.: I was blaming Sarah, so I would say I was overcompensating.

T: To wrap up, it's important that both of you try to regain balance by connecting with the "blocked leg" during the conflict—that is, by reflecting on the need that was left in the background, the emotion that was blocked or hidden, and the flexible coping behavior that could have been used. Let's start with Sarah: What was the need that was left in the background for her?

(Continued)

(Continued)

S.: Her need for attachment–connection.

T: And in William's case?

G.: Also, my need for attachment–connection.

T: Okay. Now I'd like you both to reflect on your need for attachment and connection by answering the following questions: How does my partner feel about this situation? What do they need from me right now? In this situation, what is my share of responsibility for the problem? Based on their life history, what is my behavior triggering in them from their past? What has my partner given up in the past to make me feel better? Do you have the answers?

S.: Yes.

G.: Yes.

T: All right, let's move on to the emotions. William, what emotion was blocked or hidden for you?

G.: Sadness.

T.: And in your case, Sarah, what was the emotion that was blocked or hidden?

S.: Sadness as well.

T: Now connect with your blocked emotions by answering these phrases: It makes me sad that my partner... and It scares me that my partner... Have you been able to connect with these emotions?

S.: Yes.

G.: Yes.

T: Finally, reflect on the flexible coping behaviors you could have used by answering the following questions: What can I give in this situation without sacrificing myself? What can I do to ensure my partner's needs aren't frustrated? Do you have the answers?

S.: Yes.

G.: Yes.

Reflection: With which of the two partners of the couple do you consider most appropriate to begin the analysis of their needs, emotions, and coping modes?

Therapist's Advice: In general, it's recommended to start with the partner who shows the greatest emotional arousal, especially if they are in an overcompensatory or active avoidance coping mode. Working with this person first helps reduce their arousal, facilitating a more receptive connection to what the other partner presents during the exercise. However, it's essential to validate this decision with both partners, asking them if they agree to start with the person suggested by the therapist.

It's important to clarify that the questionnaires are only a working proposal; the therapist should choose the questions or strategies they deem most appropriate to help partners connect with their blocked needs, emotions, and feelings. For example, the work can be done first with one client until that partner can rebalance, and then move on to the second partner. The model is flexible with therapeutic styles; the important thing is to meet the objective of the modules. In this case, the objective is for them to stop the Mode Cycle, take time out, try to rebalance, and coexist again without addressing the topic until the next session.

Similarly, to avoid writing the case in too lengthy a manner, the therapist's approach to rebalancing is summarized, generally listening to each partner's responses. It's also important to clarify that this is a first approach to rebalancing; the next session (Module IV) will focus more on working on it in depth. In cases where there are significant blocks or difficulties in connecting with these emotions, needs, or flexible coping behaviors, specialized strategies to promote emotional rebalance will be addressed in Modules V, VI, VII, or VIII.

It is important for the therapist to clarify to the couple that they are not expected to perform the process perfectly, but that the main objective is to stop the Mode Cycle and take some time to regulate emotionally. The process of identifying the active and blocked legs, along with the respective underlying needs, child and coping modes present, and the Mode Cycle that is being repeated in the interaction, requires practice and time. As the couple progresses in therapy, these skills will be refined.

7.4 Closing the Session

7.4.1 Restore Coexistence

The therapist explains to the couple that, once the established time for re-equilibration in separate rooms has elapsed, it will be time to resume daily life, setting aside any attempt to discuss the problem. The recommendation is to postpone the discussion until the next couples therapy sessions.

It's essential for the therapist to emphasize that, after the agreed-upon time, there's no need to attempt to reconnect emotionally or resolve the conflict immediately. Instead, it's suggested that both partners treat each other cordially and respectfully, similar to how they would treat a neighbor, coworker, or friend. This helps the couple avoid further disagreements and maintains a calm and cooperative atmosphere.

Before concluding, the therapist should ask the couple if they have any questions or concerns regarding this point. The couple's willingness to limit the conflicts and temporarily stop them while they cool down their emotional arousal constitutes a significant and essential change. This adjustment represents the first step toward rebuilding the relationship and allows them to move on to the next phase of rebalancing.

If, at the end of the time-out, one partner is unable to regulate their emotions, it is suggested that they inform the other and continue in a separate room, taking another 30 minutes to rebalance. This process can be repeated as many times as necessary until the person calms down and is ready to resume the interaction constructively.

To illustrate this step, the case of William and Sarah is reviewed below. The therapist explains that the final part of the process involves returning to their daily routine without addressing the conflict again until the next couples therapy session.

Sarah and William, 35 years old

T: Now that you've both worked separately on trying to rebalance, I'd like to ask: Do you feel any different compared to when you stopped the Mode Cycle?

S.: Yes.

G.: Yes.

T: Very well. Now I ask you to move your chairs back and face each other. This symbolizes that, once the agreed-upon time for rebalancing is over, you can both leave the rooms and resume living together. It's important to remember that during this time, you should not revisit the topic of conflict. This will be addressed only during our next session together. In the meantime, I recommend that you treat each other with cordiality and respect, even if one of you seems a little distant. If at any point you feel you need more time to rebalance, it's important to communicate this clearly to your partner and return to the room. In the meantime, the other partner can continue with their daily life, respecting the space of the person who is still working on rebalancing, as we did today in the session, and avoiding entering their space. Does this approach make sense to you?

S.: Yes.

G.: Yes.

Reflection: Why does the therapist ask the couple not to discuss the problem if this could be interpreted as a form of avoidance? Wouldn't it be better to encourage the couple to try to resolve the conflict once they're both calmer?

Therapist's Advice: It is essential to understand that the modules represent structured steps in a gradual process that the couple must go through. At this stage, the couple is just beginning the rebalancing process, and this will be consolidated in the next session (Module IV) before moving on to the reconnection stage (Modules IX–XII). The objective at this point is not to resolve the conflict immediately, but to allow both partners to rebalance. In the next session, the therapist will assess whether there is sufficient evidence that both partners are ready to move to the reconnection stage. If this is the case, Modules IX–XII will be worked on. However, if either partner is still having difficulty rebalancing, it will be necessary to work on Modules V–VIII, which are designed to strengthen this process before moving on to the reconnection stage.

To summarize and facilitate the explanation of the entire process to the couple, from the interruption of the Mode Cycle to the resumption of cohabitation, a reference script is presented below that can serve as an example.

Example 7.1 Script to Highlight the Negative Consequences of Not Stopping the Mode Cycle

It doesn't matter who initiates the Mode Cycle; the important thing is that both of you contribute to maintaining it. If neither of you is able to stop it, this can lead to the erosion of the relationship and/or an emotional disconnect between you, putting your continued relationship at risk. For this reason, I want to emphasize the importance of stopping the Mode Cycle. The good news is that you both have the power to do so. Therefore, I would like to ask you, right now, to agree on a specific signal you can use to indicate that you have identified the activation of the Mode Cycle. It is crucial that, when either of you displays this signal, you both commit to honoring it and stopping the argument immediately. The partner displaying the signal will be the one who defines how much time will be necessary before living together again. During that time, each of you should go to a different space in the house, preferably a bedroom, to dedicate yourself exclusively to emotional rebalancing. This involves working on activating the blocked emotion and need, making the corresponding "leg" change. After the established time, you can interact again, but without discussing the conflict. It's important to respect if either of you isn't ready for close contact at the moment and maintain a cordial and respectful interaction.

7.4.2 Therapeutic Task: Stopping the Mode Cycle Themselves

As homework, the couple is asked to stop as many fights as possible. It is essential for the therapist to motivate the couple by recognizing their achievements and reinforcing their commitment to the process, emphasizing that therapy is a journey with advances and setbacks.

At this point, the therapist can explain that establishing new patterns involves neurological challenges, due to the brain's natural tendency to cling to previously established patterns. This process requires dedication, energy, and constant motivation to consolidate the change. Highlighting these aspects helps normalize the difficulties and encourages the couple to continue working toward their progress.

Below is how the therapist explained to William and Sarah the therapeutic task of stopping the Mode Cycle on their own, practicing the process presented in the session.

Sarah and William, 35 years old

T: Very well, I congratulate you on the work you've done. I think you're now ready to identify the emotional arousal you're feeling and manage it by calling a time-out when you detect a pattern starting. Therefore, as homework, I ask you to work on stopping as many Mode Cycles as possible, following the procedure we practiced in the session: give the agreed-upon signal, retreat to separate rooms, and work on rebalancing yourselves emotionally. Once the agreed-upon time has passed, return to your normal routine, but without resuming the topic of the conflict until our next meeting. Is that okay with you?

G.: Yes.

S.: Yes.

T: I ask you to be patient with yourself and work hard at applying these strategies. Remember, this is a new skill that requires practice and conscious effort. If you don't get it right the first time, don't worry; the important thing is to keep trying and learning in the process.

To summarize the steps applied for the development of Module III, the steps recommended during the session are presented below.

Beginning of the Session

- **Identification of the Problem to be Worked On:** The couple is asked to identify the conflict to be worked on in the therapy session.

- **Beginning of the Mode Cycle:** Both partners are asked to try to resolve the problem by discussing it directly with each other.
- **Stop the Mode Cycle:** Once detected, the therapist stops the Mode Cycle as soon as it starts.

Cognitive Work

- **Observer Team Work:** The therapist asks the couple to stand and follows these steps:
  - **Disadvantages of the Mode Cycle:** The therapist explains the negative consequences of not stopping the Mode Cycle.
  - **Stopping the Mode Cycle themselves:** The therapist tells them that from now on, they will have to stop as many Mode Cycles as they can on their own.
  - **Set a Signal:** The couple agrees on a common signal to stop the Mode Cycle.
  - **Set a Time to Reconnect:** The therapist specifies that whoever requests a "time-out" must set a duration for the time-out.
  - **Separate into Different Rooms**: Once the time-out is established, the therapist instructs them to retreat to separate rooms.
- **In-session Work to Support Rebalancing:** The couple will attempt to rebalance by standing up and bringing awareness to their active need. Then, a chair will be placed to represent their active coping mode. Next, a second chair will be placed behind the first one, symbolizing their active child mode (and, if possible, also their partner's). With this setup, the "leg" on which they are currently leaning will be identified. Afterward, the therapist will help explore the need that was left in the background, the blocked or hidden child mode and emotion, as well as the flexible coping behavior that could be used to support the leg switch.

Closing the Session

- **Reestablishing Coexistence:** The therapist indicates that once the rebalancing period has passed, they should return to living together, but without discussing the problem until the next therapy session.
- **Therapeutic Task:** The therapist encourages each partner to identify and stop the Mode Cycle when it occurs.

8

Rebalancing After Separation: Entering Healthy Adult Mode (Module IV)

8.1 Introduction

At this point in therapy, the couple should be able to interrupt a Mode cycle on their own whenever it arises. This involves recognizing the trigger, separating into different rooms to rebalance emotionally, and then resuming their relationship without reactivating the conflict.

The next step in the therapeutic process is to work on establishing a stronger emotional balance, which will serve as the basis for later seeking reconnection.

Regardless of the type of Mode Cycle the couple enters, these cycles often lead to disconnection between partners. For this reason, this module will encourage each partner to reconnect with their attachment needs once the couple has separated, calmed emotionally, and rebalanced. During this module, the therapist encourages the couple to connect with their attachment needs through exercises designed to facilitate this process and help both partners become aware of how it feels to have that need met.

8.1.1 General Objective

The couple can connect with their healthy adult and their basic needs, establishing flexible coping behaviors to be able to satisfy them (taking the initiative, being firm and cooperating, and giving in).

8.1.2 Specific Objectives

- Both partners can find balance by connecting with their need for assertiveness and autonomy and seeking to satisfy it through the flexible coping behavior of initiative and firmness by asking for what they expect from their partner through the exercise of connection dialogues.

- Both partners manage to detect their need for attachment–connection by finding positive memories of their partner and seek to satisfy it through the flexible coping behavior of cooperating-yielding by offering something to their partner through the exercise of connection dialogues.
- Promote the importance of balancing the use of both legs by highlighting the role of the blue leg in facilitating reconnection.
- Let the couple identify the advantages of using the blue leg to resolve relationship problems.

8.2 Beginning of the Session: Identify the Problem to Be Worked on and Start and Stop the Cycle

The session begins like the previous ones: the therapist asks the couple what they would like to "bring to the session." Once the problem is identified, the therapist asks them to discuss it directly (chairs 2A and 2B in Figure 3.5). Depending on the case, the therapist can move on to the next step or wait for the cycle to begin before stopping it.

Below is how the therapist begins the fourth session with William and Sarah, and details the issues that will be addressed during this session.

Sarah and William, 35 years old

T: I would like to know, what are you bringing to work in therapy today?

G.: I would like us to discuss today how Sarah has neglected the children because she is too concerned about her mother's health.

T: Sarah, do you think it's okay for us to work on this topic?

S.: Yes, that seems fine to me.

T: Okay, then I would ask you to turn your chairs so you are facing each other and speak directly to each other.

G.: You are neglecting the children because you spend too much time taking care of your mother.

S.: That's not true, the children are fine.

G.: No, our son told me that you came home in a bad mood and yelled at him the other day.

S.: This isn't easy for me. Our son should also understand that I'm going through a difficult time and not push me so hard. Besides, you're not supporting me by helping them understand that "Mom needs space because she's so stressed."

(Continued)

(Continued)

G.: But your main responsibility is to your children, not to your mother. You have other siblings who could help you.

S.: God forbid your mother gets sick, and you need my help, because...

T: I'd like to stop you here, because I think your Mode Cycle has already started.

Reflection: Do you think it is always necessary to start the Mode Cycle at the beginning of the session so that the therapist can intervene?

Therapist's Advice: At this stage of couples therapy, since both partners have already developed the ability to stop the Mode Cycle and regulate themselves emotionally, the therapist may choose to move directly into balancing work once the Mode Cycle has been identified and put in place. As the couple progresses through the reconnection modules, the therapist can facilitate the transition directly from conflict to dialogue, allowing both partners to use both legs in a balanced way to manage and resolve their disagreements more effectively.

8.3 Cognitive Work

8.3.1 Observer Team Work

Once the therapist stops the Mode Cycle, they ask the partners to stand and begin working from the observer position. In this exercise, the observer team analyzes "from above" what happened "below" in the chairs during the conflict.

From this perspective, the therapist guides the couple through the following steps:

- **Identify the coping mode:** The therapist positions one chair to represent the active coping mode. The therapist then supports each partner in identifying what these modes were during the previous coping cycle. To do this, the therapist stands in position 1B, while the partners stand in positions 4A and 4B, observing the chairs that represent their coping modes (chairs 2A and 2B in Figure 3.5).
- **Identifying the Child Mode:** The therapist points to another chair to symbolize the active child mode. The therapist then guides the couple in determining how that child mode manifested in the Mode Cycle they just experienced. From the same positions as before, the partners observe the chairs representing the child modes (chairs 3A and 3B in Figure 3.5).
- **Identifying the Mode Cycle:** The therapist invites both partners to close their eyes and reflect on the Mode Cycle that was generated during the

conflict, helping them visualize and understand the emotional dynamics that were activated.

The therapist explains that, from that moment on, whenever they interrupt the Mode Cycle and go into separate rooms, they should engage in the rebalancing work by becoming aware of their own active needs, emotions, and coping modes. To illustrate this process during the session, the therapist turns chairs 2A and 2B, following the arrangement shown in Figure 3.5, so that they face in opposite directions. In this way, the chairs symbolize that both partners are in separate rooms. Each partner is then invited to identify the need that was left in the background, the blocked or hidden emotion, and the flexible coping behavior that could have been used. In addition, they are encouraged to identify the Mode Cycle as they did during the session, reflecting on how their coping modes and those of their partner reinforce each other and create a vicious cycle.

To support the identification of the Mode Cycle and help the couple detect it when applying this strategy at home, the therapist may provide them with the card format presented in Figure 3.2.

The following example illustrates how the therapist guides the observer team's analysis of both the active coping and child modes, as well as the identification of the blocked or hidden child-mode emotion and the flexible coping behavior that could have been used. The section below presents the work carried out during the fourth session with William and Sarah.

Sarah and William, 35 years old

T: Would you like to stand up and begin the observer team's work? This will help us analyze what's happening with William and Sarah. I'd like to start with Sarah. Is that okay?

S.: Yes.

G.: Yes.

T: Let's place one chair behind Sarah's: one will represent the active coping mode. Now, tell me, how did Sarah behave? Was she overcompensating, surrendering, or avoiding? That is, was she fighting, fleeing, or submitting?

S.: Complaining, then I think I was overcompensating again.

T: Do you agree with this, William?

G.: Yes, she usually overcompensates.

T: Let's write this down on the Mode Cycle card. Now, I'd like you to think about what flexible coping behavior could have been used to switch legs.

(Continued)

(Continued)

G.: To cooperate or to give in.

T: Do you agree, Sarah?

S.: Yes.

T: Now, let's move on to William's case. We'll place one chair behind him as well, and we'll analyze what his active coping mode was. What do you think it was?

G.: I think it was overcompensation, too; he was trying to impose his point of view.

T: Do you agree with this, Sarah?

S.: Yes.

T: And what do you think was the flexible coping mode that could have been used?

S.: Giving in. William could have given in a little to what Sarah was asking of him.

T: Do you agree that the flexible coping mode William could have used was to cooperate or give in?

G.: Yes, but it's just that...

T: Let's remember that, for now, we are only describing the active behaviors and their flexible counterparts of these two people sitting "down there" in the chairs. Sorry to interrupt you, William.

G.: Okay.

T: Let's write these down on the modes cycle card. As you can see, the card is half-completed; we have both partners' coping modes. Now let's move on to analyzing the child modes. We'll use the same chairs. Let's start with Sarah. Which child mode was active in Sarah? That is, what emotion was present: anger, disgust, sadness, or fear?

S.: Anger.

T: Do you agree with this, William?

G.: Yes.

T: And what do you think was the blocked emotion?

S.: I think it was sadness, seeing that William was hurt.

T: Okay, let's write this on the mode card. Now let's move on to William's case. These two chairs behind his main chair will now represent his child modes. Which of the two was active and which was blocked?

G.: The active one was the angry boy, because he seemed very upset. And the blocked one was sadness, because he felt less important than Sarah's mother.

S.: But...

T: Remember, right now we're the observer team, and we're analyzing what we see from "above," observing those people "below." Sarah, from the observer team, do you think that William looked angry and had blocked out his sadness?

S.: Yes.

T: Okay, let's write this on the Mode Cycle card, and it will be complete for analysis. Now, I'd like to ask you to close your eyes and reflect on the Mode Cycle that was generated. William, your complaint about how Sarah spoke to your son after coming home from her mother's house in a bad mood activated her angry child mode. This led to her complaining about you not supporting her in helping her son be more empathetic to his needs, which, in turn, activated your own angry child mode. This prompted you to respond that she wasn't assuming her responsibility as a mother. Can you see how this cycle continued to feed itself?

S. AND G.: Yes.

T: Do you agree that something similar happened?

S. AND G.: Yes.

Reflection: When a partner identifies that he or she is avoiding, what type of leg does it correspond to: blue or red?

Therapist's Advice: It is important, when identifying an avoidant coping mode, to classify it as either active avoidance or passive avoidance. This distinction will allow partners to connect avoidance with its corresponding child mode: Active avoidance is often linked to the angry child, and passive avoidance is associated with the vulnerable child. This connection helps partners better understand the dynamics between their modes and their emotional responses, facilitating therapeutic work.

As seen in the previous example, the therapist chose, on this occasion, to use only one chair to represent both the coping mode and the active child mode, instead of placing two chairs behind the chair representing the person. It is important to emphasize that both options are equally valid. The therapist may choose to use two chairs to represent the active child modes and one for the coping mode, or use a single chair to work with the mode being explored at that moment. The choice will depend on the therapist's approach and the specific needs of the session.

8.3.2 Analyze the Advantages of Using the Blue Leg

Once the active coping and child modes have been analyzed, as well as the blocked or hidden emotion and the Mode Cycle, the next step in the session is to guide the couple toward emotional rebalance. To achieve this, the therapist follows these steps:

1. **Selecting the Partner to Work With:** The therapist suggests starting the rebalancing process with one of the limbs, usually the one most activated in the red leg. It is explained that the other partner will be the primary focus in the next session. If both agree, work begins with the selected limb.
2. **Advantages of Using the Blue Leg**: The therapist emphasizes the importance of using the blue leg to build a better connection with your partner, highlighting the advantages of expressing needs from a place of vulnerability (emotions such as sadness or fear).

To illustrate how to choose a partner and evaluate the advantages of using the blue leg, the case of Sarah and William is reviewed.

Sarah and William, 35 years old

T: Very well. Now I'd like to support you in your rebalancing work. To do this, we need to start with one of you. I'd like to start with you, William, and in the next session, we'll work with you, Sarah. Does that sound okay?

G.: Yes.

T: Do you agree, Sarah?

S.: Yes.

T: Before we begin, I want to remind you that now that you've learned how to stop the Mode Cycle and detach in order to rebalance, it's important to work on connecting with your need for attachment-connection, your emotions of fear and sadness, and your flexible coping behaviors, such as cooperating and giving in (your blue leg). Expressing what you need from this vulnerable stance offers a greater chance of finding balance, as humans tend to respond with empathy when we perceive vulnerability, but react with fight or flight when we perceive aggression. Does this make sense to you?

S.: Yes.

G.: Okay.

As shown in the previous case, it is essential for the therapist to encourage the couple to connect with their need for attachment and connection, explaining that compassion is a key tool for developing healthier connections. By expressing their needs and emotions from a place of vulnerability, their partner and even others are more likely to respond favorably.

To facilitate the implementation of cognitive work aimed at motivating the use of the blue leg as part of the rebalancing process, a reference script for use in the therapeutic session is presented below.

Example 8.1 Script for Performing the Cognitive Work to Explain the Need to Connect with the Blue Leg to Reconnect with One's Partner

From a neurobiological perspective, the brain releases oxytocin when it perceives vulnerability in another person. This hormone, known for its role in promoting empathy, compassion, and the wish to care, triggers a response of warmth and emotional connection. By leaning on our blue leg to express our vulnerability, we can facilitate this response in the other person. This not only calms us but also strengthens bonds and fosters emotional security in the relationship.

8.4 Experiential Work: "Best Day" Exercise

To initiate emotional connection, the therapist introduces the exercise called "The Best Day." While the couple is standing, the therapist asks them to close their eyes and then poses the following questions to each partner: How would you like your partner to behave next week? What would they do or stop doing? How does that make you feel in your body now? What are you willing to offer in return to encourage them to act that way? The active partner indicates the activity they would like to do together next week, describing it from a pleasant perspective, where both partners are enjoying the moment. The exercise is carried out in three sequential stages:

1. **With the Therapist:** With eyes closed and standing, the partner being worked with answers the questions directly as the therapist asks them. To provide a visual representation, the partner with whom the therapist is working carries out this step from the observer positions 4A or 4B, while the therapist stands in position 2B, as shown in Figure 3.5.
2. **Toward the Empty Chair:** With eyes open, the partner who is actively doing the exercise again expresses the responses to an empty chair representing his or her partner. From the previous position shown in Figure 3.5, the partner standing in positions 4A or 4B now speaks to the empty chair 2A or 2B, which represents their partner.
3. **Toward the Partner:** Sitting face to face, the partner expresses the answers directly to their partner, looking them in the eye and connecting genuinely. Following the arrangement shown in Figure 3.5, the partners sit in their respective chairs 2A or 2B, while the therapist occupies chair 1A. From this position, the partner with whom the therapist is working repeats the responses while looking at their partner.

It is important to clarify that the partner who is actively performing the "Best Day" exercise should express it toward the therapist and toward the empty chair (2A or 2B in Figure 3.5) from their flexible coping modes (taking initiative–assertiveness and cooperating–yielding). If this is not the case, the therapist should provide feedback to help the partner enter the corresponding flexible coping mode. Once the therapist verifies that the partner can do this, the exercise proceeds to expressing it face-to-face with their partner. At this stage, the chair 2A or 2B of this partner represents the flexible coping mode required to perform the leg switch.

Once the partner directly expresses their vision of the activity, the therapist asks the partner if they were able to visualize the image just described by the partner being worked on. If the response is favorable, the therapist proceeds to ask them how they see themselves in that image and how it makes them feel in their body. Similarly, the therapist asks the partner if there is anything they would like to change about that image to make it more appealing.

If the partner makes changes, the therapist establishes a negotiation process until both reach an agreement on how to spend "the Best Day." This is done by speaking face-to-face from chairs 2A and 2B in Figure 3.5, which represent their flexible coping modes.

It is important to clarify that the therapist provides feedback to help each partner respond to the other from a flexible coping mode. This involves, on the one hand, taking the initiative by asking for something and, on the other, cooperating by offering something in return. In this way, the therapist ensures that both partners remain in their flexible coping modes until they reach an agreement about the activity to be carried out during the week proposed in the "Best Day" exercise.

Once an agreement has been reached, the therapist asks about the positive emotions both partners experienced after agreeing on the activity they will do next week. They may also offer suggestions to help the partner become aware of their emotions while doing the exercise, asking questions such as: Do you feel closer to your partner or less close after doing this activity? The therapist may also ask the partners to ask each other how they experienced the exercise.

Reflection: What should you do if one partner is unable to connect with their blue or red leg and express their desires in a balanced way?

Therapist's Advice: In couples with sufficient healthy adult modes, they are likely to be able to reconnect and express their desires in a functional and balanced way after working on their rebalancing. In other cases, they may simply be able to resume daily life more calmly, which also represents significant progress. However, if one or both partners struggle with emotional rebalancing or expressing their desires appropriately, it will be necessary to work with them in Modules V–VIII, adapting the intervention according to the specific needs of each case.

To demonstrate how the therapist can implement the "Best Day" exercise, a reference script is presented below to facilitate its application in the therapy session.

Example 8.2 Script for the Best Day Image

"How would you like your partner to behave next week? What do you imagine him/her doing? What doesn't he/she do? What do you feel in your body when you imagine your partner like that? What are you willing to do for your partner in return for him/her to behave that way?"

To illustrate the application of the exercise in the therapeutic session, we return to the case of Sarah and William at the moment when the therapist implements the "Best Day Technique."

Sarah and William, 35 years old

T: I'd like to do an exercise with you, William. Imagine that after leaving this session, you're having the Best Day with Sarah. How do you imagine she'll behave?

G.: She's with us and the children, living together. She seems happy, not distressed or sad.

T: What does she do specifically?

G.: She laughs with the children, plays with them, and asks me how my work went.

T: How does that make you feel in your body now?

G.: I feel happy, it excites me.

T: And what would you be willing to offer her in return to encourage her to act this way?

G.: No more arguing with her.

T: It's a good intention, but, in theory, it should happen naturally if you both feel more connected. What do you think she needs from you that you could offer her in return?

G.: I'm not sure.

T: What do you think about offering on alternate Sundays? Going to her mom's house every other Sunday, in exchange for her being more connected to you and the kids during the week.

G.: It could be.

T: Okay. Now, open your eyes and, standing up, I'd like you to tell your partner what you'd like from them and what you're willing to offer them in return.

(Continued)

(Continued)

G.: Sarah, I'd like to see you happy, connected with the kids and me. I'd like you to ask me how work went, and in return, I'd like to spend Sundays with your mom every two weeks.

T: How do you feel about expressing it this way and from a more vulnerable place?

G.: I feel good.

T: Perfect. Now, Sarah, open your eyes, please. I'd like you both to sit in your respective chairs. William, now I want you to say the same thing to Sarah, but looking her directly in the eyes.

G.: Sarah, I want to see you more connected to us. I want to see you happy and for you to ask me how my work went. In return, I want to support you and accompany you to your mom's house every other Sunday.

T: William, how do you feel about expressing this directly?

G.: I feel good.

Reflection: What do you think the therapist should do when the client is unable to propose something reasonable in exchange for what he or she is asking of his or her partner?

Therapist's Advice: If the client is unable to offer anything attractive to their partner in exchange for desired behavior, the therapist can offer reasonable options that will allow for fair treatment. If the client is unwilling to compromise, it is necessary to work on the appropriate Modules V–VIII to facilitate rebalancing.

8.5 Closing the Session: Therapeutic Task: Identify the Active Leg, Bring a Positive Image, Reconnect with Your Partner, and Do the Best Day Activity

To conclude the session, the therapist assigns the couple homework: after stopping the Mode Cycle and moving to separate rooms, in addition to the rebalancing work outlined in the previous session, they must identify their Mode Cycle (if possible, by filling out the Mode Cycle card) and make a conscious effort to lean on their blue leg. As part of this exercise, they are asked to bring to mind a positive image of their relationship that generates warm and connective feelings, for example, remembering how, at the beginning of the relationship or during its best moments, they had positive emotions and desired to spend time with the other person. They can also make a list of "pluses" about their partner and read them during those moments to reinforce contact with their blue leg and their need for attachment and connection.

Finally, the therapist asks them to carry out the activity agreed upon during the Best Day exercise, reminding them that they may also consider doing more activities like this together during the week, taking turns choosing what to do.

The therapist reminds them that the same exercise will be performed in the next session, but with the partner who wasn't the main focus this time, ensuring that both partners work equally in the process.

To see how the session ends, the case of William and Sarah reviewed above is presented below.

Sarah and William, 35 years old

T: To end the session, I'd like to propose a task for this week. In addition to continuing to stop the Mode Cycle as we've practiced, when you're in separate rooms and working on rebalancing, if you're struggling, I want you to fill out the Mode Cycle card and take it a step further. Before returning to your daily tasks, I ask you to lean on your blue leg, bringing to mind a positive event in your relationship that generates warm feelings toward your partner, as well as making a list of positives you see in your partner. This will help strengthen your emotional connection. Do you agree?

G.: Yes.

S.: Yes.

T: You also have to do the homework agreed upon in the "Best Day" exercise. That is, one day a week, Sarah, you make an effort to disconnect from worrying about your mother and allow yourself to enjoy spending time with your children in the present. You ask William how work went. In return, William will visit your mother this Sunday or the next. Does that sound okay?

G.: Yes, that seems fine to me.

S.: Yes, me too.

Upon completion of Modules I–IV, if the therapist determines that the couple has sufficient emotional resources, appropriate skills, and a sufficiently developed healthy adult, as well as a solid foundation of emotional connection and willingness to collaborate, it will be possible to advance directly to the reconnection and coaching phase (Modules IX–XII). In these cases, the entire therapy may last between 12 and 15 sessions.

On the other hand, if one partner displays greater rigidity, whether by constantly justifying their behavior, questioning the therapeutic approach, or remaining trapped in automatic coping modes, it will be necessary to work on the intermediate modules (V–VIII) before moving forward. These intermediate modules will address these difficulties and facilitate progress toward emotional reconnection.

As a way to structure the work done in Module IV, the essential steps to put into practice during the session are described below.

Beginning of the Session

- **Identification of the Problem to be Worked On:** The couple is asked to identify the conflict to be worked on in the therapy session.
- **Beginning of the Mode Cycle:** Both partners are asked to try to resolve the problem by discussing it directly with each other.
- **Stop the Mode Cycle:** Once detected, the therapist stops the Mode Cycle as soon as it starts.

Cognitive Work

- **Observer Team Work:** The therapist and partners stand and become aware of the following.
  - **Child Modes:** Their angry or Vulnerable Child Mode is active and blocked.
  - **Coping Modes:** Their overcompensation, surrender, and avoidance are active coping modes and flexible coping behavior that represents its counterpart.
  - **The Mode Cycle:** How the interaction between each partner's child and coping modes perpetuates a Mode Cycle that maintains their problems as a couple.
- **Analyze the Advantages of Using the Blue Leg:** The therapist and the partners.
  - **Choosing the Partner to Work With:** The therapist and the couple agree on which partner will begin the rebalancing work.
  - **Advantages of Using the Blue Leg:** The therapist highlights the advantages of using the blue leg to establish rebalancing.

Experiential Work

- **"Best Day" Exercise:** The therapist applies the Best Day exercise, in which one partner reflects on a good moment they can experience with their partner in the coming week, becoming aware of what they need from their partner to make that moment a reality and what they can offer in return to motivate them to behave in the expected manner. This is done first toward the therapist, then toward the partner's chair, and finally directly to their partner.

Closing the Session

- **Therapeutic Task:** After stopping the Mode Cycle and moving to separate rooms, the therapist asks each partner to identify their Mode Cycle (preferably by filling out the Mode Cycle card) and make a conscious effort to lean on their blue leg, bringing to mind a positive image of the relationship and reading their partner's "pros" list. Finally, they must do the agreed-upon activity during the Best Day exercise.

Part III

Rebalancing

The initial modules lay the foundation for couple schema therapy: stopping the mode cycle, identifying the needs, emotions, and coping modes (red or blue leg) of each partner, and restoring balance by activating blocked needs and emotions and expressing them from a vulnerable perspective (blue leg). If the couple demonstrates sufficient emotional resources, they can move directly to the reconnection and coaching modules (Modules IX–XII). However, if either partner displays rigidity or struggles to move forward, it will be necessary to work on these intermediate modules (V–VIII).

In the intermediate modules, the approach may seem more individual, although the work is conducted in the presence of the partner. This work allows for addressing the rigid coping patterns and dysfunctional dynamics that arise in the mode cycle. It is essential for the therapist to actively engage the observing partner, asking them to connect emotionally with the other partner during the session. This prevents the observer from becoming disconnected or losing interest and teaches them how to interact more empathetically.

These modules seek to strengthen emotional connection through exercises that foster closeness, such as ending each session with a hug. They also generate a sense of unity that helps create a sense of connection throughout the session.

If one partner remains stuck in rigid coping modes, individual sessions may be necessary. This occurs when the person's activated schemas distort their perception of their partner, viewing them as a "caricature" through the lens of their schemas. This distortion affects their ability to be emotionally present, leading to maladaptive behavior.

In these cases, working individually allows the therapist to provide emotional security and help the client emerge from their protective coping mode. The trust developed in individual therapy is a prerequisite for the client to open up emotionally. This process includes:

- **Active therapist presence:** Being physically present, validating emotions and behaviors.
- **Building trust:** Making the client feel seen, heard, and understood.

When the client manages to leave their protective coping mode and experience a more open state, they acquire an "emotional map" of how this change feels, which makes it easier to work with later in couples sessions.

The intervention in these intermediate modules has three fundamental steps:

- **Stopping dysfunctional cycles:** Identifying and stopping conflict dynamics before they escalate.
- **Creating emotional connection:** During sessions, the therapist helps the couple spend quality time together, fostering a positive emotional connection. Between sessions, they are assigned tasks to create enjoyable moments in their daily lives.
- **Learning to communicate functionally:** Teaching them to speak from a place of vulnerability (need for attachment–connection) rather than a defensive or combative one (need for assertiveness–autonomy).

For a couple to effectively resolve conflicts, it is crucial for each partner to be aware of their emotional arousal (sympathetic nervous system) and learn to shift it to a calm state (parasympathetic nervous system). This process of emotional self-regulation allows the couple to be present and facilitate solutions.

It's important to clarify that, throughout these chapters dedicated to the intermediate modules, the terms "externalizing" or "internalizing" are used to refer to partners who struggle to find balance, as they tend to be overly fixated on one of their legs. However, this adjective should not be interpreted as a permanent label, as, depending on the situation and context, individuals can fluctuate between a more internalizing or externalizing stance.

The exercises presented in the following chapters (corresponding to Modules V–VIII) end by seeking rebalance where the partner who has shown difficulties in finding rebalance in the use of their legs asks something from their partner and offers something in return. If they do so in a balanced way and the other partner responds well, this can open the way for the therapist to apply the connection dialogues of Chapter 14 (Module XI). If the partners are not interested in rebalancing, it is recommended to work on the blocking patterns in individual sessions; if there is still no favorable response, preparation for separation can be addressed in the individual session, as discussed in Chapter 16 (Module XIII).

By teaching partners the techniques used in these leg rebalancing modules, both partners can apply them outside of the session, especially when they are in separate rooms and seeking to restore their balance.

9

Externalizing Partner (Module V)

9.1 Introduction

Modules V and VI addressed in this chapter are designed to provide tools for those partners who are excessively focused on the need for assertiveness and autonomy (self-centered), on emotions such as anger or disgust, and on coping modes such as overcompensation (controlling, dominant, bossy) or active avoidance (self-soothing behaviors such as addictions or passive-aggressive behaviors).

These individuals often have difficulty connecting with their blue leg, which represents the need for attachment and connection, as well as the basic emotions of fear or sadness. Connecting with this vulnerable part involves recognizing the desire to yield in order to maintain emotional closeness and connection with others.

It is important to remember that, before moving on to the reconnection modules, both partners must have worked on supporting themselves on their blue leg. This ensures that both are willing to engage emotionally and to prioritize cooperation and attachment.

The exercises described below are designed to help partners move out of the stagnation they experience when they remain rigidly on their red leg, and to guide them toward using their blue leg, thus fostering emotional and behavioral balance within the relationship.

Reflection: How can you determine whether a partner is acting from their red leg or their blue leg during the session?

Therapist's Advice: It is essential that, as a therapist, you learn to identify "reddish energy" in clients. This energy often manifests itself through behaviors such as a tendency to fight, dominate, or express anger and displeasure. A key sign is that you may feel a natural inclination to distance yourself or avoid interaction due to the intensity of their responses. However, it is crucial to maintain a professional, empathetic, and balanced stance. Recognizing this energy does not mean judging it, but rather understanding it as part of the client's active coping mechanisms.

When working with clients whose red leg is dominant and who have difficulty connecting with their blue leg or vulnerable side, the therapeutic process must be approached on two complementary levels: cognitive and emotional.

9.1.1 General Objective

Emotionally activating the need for attachment-connection in the externalizing partner.

9.1.2 Specific Objectives

- Triggering the externalizing partner's need for attachment and connection, and their negative emotions of fear or sadness, by imagining their partner leaving their life forever.
- Emotionally activating the externalizing partner's need for attachment and connection, as well as positive emotions, by recalling the good moments of the relationship.
- Helping the externalizing partner to express directly to their partner their need for attachment-connection and their emotions of fear or sadness.
- Facilitating the couple's ability to connect with the positive emotions generated by the expression of the externalizing partner's vulnerable side.
- The therapist encourages reconnection within the couple by setting up appointments to look at past photos, reminisce about good times, and provide positive feedback outside of the session.
- Reinforcing the couple's shift from the red leg to the blue leg by helping them identify how they feel before and after applying the exercises for externalizers.
- The therapist guides the externalizing partner to become aware of the positive value of the flexible coping behavior of having initiative-assertiveness.
- The therapist helps the externalizing partner become aware of the negative consequences their coping style has on their partner, motivating them to try a new alternative.
- Helping the couple reconnect physically and emotionally.

Below are key steps for guiding clients toward their Vulnerable Child Mode, particularly when they are overly focused on the child and coping modes associated with their red leg.

9.2 Beginning of the Session: Identifying the Problem to Be Worked on and Identifying That One of the Partners Is Too Focused on Their Red Leg

As in the previous modules, the therapy session begins by greeting the couple and identifying a problem they wish to work on, asking something like: "What are you bringing to the session today?" Once the conflict is defined, they are invited to discuss it directly among themselves (chairs 2A and 2B in Figure 3.5). If, during the interaction, they detect that one partner is stuck on their red leg, the therapist stops them. To do so, they may comment, such as: "Excuse me for interrupting the discussion, but I've just detected that you are not balanced enough to be able to negotiate between yourselves. That's why, before continuing, I'd like to do some exercises to find balance. But first, I invite you to see together which leg you are too fixed on and which one you need to move on to."

It is important to clarify that sometimes it is not evident that one of the partners is too fixated on their red leg until the mode cycle starts. In that case, the therapist interrupts the interaction once the cycle is triggered.

To illustrate this step related to the detection of stagnation of one of the partners of the couple on the red leg, the case of Beatrice and Bartholomew is presented below.

Clinical Case 21 Beatrice and Bartholomew, 35 years old

T: Very well, I would like you to tell me, what are you "bringing" to couples therapy today?

BEATRICE (BE): I want to say that I feel tired that Bartholomew spends so much time in his studio listening to music, while he doesn't help me do the weekend shopping, tries to spend quality time with me, or helps me take care of our pets.

T: Bartholomew, do you think we should address this topic?

BARTHOLOMEW (BA): Whatever.

T: I'd like to discuss this topic if you're in agreement. If you're not, that's fine too. But I'd like to know, what topic do you think you'd like to discuss in this session? And then we'll negotiate and decide. What do you think about what I'm telling you?

BA.: Yes, I also want to talk about that topic.

T: Okay, so I'd like you to try to talk about it directly.

(Continued)

Clinical Case 21 (Continued)

BE.: You never help me, you always spend your time locked in your damn room, I hate that place so much, one of these days I'm going to throw away all your records so you'll stop being obsessed with them.

BA.: If you throw away the records I'll buy more or charge you for them.

BE.: I'm tired of doing things alone, you can perfectly accompany me when I go shopping and instead you prefer to stay, but I'm tired of doing things alone, it seems that I don't have a husband, you don't help me at all. What's the point of us living together? 'You're like a piece of furniture.

BA.: Join you so I can listen to your complaints? No, thank you.

T: Sorry to interrupt the session, but for a good conversation that allows you to reconnect, you first need to be balanced, and I'm seeing that those conditions don't exist. Would you mind taking a closer look at this perception?

BA.: Yes.

BE.: Yes.

9.3 Cognitive Work

9.3.1 Observer Team Work

As soon as the interaction stops because one partner is stuck on their red leg, the therapist asks both partners to stand up and analyze what happened from an observer's perspective.

Then, the therapist places two chairs facing each other and explains that each one will represent one of the partners during the discussion. From these chairs, the following elements will be identified:

- **Coping Modes:** The therapist guides each partner to identify, from their respective chair, the active coping mode they used during the discussion (From positions 4A and 4B in Figure 3.5, the partners observe chairs 2A and 2B). Once identified, the other partner is asked whether they agree with this interpretation. If either partner has difficulty recognizing their coping mode, the therapist provides feedback to support the process.
- **Child Modes:** Next, the therapist indicates that each chair will also represent the child mode that was active during the discussion (from the previous position, the partners observe chairs 3A and 3B in Figure 3.5). Once each partner has identified their child mode, the other partner is asked whether they agree with the interpretation. If there are difficulties in identifying the child mode, the therapist offers support and feedback.

Once the coping and child modes of both partners have been identified, the therapist explains the identified mode cycle and how it perpetuates problems in the relationship, showing the interaction between the needs, emotions, and coping modes of both partners.

To see another way in which the therapist can explain the relationship between coping modes and their flexible version, below is a reference script that can be used during the therapeutic session.

Example 9.1 Adapted Script to Explain Coping Modes with Clients Who Are Highly Focused on Their Red Leg

Let's remember that there are three social roles. The first is to be active, to take the initiative, and to try to make something happen, or to dominate. If we try to take responsibility and try to make something happen, that's healthy. The second is to cooperate, give in, sacrifice, or submit, which is fine even with someone who is dominant. The third option is to withdraw to find balance before continuing.

Reflection: How should a therapist approach a client who perceives their red leg as a central part of their personality and essence?

Therapist's Advice: A client with a red leg leaning often identifies with the positive aspects associated with it, such as being active, taking initiative, and taking responsibility for making things happen. It is important for the therapist to validate this perception, recognizing these traits as strengths when expressed in a balanced way. By presenting the dominant role from a positive and balanced perspective, the client will be more receptive and less defensive. This lays the groundwork for inviting them to explore and connect with their vulnerable side, or their blue leg. It is crucial to emphasize that this shift does not mean giving in to submission or self-sacrifice, but rather finding a balance between both legs that fosters flexibility and adaptability.

To verify how the therapist, after stopping the interaction, analyzes the couple's coping and child modes and the mode cycle to demonstrate the excessive use of the red leg by the externalizing partners, the case of Beatrice and Bartholomew is reviewed below.

Beatrice and Bartholomew, 35 years old

T.: So I'd like you to stand up and form the observer team again. Now, let's look down at Beatrice's coping mode chair and ask ourselves: During the discussion a moment ago, did Beatrice overcompensate, surrender, or avoid?

BA.: I think the overcompensating.

T: Do you agree with this perception, Beatrice?

(Continued)

(Continued)

BE.: Yes.

T: And in Bartholomew's case, what kind of coping mode was he in?

BA.: In surrender mode.

T.: Yes, I'm sure he acted that way. However, it seems to me that his behavior was more avoidant—he didn't directly confront the situation with Beatrice. He also sounded a bit sarcastic and defiant, so I believe the visible coping behavior was active avoidance. Therefore, the leg he used was the red leg. But I'd like to know your opinion, Beatrice. What do you think about what I mentioned to Bartholomew?

BE.: Yes, it felt like he was challenging Beatrice when he said that if she throws the records, he'll just buy new ones, instead of confronting her directly. So I guess the behavior he showed was active avoidance.

T: What do you think of these ideas, Bartholomew?

BA.: Yes, I think in the end, what Bartholomew wasn't completely submitting, but rather he was challenging her.

T.: Now that we've identified the coping modes, let's move on to analyzing the child modes. Down there, in Bartholomew's child mode chair, what was activated during the session? Was it Angry Child mode or the Vulnerable Child Mode?

BA.: I think it was Angry Child mode mode.

T.: Beatrice, do you agree with that interpretation?

BE.: Yes.

T.: Now let's look at Beatrice's child mode chair from the recent discussion. What emotion did she express? Was it anger or disgust? Or was it sadness or fear?

BE.: She looked upset.

T.: So, what child mode would that be?

BE.: Angry Child.

T.: Bartolomeo, do you agree?

BA.: Yes.

T: So we see the mode cycle that happened in this couple as follows: Bartholomew, in active avoidance, ignored Beatrice by locking themselves in his room to listen to music. This triggered Beatrice's angry child mode, and she reacted with overcompensatory coping mode, complaining that she wasn't paying attention to him and that she was going to throw his CDs at him. This triggered Bartholomew's angry child mode, and he reacted with active avoidance coping mode, being sarcastic or seemingly indifferent to Beatrice's threats, which triggered her angry child mode, thus perpetuating the cycle. Does this make sense to you?

9.3.2 Analyze the Advantages and Disadvantages of Using the Red Leg

It's common for clients with difficulty getting out of their red leg to have experienced situations in the past in which, by being kind, giving in, or showing vulnerability, they didn't receive a favorable response from those around them. These experiences led them to associate vulnerability with a risk of abuse or manipulation, which motivated them to develop overcompensation or active avoidance strategies as a way to protect their emotional safety. The red leg, with its overcompensatory coping mode, then becomes a resource that gives them a sense of control and protection, avoiding the pain of being abused again.

The cognitive approach facilitates the process of overcoming this pattern, recognizing that overcompensation or active avoidance, although functional in the past, may be dysfunctional in the present.

After identifying the child and coping modes, in addition to the couple mode cycle, it is important to encourage rebalancing by working with the overcompensation or active avoidance coping mode by performing the following actions:

1. **Advantages of the Coping Mode:** The therapist begins by recognizing and validating the positive consequences of the red leg coping behavior in its flexible form: initiative and assertiveness. This behavior implies initiative and responsibility, and can be beneficial in the relationship if kept balanced.
2. **Disadvantages of the Coping Mode:** The therapist seeks to have the client reflect on whether his or her coping mode of overcompensation or active avoidance is fulfilling its main objective: satisfying his or her need for assertiveness-autonomy. This involves analyzing whether this strategy actually gets your partner to cooperate and do what is expected of them. Some key questions that can facilitate this exploration are: Are you achieving the results you want with this strategy? Is your partner cooperating the way you expect when you act this way, or is the opposite occurring?
3. **Propose a Change in Strategy:** The therapist suggests trying a new approach that involves connecting with their most cooperative and vulnerable side. It is essential to assure the client that, if this change doesn't work, they can always return to their previous strategy, which has been helpful in the past. This step reinforces the client's confidence, providing them with a "safe harbor" to return to if they feel that vulnerability puts them at risk.

If the person is more open or needs to connect more deeply with their emotions, the therapist may choose to move directly to rebalancing using some of the techniques for externalizers described in experiential work.

Reflection: What should be done if one partner claims to be operating from their blue leg, but both the therapist and their partner perceive them as operating from their red leg?

Therapist's Advice: When a client with an overcompensatory or actively avoidant coping mode states that they are being cooperative or feeling vulnerable, it is important to avoid directly contradicting them. Instead, validate their perception by saying something like, "I understand that a part of you is trying to be cooperative or is feeling vulnerable." At the same time, empathically point out that there is likely another side to their behavior that is being bossy, annoying, or controlling. Next, invite the partner to share their perspective by asking, "How do you perceive this situation?" If the conversation becomes conflictual, use the cell phone metaphor as a reminder that both perceptions represent complementary parts of the same reality. You can point out at the end, "I understand that you are feeling vulnerable, but your partner and I see another side right now."

To illustrate how to apply this cognitive approach, the case of Bartholomew and Beatrice is reviewed, in which the therapist guides Bartholomew (focused on the red leg) to recognize and validate his coping strategy, explore its dysfunctionality, and consider a new approach.

Beatrice and Bartholomew, 35 years old

T: I'd like to tell you, Beatrice, that I think it's a good idea for you to actively seek to talk with Bartholomew about what you don't like and what you'd like to achieve in the relationship. However, I'd like to ask you: How would you like Bartholomew to react to these requests: by cooperating, fighting, or fleeing?

BE: Cooperating.

T: Exactly! And the way you're expressing things is getting Bartholomew to use his blue leg in cooperation with you?

BE.: No.

T: I agree with you. Despite your repeated attempts to annoy him and urge him to change, he keeps locking themselves in his studio to listen to music. That's why I'd like to propose something new. You have nothing to lose: if it doesn't work, you can always go back to the way you've been behaving. What do you say we try it?

BE.: Yes.

Reflection: What can the therapist do when a client is so focused on their red leg that they cannot access their Vulnerable Child Mode?

Therapist's Advice: For many clients dominated by their red leg, accessing their Vulnerable Child Mode can be a completely new experience. This occurs because they are often in a state of precontemplation, where they are unwilling to explore other perspectives or emotions. To facilitate this shift, the therapist can use the technique of inviting the client to adopt a standing posture. This physical adjustment can stimulate, at the brain level, a greater willingness to open emotionally and cognitively. By changing their body posture, the client activates new processing pathways that help them explore blocked emotions, such as the vulnerability associated with their blue leg.

To facilitate the application of cognitive work in the rebalancing of the red leg, a reference script is presented below, which can be adapted to the therapist's personal style for use in session.

Example 9.2 Adapted Script to Explain the Cognitive Work to Make the Use of the Red Leg More Flexible

When you're adopting a firm coping strategy, proposing something in the relationship, I think you're hoping she'll cooperate. That's why I'd like us to reflect together: Are you making this happen? Is your partner cooperating? I think it's not working, and when the desired outcome and the actual outcome are different, it might be worth changing your strategy. That's why I'd like to propose something different. What do you think if I offer you this Plan B and you try it out? I want to make it clear that if putting this proposal into practice doesn't work, you can return to the previous strategy. You're not sacrificing anything; you're just gaining a second option, and then you can choose. If your brain has more options, it can be more flexible.

Reflection: How do you think we should work with clients who have a high resistance to experiential work in therapy?

Therapist's Advice: When working with clients who are more skeptical or who exhibit narcissistic traits, it's advisable to start with a cognitive approach before introducing emotional work. Addressing emotions directly can generate resistance, while a gradual approach allows for building trust and a willingness to open up emotionally. In these cases, it's helpful to frame interventions in a way that connects with their desire to improve and maintain control. For example, you can say, "You're doing great on your red leg, but I can teach you how to be even better." This type of statement appeals to their need to excel and can be particularly effective in capturing their attention. You can then reinforce the message by adding something like, "I can teach you something else, so you have more options. In the end, it's your decision, because you're the one in charge." This approach not only validates their need for control but also allows them to feel empowered to choose how to proceed. Once this openness is achieved, you can gradually move toward emotional work, integrating the necessary tools to connect with their more vulnerable side.

9.4 Experiential Work to Rebalance the Red Leg

For the experiential rebalancing of the red leg, depending on the characteristics of the session, the therapist may choose between the following two exercises to help balance the externalizing partner:

1. **Gaining Access to the Vulnerable Side** (Module V): Here, the client is invited to reflect on how they would feel emotionally upon realizing that their red leg behavior is pushing their partner away.
2. **Emotionally Reconnecting by Floating Back to a Honeymoon Scene** (Module VI): This exercise helps the client connect with positive emotions associated with closeness and cooperation with their partner.

The common goal is to facilitate the partner's connection with their need for attachment and connection, their vulnerable emotions (sadness or fear), and their desire to cooperate or compromise in the relationship.

Reflection: What aspects are addressed in individual therapy when these sessions are necessary during the rebalancing phase?

Therapist's Advice: When specific needs are identified that require individual sessions, these focus on exercises that help the client connect with their vulnerable side (blue leg) and understand how to do so in their relationship as well. In this context, it is crucial for the therapist to address the impact of the overcompensatory coping mode, explaining to the client how it can create emotional distance, both in the therapeutic relationship and with their partner. It is essential to convey this information empathetically, validating the positive intention behind their behavior but pointing out its consequences. Furthermore, the therapist should reinforce the importance of expressing emotions and needs from the blue leg, highlighting its positive impact.

Below is a reference script that illustrates how the therapist can empirically confront the overcompensatory coping mode in a client with an externalizing behavior pattern.

Example 9.3 Script for Empathically Confronting the Overcompensatory Coping Mode in Individual Therapy

I realize that your overcompensatory behavior is a way of protecting yourself and trying to get your needs met. However, this behavior can also cause both you and your partner to feel emotionally detached, making it difficult to connect with them as you truly desire.

To highlight the benefits of communicating from a place of vulnerability, a reference script is included below, which can be adapted to the therapist's personal style and applied in couples therapy.

Example 9.4 Script for Highlighting the Positive Consequences of Speaking from a Position of Vulnerability

When you share your emotions and needs from your vulnerable side (blue leg), I notice that it awakens in me, and probably also in your partner, a genuine impulse to reach out and collaborate with you. This shift not only makes connection easier, but also increases the likelihood that others will respond more positively to your needs.

Reflection: What to do if a client moves to his red leg again during exercise?
Therapist's Advice: In this and the other experiential exercises, when the client returns to their overcompensatory coping mode, with their anger or disgust, their critical mode, and begins to blame or justify themselves, it is import ant to reflectively interrupt that pattern.

To illustrate how to set limits on the use of the red leg during therapy exercises, a reference script is presented below, which can be adapted and used in the therapy session.

Example 9.5 Script to Stop Use of the Red Leg and Reorient to the Blue Leg

Pause for a moment. Do you realize which leg you're leaning on right now? Return to the leg that represents your healthiest and most vulnerable side. From there, let's try to answer again.

9.4.1 Gaining Access to the Vulnerable Side (Module V)

In this exercise, the therapist seeks to access the "Vulnerable Child Mode" of the externalizing partner through the following sequence of steps:

- **Fostering Empathy Toward the Other:** The externalizing partner is invited to become aware of how their "red leg" (overcompensating or avoidant mode) negatively impacts the relationship.
- **Connecting with the Vulnerable Child Mode:** The externalizing partner is encouraged to reflect on how they feel emotionally upon realizing that their red leg behavior is pushing their partner away.
- **Speaking from Vulnerability:** The partner is guided to express their need for attachment and connection from their most vulnerable side. If resistance to connect with the "blue leg" arises, the therapist may use the abandonment imagery technique (imagining that their partner leaves them).
- **Reconnection:** Once the externalizing partner has connected with the emotions associated with their blue leg (fear–sadness) and expressed their need for attachment and connection to their partner, the therapist facilitates emotional reconnection between both partners.

9.4.1.1 Fostering Empathy Toward the Other Side

The experiential process begins by helping the externalizing partner become aware of themselves, their behaviors, and how these directly impact their partner, triggering an emotional reaction in them. To achieve this, the following steps have been developed:

- **Describing the Externalizing Partner's Behavior:** From the observer position (therapist in position 1B and partners in positions 4A and 4B in Figure 3.5), the therapist invites both partners to look toward the externalizing partner's chair as if watching a video recording of the interaction. From this vantage point, they describe the reactions and behaviors the externalizing partner displayed during the discussion while addressing the issue directly with their partner. The therapist may guide the process with questions such as: What was their posture, gestures, facial expression, tone of voice, and choice of words? What do you see in their eyes? What kind of energy do they radiate? If necessary, the therapist may supplement the couple's observations with their own to help construct a clearer image of the lived moment.
  Note: The therapist's goal in inviting the partner to observe themselves "as if in a video," together with the therapist and his partner, from the observer position, is to prevent judgment or justification.
- **Helping the Externalizing Partner Become Aware of the Emotional Impact of Their Behavior on the Other Partner:** Once the externalizing partner's communication has been described, the next step is for them to observe their own behavior "through their partner's eyes." To facilitate this, the therapist may choose between two modalities depending on the level of confrontation deemed appropriate:
  a. **Less Confrontational Option:** The externalizing partner sits in the chair representing their partner (chairs 2A or 2B in Figure 3.5). The therapist positions themselves behind the chair, and the partner stands next to the therapist. The therapist then asks: "How do you feel when you put yourself in your partner's shoes? What do you experience when you see yourself talking, looking, and moving in that way while communicating with them?" The therapist then repeats the scene description and continues: "How does your body feel when you place yourself in your partner's position—when that person in the other chair (referring to the externalizing partner) looks at you, talks to you, yells at you, or moves in that way? What do you feel inclined to do?"
     Note: If the emotional block of the externalizing partner breaks, the therapist may move on to the exercise "Gaining Access to the Vulnerable Side." If, however, the block persists, the therapist proceeds to the next, more confrontational option.

b. **More Confrontational and Intense Option:** The externalizing partner sits in the chair representing their partner's Vulnerable Child Mode (chairs 2A or 2B in Figure 3.5), while the therapist positions themselves directly behind the chair, and the other partner is asked to stand next to the therapist. All participants are invited to close their eyes, and the therapist addresses the externalizing partner with the following prompts: "From your partner's Vulnerable Child Mode chair, what do you feel in your body when you hear your overcompensating or avoidant mode activated? How does their voice sound? How do they look at you? How do they move their hands? Can you feel their energy?" After reconstructing the image, the therapist provides a complete description of the scene and then asks the externalizing partner (who is now sitting in their partner's Vulnerable Child Mode chair) to respond: "From your partner's perspective in this scene, how does your body feel? What do you feel like doing?"
Note: In both options, the therapist emphasizes that the externalizing partner's coping mode is pushing their partner away.

- **Confronting the Effectiveness of the Overcompensating or Passive Avoidant Coping Mode:** Once the externalizing partner recognizes that their red behavior drives their partner away, the therapist helps them question whether that is the outcome they actually desire in the relationship, by asking: "Is this what you want—to make your partner move away from you?" "When you speak to them this way, does it make them more interested in your needs?" and "Does it help them behave the way you want?" The goal is to help the externalizing partner recognize how their red side ultimately distances their partner.
Note: If the partner responds that this is what they want to achieve in the relationship, the therapist may move on to the module titled "Preparing for Separation."

To illustrate this first step in guiding the externalizing partner toward their blue leg and fostering empathy toward their partner, we continue with the review of the case of Beatrice and Bartolomeo.

Beatrice and Bartholomew, 35 years old
T: Very well. From this observer's perspective, I'm going to ask that we describe Beatrice's behavior a moment ago. Let's imagine that we're watching Beatrice again during the discussion – as if we were seeing her through a video camera. Beatrice, I'd like you to tell me: what was her posture?

(Continued)

(Continued)

BE: She looked leaned forward toward him.

T: What were her gestures?

BE: She looked very upset.

T: How was her facial expression?

BE: It looked rigid and tense.

T: How was her tone of voice and her words?

BE: Very loud—almost shouting—and as if giving orders.

T: What do you see in her eyes?

BE: Her gaze is full of anger.

T: What kind of energy does she radiate?

BE: Fighting energy.

T: Good. Now, let's try to see these images through Bartolomeo's eyes. I'd like to ask you, Beatrice, to sit in Bartolomeo's Vulnerable Child Mode chair. I'll stand behind you, and you, Bartolomeo, please stand next to me. Does that sound okay to you both?

BE AND BA: Yes.

T: Very well. Now, I'd like to ask you—now that you're sitting in the chair that represents your partner's vulnerable part—how do you feel when you put yourself in your partner's shoes?

BE: It's something new for me.

T: From that position, what do you experience when you see yourself talking to him, looking at him, and moving in that way?

BE: I feel irritation, annoyance, and the urge to stop talking.

T: I understand. Now, putting yourself in Bartolomeo's place, seeing that Beatrice leaning toward you, very upset, with a rigid and tense facial expression, almost shouting and giving orders, with a look of anger and a fighting energy—how does your body feel?

BE: Rigid, tense.

T: What do you feel like doing?

BE: I feel like leaving, like not talking to her anymore.

T: Is this what you want—for your partner to move away from you?

BE: No.

T: When you speak to him this way, does it make him interested in your needs?

BE: No.

T: Does it make him behave the way you want?

BE: Never.

9.4.1.2 Connecting with the Vulnerable Child Mode

Once it has been identified that the coping mode of the externalizing partner is creating distance in the relationship, the next step is to help them connect with their attachment needs and the underlying emotions of fear or sadness that belong to their Vulnerable Child Mode.

To do this, the therapist sits in their chair (chair 1A in Figure 3.5) and then asks the externalizing partner to sit in the chair that represents their vulnerable part or their blue leg (chairs 3A or 3B in Figure 3.5). The therapist explains that, by sitting in this chair, they should leave the emotions associated with the red leg (anger and disgust) in another chair.

Then, the therapist asks the other partner to sit in the chair that represents their active coping mode (avoidance or overcompensation), which is placed facing away from the externalizing partner, symbolizing the disconnection generated by that mode (chairs 2A or 2B in Figure 3.5, facing away from the externalizing partner).

Next, the therapist begins the emotional activation, speaking softly to the vulnerable side of the client, saying something like: "What do you feel right now, as you realize how your coping mode (whether overcompensating or active avoidance) is pushing your partner away?, Now close your eyes and become aware of how your body feels. How is your breathing? Your chest? Your stomach?"

The positions shown previously encompass the entire process—from the moment the externalizing partner sits in their Vulnerable Child Mode chair to their partner's responses to the requests made during the strategies "Gaining Access to the Vulnerable Side," "speaking from vulnerability," and "imagining that the partner leaves."

To illustrate the application of the "Connecting with the Vulnerable Child Mode" technique, the case of Beatrice and Bartolomeo is revisited.

Beatrice and Bartholomew, 35 years old
T: Let's remember that when we experience negative emotions, some of them are active while others remain blocked. In your case, Beatrice, I think you're having difficulty connecting with the emotions linked to your need for attachment and connection—what we call your blue leg. That's why I'd like to invite you to sit in this chair, which represents your vulnerable side. If, during the exercise, emotions such as anger or irritation arise, I'll ask you to leave them in Angry Child mode chair and stay connected to your vulnerable part. Does that sound good?
BE.: Yes.

(Continued)

(Continued)

T: In your case, Bartolomeo, I'd like you to sit with your back to Beatrice, to symbolize what her overcompensating mode provokes in you. Are you willing?

BA.: Yes.

T: Now, Beatrice, as you sit in the chair representing your Vulnerable Child Mode, I'd like to ask you: what do you feel right now when you see how your overcompensating coping mode is pushing your partner away?

BE.: I feel sad.

T: Now close your eyes and become aware of how your body feels. How is your breathing?

BE.: It feels slow.

T: How is your chest, your stomach?

BE.: My chest feels tight.

T: How is your stomach?

BE.: Contracted.

9.4.1.3 Speaking from Vulnerability

The therapist validates the emotions that come from the blue side of the externalizing partner with phrases such as: "I'm glad that you can now feel this and express it in this way", "This is your vulnerability—it has always been there, and now you can experience it and show it. Congratulations", "When I see this part of you, I feel more connected to you."

Once the externalizing partner connects with their vulnerable side and recognizes how their coping mode pushes their partner away, the therapist helps them connect with their need for closeness—to express the wish that their partner not move away—and to do so in an assertive manner. The therapist might ask questions such as: "What do you need from your partner?" "What would you like them to do?" "What can they give you?" "How do you feel without them?"

Afterward, the client is invited to express these attachment needs directly to their partner from their vulnerable side. However, it is common for the tone or wording to come across as demanding, controlling, or accusatory (from the red side). In such cases, the therapist validates the underlying emotion but suggests leaving it, for the moment, on the red chair.

From there, a shaping process begins, in which the therapist helps the externalizing partner express their attachment needs from their vulnerable side. The therapist may start by suggesting some blue side phrases, so the externalizing partner can rephrase them in their own words to express their need for attachment and connection to their partner.

If the requests made by the externalizing partner sound unbalanced or somewhat excessive, the therapist helps adjust them by encouraging reciprocity, offering something meaningful in return to make it easier for their partner to respond positively. The therapist might ask questions such as: "What could you offer in return to make your partner more willing to get closer to you and meet your needs?" If the partner cannot think of a clear answer, the therapist may make a gentle suggestion, such as: "What if, in exchange for what you're asking, you offered them this...?"

If the externalizing partner succeeds in expressing their needs in a healthy way from the blue side, the session proceeds toward fostering emotional reconnection. If it remains difficult for them to express themselves from this side, the therapist applies the exercise "imagining that the partner leaves."

In the following scene, we return to the therapist working with the case of Beatrice and Bartolomeo. In this phase, Beatrice, after having connected with her need for attachment and emotional closeness, now seeks to express it to Bartolomeo with the therapist's guidance.

Beatrice and Bartholomew, 35 years old

T: I understand that you feel sad when you see Bartolomeo moving away from you because of your overcompensating coping mode. I'm glad that you're able to connect with this part of yourself—congratulations. Even as I listen to you, a part of me also feels more connected to this need of little Beatrice.

T: Now, I'd like you to express to Bartolomeo the need for connection from your vulnerable side—so that he doesn't go away. How about saying something like: "Don't go, don't move away, I need you, I miss you, I don't want to lose the connection I have with you."

BE.: Okay.

T: Good, then go ahead and express it.

BE.: I want you to stop pushing me away. It's always the same—you get upset and don't say anything to me.

T: Very good effort. Let's take it a step further and try to express it in a way that comes more from your blue side—more as a request than as a command. You could say something like: "I feel lonely when we grow distant from each other. I feel sad when you move away from me because I miss you." Does that sound okay?

BE.: Yes. You always make me feel lonely and sad. Stop moving away from me.

Note: Since Beatrice had difficulty connecting with her vulnerable side when expressing her needs, the session moved on to the exercise called "Imagining that the Partner Leaves."

9.4.1.3.1 Imagining That the Partner Leaves

This strategy is used when the externalizing partner is unable to connect with their vulnerability, even after realizing that their red side is pushing their partner away and therefore cannot express their need for attachment and connection.

The therapist guides an imagery exercise, sitting close to the partner and using a soft, calm tone to stimulate emotional connection: "With your eyes closed, imagine that your red side—the part that pushes and pressures—has driven your partner away. Now imagine that your partner stands up, walks toward the door, steps outside, and keeps moving farther and farther away."

Once this scene is established, the therapist seeks to activate the client's negative schemas to help them connect more deeply with the vulnerability of losing their partner, saying phrases such as: "You will never see them again for the rest of your life", "Now you are alone", "You have failed to maintain this relationship."

Then, the therapist reinforces the sense of attachment through questions like: "What would you miss about them?" "If you lost them, what do you feel you could never regain in the same way with anyone else?"

The therapist also encourages cooperation and the willingness to yield by inviting reflection: "What do you regret not having tried?" "If you could look back a few years from now, what would you have done differently to try to save this relationship?" Finally, the sense of attachment is strengthened by asking again: "What would you miss about them?" "What do you feel you would lose forever—something you could never get from anyone else in quite the same way?" And to encourage cooperative behavior and emotional openness, the therapist concludes with: "What do you regret not having tried? Looking back after several years, what would you have done differently to try to rescue this relationship?"

The therapist, with the goal of helping the partner connect with the negative emotions that arise in response to loss, explores physical sensations by asking questions such as: "How does it feel in your body? Does your chest expand or contract? Is your breathing easy or difficult? Do you feel tension in your stomach, or does it feel like it's collapsing?"

If the client shifts back into anger or blame, the therapist redirects them by saying, "That's your red leg again. Leave that on the red chair and return to this chair. Connect with the feeling of being alone and having failed."

The therapist may also add: "I understand, but I don't want to take that path right now. What I'd like to focus on is how that makes you feel in your body."

Once the client connects with their vulnerability, the therapist reinforces this by saying something like: "Thank you so much for opening up and allowing us to see your vulnerable side." The therapist then asks: "What do you need from your partner?" This helps the partner express their needs from a place of vulnerability.

During this process, the therapist guides the client to speak in an emotional and direct way, for example: "I need you. I need you to be with me. I need your support. This is too much for me alone. I need your closeness; otherwise, I feel alone."

Once this has been expressed, the therapist continues: "What would you like your partner to do? Would you like them to turn their chair around and be with you again?", If the client responds affirmatively, the therapist adds: "Can you ask your partner to turn around? What would you like to say to them now?"

If the client is able to make this request from their vulnerable mode, the session proceeds to the next step. If, however, the client uses a controlling or critical tone, the therapist provides feedback and models how to express needs from a vulnerable position.

The therapist then turns to the partner (who is still sitting with their back to the partner) and asks: "How does it feel to hear your partner express their needs in this way? Can you picture your partner feeling lonely?" If the partner expresses compassion, the therapist explores their willingness to reconnect by asking: "Would you be willing to move closer to your partner?" If the answer is negative, this may be a concerning indicator for the relationship, and the therapist should address it carefully.

The following section presents this technique through the case of Bartolomeo and Beatrice. It is important to note that this intervention can also be used as a complement to the strategy "Accessing the Partner's Vulnerable Mode," particularly when the externalizing partner struggles to connect with their blue leg.

Beatrice and Bartholomew, 35 years old

T: Let's remember that when we experience negative emotions, some of them are active while others remain blocked. In your case, Beatrice, I think you're finding it difficult to connect with the emotions related to your need for attachment and connection—what we call your blue leg. That's why I'd like to invite you to sit in this chair, which represents your vulnerable side. If, during the exercise, emotions like anger or irritation arise, I'll ask you to leave them in Angry Child mode chair and stay connected to your vulnerable part. Does that sound okay?

BE.: Yes.

T: Now, Beatrice, from the chair of your Vulnerable Child Mode, I want you to close your eyes and imagine how your overcompensating mode pushes Bartolomeo away. Visualize him standing up, walking toward the door, stepping outside, and gradually disappearing until he's completely gone. Now you're alone. You have failed to keep the relationship together. Once you can see that, focus on how it feels in your body. Does your chest expand or contract?

BE.: It contracts.

(Continued)

(Continued)

T: Is your breathing easy or difficult?
BE.: It becomes difficult.
T: Do you feel tension in your stomach, or does it feel like it's collapsing?
BE.: It feels like it's collapsing.
T: What would you miss about him?
BE.: His gaze... his body in the mornings when we wake up... his warmth.
T: What do you feel you would lose forever—something you couldn't get in quite the same way from anyone else?
BE.: I'd lose my life partner—the one I've shared so many beautiful experiences with.
T: What do you regret not having tried?
BE.: Not having made a greater effort to communicate things to him more assertively.
T: Looking back years from now, what would you have done differently to try to save this relationship?
BE.: I would have given in a little more to what he asked of me.
T: Thank you so much for opening up and allowing both Bartolomeo and me to see your vulnerable side. Now, reflect for a moment—what do you need from your partner?
BE.: I'm not sure.
T: That's okay—it's hard to find the words. What if you try saying something like this: I need you. I want you to be with me. I need your support. This is too much for me alone. I miss your closeness. Without it, I feel lonely. Once you can imagine that, let me ask—would you like Bartolomeo to turn his chair around and be with you again?
BE.: Yes, that's what I want.
T: Can you ask your partner to turn around?
BE.: Bartolomeo, would you turn around, please?
BA.: Yes.
T: Bartolomeo, how does it feel to hear Beatrice express her needs this way?
BA.: It makes me feel important. I didn't realize she felt that way.
T: Can you picture your partner feeling lonely?
BA.: Yes.
T: Would you be willing to move closer to your partner?
BA.: Yes.
T: Now, please stand up. (The therapist moves Bartolomeo's chair so that they face each other.) If you'd like, hold hands while staying connected with your vulnerable emotions—and if you feel comfortable, you may hug each other. When you're ready, you can open your eyes.

9.4.1.4 Reconnection

If the couple is willing to reconnect, they are asked to stand up. The therapist moves the chair that was previously turned away and places the chairs face-to-face. They are invited to hold hands while remaining in touch with their vulnerable emotions and, if they feel comfortable, to embrace. At the end, the therapist asks them to open their eyes.

At this stage, it is expected that before standing up to reconnect, the partner is already in a flexible coping mode. Therefore, it is essential for the therapist to provide support to both the externalizing partner and their counterpart through feedback, shaping, and modeling, in order to help them express their needs from their vulnerable side.

Beatrice and Bartholomew, 35 years old

T: Good. Now that you've been able to express your need for attachment and connection toward Bartolomeo, what would you like to do, Bartolomeo?
BA.: I'd like to hug her.
T: Beatrice, would you like to receive this hug from Bartolomeo?
BE.: Yes.
T: I'm going to remove this chair that was keeping you apart. Please stand up and give each other a hug... Now that you're embracing, open your eyes. How do you feel?
BA.: I like it.
BE.: It feels good.

9.4.2 Reconnecting Emotionally by Floating Back to a Honeymoon Scene (Module VI)

This exercise aims to help the partner, who is fixated on their red leg, balance by connecting with their need for attachment and connection and the positive emotions they have experienced in their relationship with their partner. It is especially useful when the client finds it difficult or resists connecting with vulnerable emotions toward their partner. To perform the exercise, proceed as follows:

1. **Sitting in the Vulnerable Child Mode Chair:** Both partners are asked to sit in the Vulnerable Child Mode chair and close their eyes (chairs 3A and 3B in Figure 3.5).
2. **Imagining the Best Moments of the Relationship:** The therapist guides the externalizing partner to a positive memory: "I want you to transport yourself to the beginning of your relationship, looking for an image of a moment in which you felt truly in love with your partner. Where are you? What are you doing? What do you see in their eyes?"

3. **Connecting with Positive Emotions:** The therapist guides the client to explore the emotions associated with that memory: How does this moment make you feel? What do you feel in your body?
4. **Activating the Attachment–Connection Need:** Once the client is connected to the image and the emotions it evokes, the externalizing partner is asked: What would you like to say or do to your partner right now? They are here and can hear you. The client is encouraged to express these words directly to their partner. The therapist reinforces the moment by asking: "How does it make you feel to speak from this emotion and connection?" They are invited to remain connected to those feelings for a moment.
5. **Partner's Response to Externalizing Partner's Requests:** The therapist turns to the other partner and asks: How does it make you feel to hear your partner express these things in this way? What would you like to say to him or her? The client is encouraged to respond directly and, if willing, to speak from his or her own vulnerability: The client is asked something like: How does it make you feel to talk to your partner like this? Is there anything else you would like to say or do?
6. **Reconnection:** If both partners seem ready to reconnect physically, the therapist asks them to stand while keeping their eyes closed. Guiding them, they are positioned facing each other. They are encouraged to hug each other while staying connected to their vulnerable emotions. The therapist asks the partner in overcompensating mode, "How does it feel to hug your partner?" and then asks their partner, "How do you feel?" The therapist asks them to open their eyes while still hugging and says to the partner in overcompensating mode, "Look, after all these years, your partner is still the one for you."

If in the previous steps the partners are unable to demonstrate these behaviors, the therapist intervenes by offering suggestions, providing feedback, or modeling, until the couple is able to express flexible coping behaviors.

To illustrate the steps of this technique and show a third alternative that the therapist could have used in the experiential rebalancing of Beatrice's red leg, her case is presented again.

Beatrice and Bartholomew, 35 years old
After completing the cognitive work with Bartholomew to motivate the change from the red leg to the blue leg, the therapist applied the exercise: "Reconnecting emotionally by floating back to a honeymoon scene." This exercise is designed to help Beatrice reconnect with her need for attachment and connection, as well as with Bartholomew's importance in her life.

T: I'd like both you, Beatrice, and you, Bartholomew, to sit in your Vulnerable Child Mode chair and close your eyes. Beatrice, I want you to imagine that you can travel back to the beginning of your relationship, searching for a memory in which you truly felt in love with Bartholomew. Can you get a picture?

BE.: Yes.

T: Where are they located?

BE.: On our honeymoon.

T: What are they doing?

BE.: We are walking along the walkway while there are stages with bands playing music that we both like.

T: What do you see in his eyes?

BE.: They are full of love when he looks at me.

T: How does that moment make you feel?

BE.: I feel very happy.

T: What do you feel in your body?

BE.: I feel agitated, full of life.

T: What would you like to say or do to your partner right now? She's here and can hear you.

BE.: That I love him.

T: How does it make you feel to speak from this emotion and connection?

BE.: I feel happy and a little nostalgic at the same time.

T: Stay connected to those emotions while I talk to your partner. Bartholomew, how does it feel to hear your partner express these things in this way?

BA.: I feel happy.

T: What would you like to say to him?

BA.: That I love her too.

T: Tell him straight.

BA.: I love you, Beatrice.

T: How does it make you feel to talk like this with your partner?

BA.: I feel good.

T: Is there anything else you would like to say or do?

BA.: Yes, I want to get back what we had.

T: I'd like you to stand with your eyes closed (as you guide them and position them facing each other). Now I want you to hug each other, staying connected to your emotions. Beatrice, how does it feel to hug your partner?

(Continued)

(Continued)

BE.: I feel very good.
T: And you, Bartholomew, how do you feel?
BA: I feel sad. I've been wanting her to hug me for a long time.
T: Now, open your eyes and look at each other. Beatrice, I think that after all these years, Bartholomew is still important to you, don't you?
BE.: Yes.

If partners manage to feel emotionally connected during the visualization, it means that neural connections still exist that allow them to feel something positive for each other. These connections can be strengthened with practice. A complementary exercise to reinforce this work is to ask them to look at photos together of happy moments. This helps revive positive memories, generating "sparks" that can rekindle the emotional connection between them. It's important to emphasize that, although they may have changed over time, the essence of the person remains the same, and the connection can be renewed by focusing on those meaningful moments.

To provide guidance to the therapist in applying the "Honeymoon" technique, a reference script is presented below, which can be adapted and used in the therapeutic session.

Example 9.6 Script for the Honeymoon Exercise

Relax deeply, connect with your body. Feel the air moving in and out of your chest, gently moving with the rhythm of your breathing. Allow that connection with your body to take you to your inner world and your personal life. Once you're there, imagine yourself floating back in time, returning to that moment when you were on your honeymoon or deeply in love with your partner, to that place and time when you had a wonderful time together. Visualize that moment. Notice where and when it was. Hold that image in your mind. Can you see your partner? What do they look like? What's their hair like? What are they wearing? What does their voice sound like? Listen to their words carefully. What are they doing at that moment? Are they walking, sitting, or enjoying some scenery? Imagine the place in all its details. You are there again. Listen to the sounds around you, feel the weather on your skin, and perceive everything with all five senses. Now, observe your partner. Can you look into their eyes? What do you see there? What emotions arise in your body when you connect with their gaze? Do you want to feel their body next to yours? Can you perceive their scent? Connect with that feeling of closeness. Perhaps you can feel their arms around you and yours around them. How does your body feel now? What impulse arises in you at this moment? Stay with that feeling for a moment. If you are fully connected to all these channels of perception, allow those intense emotions to emerge. Open yourself to them, let yourself be immersed. If you let go of all your thoughts and surrender to this moment, you will feel that you are truly there, as if the past returns to the present reality. Pay attention to the intensity of these emotions. Now, little by little, imagine yourself returning to the present, but keep that emotional connection alive. Visualize your partner as they are now, but without losing the connection with the emotions you have just experienced. Realize that the person in front of you is the same, that all those shared experiences are part of the memories you both have. These memories are small treasures you can share together. Try to connect the person your partner is today with those memories from the past. Recognize that your brain has the capacity to make this journey, to unite the present with the past. Now, ask yourself: How do you feel around your partner after reconnecting with those old feelings? Compare these emotions with the ones you had before starting the session. Both feelings are real, and you have a choice about which one you want to prioritize.

9.5 Closing the Session

9.5.1 Reinforce the Benefits of Leg Switching

In this step to conclude the experiential exercise, the therapist guides the couple in a reflection on the emotional change achieved, inviting them to compare how they felt at the beginning and end of the session: "What differences do you notice?" The therapist emphasizes that this change was made possible by the transition from the red leg to the blue leg, highlighting the importance of connecting with the need for attachment and connection.

To consolidate this learning, the therapist poses questions such as, "Do you realize that you can still experience good feelings for each other when you make this change?" Finally, the therapist reinforces their control over their emotional experience, emphasizing, "This is in your hands. You have the power to generate and strengthen these images, thoughts, and feelings within yourself."

To illustrate this step on how to conclude experiential exercises, helping the couple connect their experience before and after the exercise, the case of Beatrice and Bartholomew is reviewed.

Beatrice and Bartholomew, 35 years old
T: I'd like you to reflect together. Compared to how you felt before the exercise, do you notice any difference? BE.: Yes, I feel more connected to Bartholomew. BA: I feel moved, and I also feel more connected to her. T: Remember, you have control over your emotional experience. You can evoke these positive images, generate and strengthen the feelings they evoke in you toward your partner. This is in your hands. What do you think? BA. AND BE.: Yes!

9.5.2 Therapeutic Task: Meet with the Couple to Look at Past Photos, Remember Good Times, Give Positive Feedback, and Use the Technique Learned in Session

To conclude the session, the therapist assigns the couple a homework assignment: in the coming days, they will schedule a special time together to look at photos from their past or recall significant experiences. During this activity, they are invited to reflect and discuss how they felt during those moments, with the goal of reinforcing positive emotions and strengthening the emotional connection.

They are also asked to practice deliberate physical connection, hugging at least once a day. Finally, the therapist assigns them the task of providing the other partner with positive feedback, a compliment, thanking them for something, or telling them why they like it once a day. They are also instructed to try practicing the blue leg reconnection technique learned in therapy when the externalizing partner is in the separate room at home after the time-out.

Below is how the therapist ends the session with Beatrice and Bartholomew, leaving the task of reconnection as a key step in strengthening their bond.

Beatrice and Bartholomew, 35 years old
T: Ok, to end the session, I want to leave you with a task for this week. I'd like you to plan a special date of at least 30 minutes, where you can meet to look at photos or reminisce about meaningful and happy moments in your relationship. During this activity, I invite you to connect with the positive emotions that arise from these memories and maintain that feeling of emotional connection with your partner for the rest of the week. What do you think?

BE.: Yes.
BA.: Yes.
T: I also suggest that you practice deliberate physical connection, hugging at least once a day, and saying positive comments about what you like about the other partner. Does this make sense to you?
BE.: Yes.
BA.: Yes.
T: In the same way, Beatrice, I suggest that at home, when you stop the mode cycle and go to the rooms, you try to reconnect with your blue leg by doing this imagination exercise. Does that sound good to you?
BE.: Yes.

Below, a summary of the steps to be taken with externalizing partners who are stuck in their red leg is presented:

Beginning of the Session

- **Identification of the Problem to Be Worked On:** The couple is asked to identify the conflict to be worked on in the therapy session:
- **Identifying That One Partner Is Overly Fixated on Their Red Leg:** Either when both partners are asked to try to resolve the problem by talking it over directly with each other, or as the cycle develops, the therapist detects that one partner is overly fixated on their red leg.
- **Stop the Interaction:** Once it is detected that one of the partners is stuck on his or her red leg, the therapist stops the interaction.

Cognitive Work

- **Observer Team Work:** The therapist and partners stand and become aware of:
  - **Coping and Child Mode in the Externalizing Partner:** The therapist analyzes the overcompensation or active avoidance coping mode and Angry Child mode mode in the externalizing partner.
  - **Coping and Child Modes in the Couple:** The therapist identifies the child mode (angry or Vulnerable Child Mode) and the overcompensation, surrender, or avoidance coping modes that are active in the couple.
  - **The Mode Cycle:** The therapist points out how the interaction between each partner's child and coping modes perpetuates a cycle of modes that maintain their problems as a couple.
- **Analyze the Advantages and Disadvantages of Using the Red Leg:** The therapist helps clients to:

  - **Advantages of the Coping Mode:** The Externalizer who takes the initiative is validated.
  - **Disadvantages of the Coping Mode:** It is questionable whether the coping mode gets your partner to cooperate.
  - **Propose a Change of Strategy:** It encourages exploration of a new strategy.
- **Experiential Work:** The therapist evaluates what type of experiential approach is appropriate for this particular case and the externalizing partner.
- **Gaining Access to the Vulnerable Side (Module V):** This exercise allows the externalizing partner to reflect on how their red leg is pushing their partner away, and—through the emotions generated by that realization—to ask their partner for the connection they need from them.
  - **Sitting in His/Her Vulnerable Child Mode Chair:** The externalizing partner sits in the Vulnerable Child Mode chair, while the other partner sits in front of them with their back turned toward them.
  - **Imagining That the Partner Is Leaving Their Life:** The Externalizing partner imagines that the partner is leaving their life while activating their negative schemas.
  - **Connecting with Emotions of Sadness or Fear:** The Externalizing partner is helped to connect with their negative emotions by asking about their bodily sensations.
  - **Activating the Need for Attachment–Connection:** The therapist activates the need for attachment-connection by giving the client suggestions of what he or she needs from his or her partner and inviting him or her to express it directly.
  - **Partner's Response to the Externalizing Partner's Requests:** The partner, with their back to the externalizing client, is asked how they feel about hearing the externalizing client express their needs in this way and whether they are willing to get closer to them.
  - **Reconnection:** The couple is asked to stand, hold hands, and open their eyes.
- **Reconnect Emotionally by Floating Back to a Honeymoon Scene:** It helps you connect with positive emotions associated with closeness and cooperation with your partner.
  - **Sitting in the Vulnerable Child Mode Chair:** Both partners sit in the Vulnerable Child Mode chair and close their eyes.
  - **Imagining the Best Moments of the Relationship:** The externalizing partner recalls a positive memory in which they felt very much in love with their partner while exploring the emotions and bodily sensations associated with it.

- **Connecting with Positive Emotions:** The therapist guides the externalizing partner to explore the emotions associated with that positive memory by identifying their bodily sensations.
- **Activate the Need for Attachment–Connection:** The externalizing partner is encouraged to identify what he or she would like to say to his or her partner and is invited to say it directly.
- **Activate the Use of the Couple's Blue Leg:** The therapist addresses the partner of the externalizer and asks how they feel when listening to what they say, and asks them to express it directly.
- **Reconnection:** Ask them to stand and encourage them to hug each other while asking them how they feel about doing so. Finally, ask them to open their eyes.

Closing the Session

- **Reinforce the Benefits of Changing Legs:** The therapist points out the differences between before and after doing the exercise.
- **Therapeutic Task:** Meet with your partner to look at past photos, reminisce about good times, and provide positive feedback. The externalizing partner is also allowed to try to put the technique learned in the session into practice at home, while taking a time-out and trying to reconnect with their blue leg.

10

Internalizing Partners (Module VII)

10.1 Introduction

This chapter describes Module VII, which is focused on providing balance for the leg-switching process in those clients who are centered on their need for attachment and connection, on their emotions of sadness or fear, and on their coping modes of surrender (passive, obedient, submissive) or passive avoidance (disconnection from their own emotions, from their partner's emotions, or from reality).

When clients experience difficulty activating their red leg—that is, their need for assertiveness and autonomy and their emotions of anger or disgust—it is necessary to help them take the initiative to express what they need, demonstrating firmness in who they are and what they desire. Proactively expressing personal needs in a clear and assertive manner can help the other partner better understand what is happening and be more empathetic to the needs of the internalizing partner.

It's important to note that before moving on to the reconnection modules, both partners must have been able to assertively express what they want using their red leg. This allows both partners to be clear about what their partner needs from them.

The following exercises were developed to help clients break out of the trap they find themselves in due to overuse of their blue leg, creating a balance between needs in the relationship.

General objective: To emotionally activate the need for assertiveness–autonomy in the internalizing partner.

Specific objectives:

- Help the internalizing partner analyze the advantages and disadvantages of their coping style through the metaphor of the castle wall.

- Facilitate the internalizing partner to connect with their assertive side through empowering images.
- Encourage the internalizing partner to find a balance in expressing their needs by taking the initiative and being clear and firm, but at the same time offering something in return.
- Demonstrate the emotional benefits of putting into practice your flexible coping method of taking initiative and assertiveness in your relationship.
- Encourage reconnection between couples.
- Develop positive interactions in the couple's relationship outside of the therapeutic session.

Reflection: How can the therapist identify clients who are using their blue leg during the session?

Therapist's advice: It is important to learn to recognize "blue energy" in clients with these characteristics. These clients often present with behaviors that reflect passive avoidance, such as emotional detachment or depressive symptoms, or with attitudes of submission or surrender, which are often accompanied by anxiety. In cases where clients are submissive, the partner often does not come to therapy unless they perceive that the passive partner is not giving enough to the relationship. As a therapist, it is common to feel an inclination to protect or defend these partners due to their apparent vulnerability. However, it is essential to encourage them to express their thoughts and desires clearly and firmly, fostering authentic and assertive communication.

10.2 Beginning of the Session: Identifying the Problem to Be Worked On and Identifying That One of the Partners Is Too Focused on Their Blue Leg

As in every session, the therapist begins by asking the couple to identify a problem to work on in therapy, with a question such as: "What are you bringing to this session today?" They are then invited to discuss it directly with each other (chairs 2A and 2B in Figure 3.5). If, during this dialogue, the therapist identifies that one partner is stuck on their blue leg, the therapist stops the interaction by saying something like: "I don't want to seem rude, but I need to stop this session right now because I just realized something important is happening between you. I think there is still a lack of balance between the use of your legs at this moment, so before continuing the dialogue, I need to try to balance you both. But before that, would you mind if we see which leg each of you is on?"

Sometimes the mode cycle will have to develop in the couple so that it becomes evident that one of the partners is too focused on their blue leg. In that scenario, the therapist stops the session until the mode cycle begins.

On other occasions, after the education phase, if at any point in the session the therapist realizes that one of the partners is stuck in their blue leg and cannot find rebalance before moving on to dialogue and negotiation (reconnection phase), the therapist should apply some of the interrogator strategies.

To illustrate the first steps of the session, we present the case of John and Rachel, a 45-year-old couple who have faced difficulties in their relationship due to Rachel's lack of assertiveness.

Clinical case, 22 John and Rachel, 45 years old

T: I would like to start the session by asking you, what are you "bringing" to work on today?

JOHN (J): I would like to work on Rachel's lack of consideration; she is always late...

T: Sorry to interrupt you, John, but I'd like you to tell us about a specific, recent situation that occurred since the last session. Something concrete will help us work through it better.

J: Well, the other day we were supposed to go to a get-together with friends, and I asked Rachel to be ready when I picked her up. She said yes, but when I got there, she was just showering.

T: Thanks for sharing, John. That's a very good example of a specific situation. Rachel, do you think it's a good idea to address this topic?

RACHEL (R): Yes.

T: Perfect. Then I ask you to address this issue directly among yourselves.

J.: Why, if we had already agreed, were you not ready?

R.: Sorry.

J.: Sorry, sorry (imitating sarcastically). You always say the same thing, but you end up doing the same thing.

R.: Forgive me, I won't do it again.

J.: But if we had already talked about it, why didn't you follow through?

R.: I don't know.

T: Excuse me for interrupting, but I'd like to stop the conversation here because, as we've reviewed previously, this is what to do when the mode cycle starts in you.

10.3 Cognitive Work

10.3.1 Observer Team Work

Once the problem and the coping modes have been identified, the therapist invites everyone to stand up to begin the meta-analysis work, in which the following aspects become apparent:

- **Coping modes:** The therapist examines the active coping mode used during the discussion, represented by each partner's chair (from this position, with the therapist in position 1B and the partners in positions 4A and 4B, the partners observe chairs 2A and 2B, respectively, in Figure 3.5). Once identified, the therapist asks the other partner if they agree with this perception. If necessary, the therapist provides feedback to help accurately identify the coping mode.
- **Child modes:** The therapist instructs each partner to identify their own child mode while standing by their respective chair (from this position, the partners observe chairs 3A and 3B in Figure 3.5). Once identified, the therapist asks the other partner for their opinion on this perception. If necessary, the therapist provides feedback regarding the emotions that were reflected during the discussion.

Once the coping modes and child modes of each partner have been identified, the therapist explains the mode cycle that is established in the interaction and perpetuates the problem, highlighting the interplay between each partner's coping and child modes.

At this point, the therapist has two options: first, to continue with cognitive work; or second, if deemed necessary, to move directly to experiential work using some of the techniques for internalizing partners.

To demonstrate the specific steps of cognitive work to help couples become aware of their child and coping modes and their mode cycle, we will continue to use the case of John and Rachel.

John and Rachel, 45 years old
T: Now we're going to stand up and look at the chairs below. Let's analyze: What coping mode was Rachel in? J: On her blue leg. T: Correct, but within the blue leg, were you submitting or passively avoiding? J: I think she was submitting.

(Continued)

(Continued)

T: Definitely. But tell me, do you think he did it out of conviction and reflection, or was it an automatic reaction to avoid problems?

J: I think it was automatic; he disconnected from the commitment.

T: Rachel, what do you think?

R: I agree.

T: Can you explain it in your own words?

R: I don't know.

T: I think your mind isn't fully present. What were you thinking about while we were talking?

R: I don't want to have problems with John anymore.

T: On a scale of 1–10, how frequent is this disconnection when you argue with John?

R: I think a 9.

T: So, if this disconnection happens so often, we can say that Rachel was in passive avoidance mode. Do you agree?

R: Yes.

J: Yes.

T: And what would be the flexible coping mode that Rachel could have used?

R: Take the initiative and assert myself.

T: I think so too. What do you think, John?

J: I agree.

T: Now let's analyze what happened with John. What coping mode was he in? Was he overcompensating, giving in, or avoiding?

J: I overcompensated.

T: I agree. Rachel?

R: Yes, he was demanding a lot from me.

T: So, if John's mode was overcompensation, then his blocked flexible behavior that he could have used would be to cooperate or give in. Am I understanding that correctly?

J: Yes.

R: Yes.

T: Now the chairs will represent your child mode. In Rachel's case, what emotion was active at that moment?

R: Fear.

T: I agree. Rachel was in Vulnerable Child Mode, experiencing fear. Do you agree, John?

J: Yes.

T: And what would be the blocked child mode?

R: Angry Child mode.
T: Correct. What do you think, John?
J: I agree.
T: And what was John's active child mode?
J: Angry Child mode.
T: Do you agree, Rachel?
R: Yes, he was clearly angry.
T: And what would be your blocked child mode?
J: Vulnerable Child Mode.
T: Exactly. Rachel, do you also think that John didn't actively express his fear or sadness?
R: Yes.
T: To summarize, we've identified the following: John complained to Rachel about not being ready, which activated his Angry Child mode, leading him to overcompensate. This triggered Rachel's Vulnerable Child Mode, experiencing fear, which led her to shut down and enter passive avoidance mode. Rachel's disconnection intensified John's anger, reinforcing his Angry Child mode and perpetuating the cycle. Does this analysis make sense to you?
J: Yes.
R: Yes.

As can be seen in the previous case, the therapist not only identifies the active modes but also points out the blocked or hidden child modes, as well as the flexible coping modes that were not used. In the intermediate rebalancing modules, the therapist can choose to identify the flexible coping behavior that could have been used during the observer team work or postpone it for later in the session, either during the analysis of the advantages and disadvantages of using the blue leg or during the experiential work.

10.3.2 Analyze the Advantages and Disadvantages of Using the Blue Leg

Internalizing partners frequently have had experiences in the past where expressing their need for assertiveness and autonomy resulted in rejection, criticism, or violence of some kind. These experiences led them to associate showing who they are or what they want with the likelihood of being abused or repressed, which led them to develop strategies of surrender or disengagement as a way of protecting themselves. The blue leg, in its coping mode of surrender or passive avoidance, is a resource that allows for a sense of protection by avoiding confrontation and the pain associated with it.

It is essential to help the client understand the negative effects of surrender and passive avoidance. While these strategies may offer an initial sense of protection, they also create the risk of emotional isolation and disconnection from others. This approach develops in the following steps:

1. **Advantages of the coping mode:** The therapist invites the internalizing partner to sit in a chair representing their Vulnerable Child Mode (chairs 3A or 3B in Figure 3.5), while placing a chair facing away from them (symbolizing their passive avoidant mode). The couple sits in the chair representing their coping mode (chairs 2A or 2B in Figure 3.5). Next, the therapist asks the internalizing partner: "If you feel vulnerable, how does it make you feel to be behind this protective wall?" Most clients respond that they feel "safe" or "good." This step validates the initial positive intention of the coping mode, acknowledging that it provides a sense of safety.
2. **Disadvantages of coping mode:** The therapist guides the client to become aware of the dysfunctionality of their coping mode by asking something like, "Would you like to remain isolated for the rest of your life?" To further this idea, the therapist uses the metaphor of a castle: He explains that although a protective wall may provide initial security, if it does not allow access to the outside, it becomes an emotional prison.
3. **Propose a change of strategy:** Using the castle metaphor, the therapist proposes an alternative: placing a door in the wall. This door allows the client to exit and enter as needed, transforming the castle into a space that provides security without becoming a prison. This approach gives the client the confidence of knowing they can return to their safe place if being vulnerable to the other person puts them in danger. This process allows the internalizing partner to feel more motivated to leave their safe place, knowing they can return to it at any time.

Clients with internalizing tendencies tend to open up and trust only when they feel safe and in control of the situation. For this reason, it is essential to use tools that foster these two key elements. One effective strategy is to use the castle metaphor, which can help the client visualize a safe and controlled space where they can explore and share their emotions without feeling vulnerable or threatened.

To illustrate how to explain the castle metaphor during the session, a reference script for the therapist is presented below.

Example 10.1 Script for Explaining the Castle Metaphor in Internalizing Partners

This is a protective wall for you. However, if you want to connect with the person on the other side: How does that part of you that wants to connect feel behind the wall? I think for that part, this wall is a prison. Let's imagine this wall is a castle, and these types of buildings have a door that allows you to enter and exit it. The door, then, combines protection with the option to cross the wall. Your healthy adult will decide when it opens for connection and when it closes for protection. How does this sound? Because this gives you two options: you don't sacrifice your wall, but you gain the option to connect with others, and you decide.

To demonstrate the specific steps of cognitive work with partners who tend to be internalizers, the case of John and Rachel is reviewed.

John and Rachel, 45 years old

T: Now I would like to work with you if that's okay with you, Rachel.

R: Yes.

T: I'd like you, Rachel, to sit in the vulnerable child's chair and you, John, to sit in the chair that represents the coping mode. Now, I'm going to turn this chair in front of you so that it faces away from John, which will represent your passive avoidance coping mode. If you think about it, this chair in your coping mode can seem like a protective wall. How does having this protective wall make you feel?

R: I feel protected.

T: Well, I think it's normal to want to feel protected, and this wall provides that. However, would you like to stay behind that wall your whole life? Remember, this protective wall becomes a prison if you can't get out of it. However, if we put a door on this place, you can go outside and return to it for protection whenever things get difficult; how about we try this new strategy, knowing that you can go back to the old one if things don't work out?

R: Yes.

10.4 Experiential Work

After applying the cognitive strategy, the next step is to implement an experiential strategy aimed at rebalancing the blue leg. In this exercise, the goal is for the internalizing partner to connect with their red leg, strengthening themselves by imagining an empowered position that allows them to express their need for assertiveness and autonomy. During the visualization, the partner is guided to imagine that a miracle occurs and their partner changes in the desired way.

From this empowered stance, the partner expresses what they need and what they can offer to their partner. To reinforce the sense of strength and empowerment, the partner remains standing throughout the exercise, instead of sitting in the chair that represents their coping mode.

10.4.1 Accessing the Assertive Side (Module VII)

This strategy is designed primarily for couples who are in a passive avoidance coping mode, characterized by emotional disconnection from their own emotions, those of their partner, and the situation. For clients with active avoidance, we suggest using the "Gaining Access to the Vulnerable Side," exercise described in Chapter 9, which is intended for externalizing partners.

Once the cycle has been identified and the cognitive work to motivate the change from the blue leg to the red leg has been performed, the exercise "Accessing the Assertive Side" is proposed, which includes the following steps:

1. **Moving past the blue leg's coping mode:** The therapist asks the internalizing partner to stand next to the chair that represents their avoidant coping mode which represents the "wall" (chairs 2A or 2B in Figure 3.5). They are invited to move the chair slightly to one side, reassuring them that they can return if needed. The other partner remains seated in their coping mode chair (chairs 2A or 2B in Figure 3.5).
2. **Imagining yourself as empowered:** The therapist asks them to close their eyes and guides the internalizing partner to visualize themselves as either a large tree, a three-meter-tall person, or a heroic figure they admire. The therapist invites the client to become that chosen image and to feel that strength throughout their body, from head to toe. Then, the therapist asks the client to imagine that a miracle happens and, the next morning, their partner behaves exactly as they wish. The therapist encourages the client to describe this behavior by asking questions such as: "What is your partner doing?" "What are they no longer doing?" "How do they act?" and "What would you like to do with them?"
3. **Activate the need for assertiveness–autonomy:** The therapist reinforces the bodily sensations generated by the imagery exercise with questions such as: "How do you feel in your body right now?" "Are you able to connect with what you desire from your partner?" and "Do you feel more strength when you are standing, being taller than your partner?" Afterward, the therapist asks the internalizing partner to keep their eyes closed and express to their partner what they truly want.

4. **Balancing the request with an offer:** To make it more appealing for the partner to respond favorably, the therapist invites the internalizing partner to offer something in return—something oriented toward meeting the partner's attachment needs. If the request and the offer are balanced, the session proceeds to the next step. Otherwise, the therapist intervenes by suggesting adjustments until the give-and-take proposals become mutually satisfying and balanced.
5. **Connecting to positive emotions:** The therapist first explores how the client feels about satisfying their assertiveness–autonomy need by expressing their desires and offerings from their red side, rather than hiding behind the wall of avoidance. The therapist then turns to the other partner and asks if they have been able to visualize the image of the empowered internalizing partner (e.g., as a three-meter tree). The therapist explores the positive emotions this generates in their body by asking something like: "How does it make you feel in your body to see your partner this way?" Partners usually find it pleasant to see their assertive, proactive side.
6. **Partner's response to the internalizing partner's requests:** The therapist asks the partner of the internalizing partner how they perceive the internalizing partner's wishes and offers, using questions such as: "Did you hear what your partner desires and what they are offering? How does this sound to you? Does it feel right, or would you like to change something?" If adjustments are needed, both partners negotiate until they reach a mutually satisfactory agreement. During this process, the therapist may rely on the strategies described in Module 11: Connection Dialogues.
   Note: If no agreement is reached—meaning the partner of the internalizing partner does not respond to their needs or shows no willingness to compromise in order to restore the connection—it is recommended to move on to Module 13.
7. **Reconnection:** Once they reach an agreement, the therapist promotes physical closeness by inviting the couple to come closer and connect emotionally. Ask the internalizing partner something like, "Can you imagine yourself getting closer to your partner?" If they answer yes, the therapist takes that partner by the hand and pulls them closer to their partner to promote physical contact. At the end, the therapist asks them to open their eyes.

It is important to clarify that, from the moment the internalizing partner stands up, while the other partner remains seated and responds to their requests and offers, and until reconnection between them is established, the therapist must ensure that both partners are in a flexible coping mode, capable of both taking initiative and yielding. If difficulties arise, the therapist may provide feedback, guidance, and modeling to facilitate this process.

Reflection: What can the therapist do if the internalizing partner fails to offer anything in return to the other partner?

Therapist's advice: If the internalizing partner struggles to express a desire or make an offer, the therapist can intervene by suggesting concrete examples that represent a balanced and fair exchange. This helps the client visualize viable options and fosters a more equitable dynamic in the relationship.

To more clearly illustrate the application of the steps necessary for the internalizing partner to connect with their red leg, the case of John and Rachel is presented as a practical example.

John and Rachel, 45 years old

T: Rachel, I'd like you to stand up and remove the chair that represents the wall separating you from John. John, on your part, remain seated in your chair, representing your coping mode. Now, I'm going to ask both of you to close your eyes. Rachel, imagine that you are a tree, that you're three meters tall, or that you are a heroic figure you admire. Try to connect with that empowered feeling from head to toe. Now, I'd like you to imagine that a miracle happens and that John adopts the behavior you desire. Can you visualize it?

R: Yes.

T: What do you see?

R: I see that he asks me if I want to go to the gathering with his friends or if I'd prefer to do something else. He also asks me if I can be ready at the time he plans to pick me up.

T: Now, I'd like you to express it directly to John, still with your eyes closed.

R: John, I want you, when you make plans for the weekend, to also ask me what I would like to do. And I want you to consult me about what time I'd prefer to go to the gatherings with your friends, instead of simply telling me when you'll come to pick me up.

T: Very good. Now, when someone asks for something, it's important to also offer something in return. What could you offer John so that he feels motivated to ask more about your wishes before making decisions for both of you?

R: I'm not sure.

T: How would you feel about offering to express more clearly what you need, regardless of whether he asks or not?

R: That sounds good to me.

T: You could also commit to being more honest with yourself, avoiding accepting agreements that you're not truly willing to keep, and making a conscious effort to follow through on the agreements you establish together. How does that sound to you?

R: Yes, I agree.

T: Then express it directly to him, standing up and with your eyes closed, just as you visualized it.

R: John, in return, I offer to be more honest when establishing agreements and to commit myself to keeping them.

T: How do you feel as you express this to your partner?

R: I feel good, confident.

T: I want you to hold on to that feeling. Now, John, have you been able to visualize Rachel from this assertive side?

J: Yes.

T: How does it make you feel, in your body, to see Rachel from this posture?

J: It makes me feel good. I like that she tells me what she wants. I didn't know many of those things.

T: And regarding what she's asking for and what she's offering – does it seem like a good deal to you, or would you like to ask for something more?

J: It seems like a good deal.

T: Perfect. This will be your agreement. We'll put it in writing, but before that—Rachel, can you imagine approaching your partner?

R: Yes.

T: Then give me your hand, and I'll place it over John's hand. John, what would you like to do at this moment?

J: I'd like to hug her.

T: Does that sound good to you, Rachel?

R: Yes.

T: Now that you're hugging each other, connect with your bodily sensations. And when you feel ready, open your eyes.

To facilitate understanding of the imagery exercises the therapist can implement when working on developing the assertive side, below are practical scripts that can be used as a guide during the session.

Example 10.2 Script for the Tree-giant Imagination Exercise to Access the Assertive Side in Internalizing Partners

Imagine that you are a huge tree with enormous roots in the ground; no hurricane can knock you down. Can you feel that power? Take this power and now imagine that you are a very tall person, maybe a warrior, a person from a movie, or a hero that you can imagine. Feel this power in your body, imagining that you are at least three meters tall. Now imagine that you tell your partner how you want your relationship to be, mention what you expect from her.

Example 10.3 Script for the Miracle Imagination Exercise to Access the Assertive Side in Internalizing Partners

Imagine a miracle happens tonight, and when you wake up in the morning, your partner behaves the way you want them to. Now describe to me: How do they behave toward you? How do you want them to be and treat you? How do you feel seeing them that way? Are you willing to try to tell them how you want your relationship to be?

Reflection: What should the therapist do if the client doubts that the internalizing partner will keep his promises due to his past behavior?

Therapist's advice: If the couple expresses doubts during the exercise, these should be validated first. Then, it is important to redirect attention to the present and help the couple recognize that these doubts are related to a social emotion of future-focused worry about what happened in the past, which is not functional in the current moment. The therapist may say something like: "I understand your past-based worries, but the past is behind us. Now we are working on building something new. How do you feel right now, in your body, as you listen to what your partner is saying?" Additionally, the therapist may introduce a positive perspective, saying something like: "Maybe something unexpected will happen, like a miracle, and your partner will actually deliver what they are promising. What would happen if you allowed yourself to open to this possibility and trust what is being worked on right now?"

10.5 Closing the Session

10.5.1 Evaluate the Benefits of Leg Switching

In this step, the therapist highlights the progress made during the exercise, reinforcing the positive impact of the interaction and promoting reflection on the benefits of switching from the blue leg to the red leg by asking questions like: "Can you notice any differences between before and after the exercise? Could you share what they are? Do you realize that both of you can express what you need without one of you having to submit or be at a disadvantage?" Finally, the therapist emphasizes that they have the power to make the leg switch and generate these types of experiences in their relationship.

To illustrate how to close the session by highlighting the positive changes achieved by switching legs, we use the case of John and Rachel as a reference.

John and Rachel, 45 years old

T: Do you notice any differences in your emotions and how you feel physically between before and after exercise?

J: Yes.

R: Yes.

T: What are those differences?

J: I feel like I understand Rachel more.

R: I feel more confident expressing things to John.

T: Do you realize that you can both express what you need without either of you having to submit or be at a disadvantage?

J: Yes.

R: I realize that now.

T: Remember that you have the power to make this change and generate positive experiences in your relationship.

10.5.2 Therapeutic Task: Meet with the Couple to Look at Past Photos or Remember Good Times, Give Positive Feedback, and Apply the Technique Learned in the Session

As with partners with externalizing tendencies, the session's homework is to dedicate time during the week to recalling significant moments through conversations, photographs, or videos. During this activity, the goal is to connect with the positive emotions and sensations associated with those memories. They are also asked to increase their physical expressions of affection and to tell each other things about their daily lives that they like and are grateful for in their partner (for example, their appearance, their efforts in contributing to household chores or family finances, etc.) with the goal of strengthening the emotional closeness between them. Similarly, the internalizing partner is instructed to practice the rebalancing technique learned in the session during the time-out, when they are in a separate room trying to reconnect with their red leg.

To illustrate how the therapist assigns this task in the case of John and Rachel, the closing of their therapy session is described below.

John and Rachel, 45 years old

T: To conclude the session, I'd like to propose a task. Before our next meeting, you'll schedule a 30-minute time slot. During this time, you'll talk about significant moments in your relationship, whether through photos, videos, or simply sharing memories. It's important that, as you do this activity, you try to connect with the positive emotions those moments generate in you. Does this make sense?

J: Yes.

R: Yes.

T: Likewise, I'd like you to try to increase your physical closeness by hugging, kissing, or lovingly caressing each other throughout the day. Is that okay with you?

J: Yes.

R: Yes.

T: Okay, Rachel, lastly, I'd like to ask you, the next time you and John take a timeout and you find yourself in a separate room trying to reconnect with your red leg, to try putting the technique you learned today into practice. Is that okay with you?

R: Yes.

It's important to remember that once the client successfully activates their assertive side, they're ready to take the next step, which is to move toward the reconnection phase. In this stage, we work directly on a daily life problem, applying the newly developed skills to foster a more balanced and functional interaction in the relationship.

Before ending the chapter, as a summary, the therapeutic approach that must be carried out once the therapist has identified that it is necessary to rebalance one of the partners that is focused on their blue leg is presented:

Beginning of the Session

- **Identification of the problem to be worked on:** The couple is asked to identify the conflict to be worked on in the therapy session.

- **Identifying that one partner is overly fixated on their blue leg:** Either when both partners are asked to try to resolve the problem by talking it over with each other or as the mode cycle unfolds, the therapist detects that one partner is overly fixated on their blue leg.
- **Stop the interaction:** Once it is detected that one of the partners is stuck on their blue leg, the therapist stops the interaction.

Cognitive Work

- **Observer team work:** The therapist and partners stand and become aware of their:
  - **Coping modes:** The therapist analyzes the surrender or passive avoidance coping mode in the internalizing partner and their significant other.
  - **Child modes:** The therapist identifies the angry or Vulnerable Child Mode that is active in both partners.
  - **The mode cycle:** The therapist explains how the interaction between each partner's child and coping modes perpetuates a mode cycle that maintains their problems as a couple.
- **Analyze the advantages and disadvantages of using the blue leg:** The therapist helps partners to:
  - **Advantages of the coping mode:** The internalizing partner is validated and wants to feel protected.
  - **Disadvantages of coping mode:** He questions how the wall that protects him imprisons him and isolates him from his partner.
  - **Propose a change of strategy:** It encourages exploration of a new strategy (putting a door in the wall).

Experiential Work

- **Accessing the assertive side**
  - **Moving past the coping mode of the blue leg:** The internalizing partner is asked to stand up and remove the chair representing the coping mode, which symbolizes a wall.
  - **Empowered imagery:** The internalizing partner imagines themselves as a tree, a powerful figure, or a person three meters tall and visualizes how their partner's behavior would look if a miracle caused them to act in the desired way.
  - **Activating the need for assertiveness–autonomy:** The internalizing partner directly expresses their needs to their partner.
  - **Balancing the request with an offer:** The internalizing partner offers something in return for what they are asking from their partner.

- **Connecting with positive emotions:** The therapist asks the internalizing partner how they feel after expressing to their partner what they need and what they are offering. Then, the therapist turns to the other partner and asks how they feel seeing their partner's assertive side.
- **Partner's response to the internalizing partner's requests:** The therapist facilitates balance by asking the partner whether they agree with what the internalizing partner is offering or if they would like to request something more in return, and a dialogue begins until they reach an agreement.
- **Reconnection:** The therapist encourages the session to conclude with both partners standing up and sharing a hug.

Closing the Session

- **Reinforce the benefits of changing legs:** The therapist points out the differences between before and after doing the exercise.
- **Therapeutic task:** Meet with the couple to look at photos from the past, remember good times, and give positive feedback. The internalizing partner is asked to apply the technique learned in session to reconnect with the red leg.

11

Facing Critical Voices (Module VIII)

11.1 Introduction

This exercise helps strengthen the bond within a couple by challenging and eliminating critical voices directed at both oneself and one's partner, which reinforce coping patterns.

Typically, critical voice patterns that interfere with a couple's relationship are addressed in individual sessions. These sessions focus on the negative schemas activated within the relationship due to past experiences in which core emotional needs were frustrated.

In the dimensional model, the treatment of negative schemas and their associated critical voices is not the primary focus of couples therapy. Instead, the emphasis is on addressing needs, emotions, and behaviors, leaving deeper work on schemas and self-criticism to individual therapy as part of a comprehensive approach.

The dimensional model classifies critical internal voices into two categories: those directed toward oneself and those directed toward others. The former are associated with emotions of sadness or fear, the need for attachment/connection, and the passive avoidance or surrender coping mode, which corresponds to the blue leg. The latter are linked to emotions of anger or disgust, the need for assertiveness/autonomy, and the overcompensation or active avoidance coping mode, which are related to the red leg.

As explained in Chapter 1, negative schemas reflect distorted perceptions about oneself and others. Critical internal voices often represent two or more schemas and can be directed toward both the self and the partner. During couples therapy, both voices may be present, one active and the other blocked.

When critical voices interfere with therapy, impacting the therapist's work and hindering emotional rebalance between partners, it is sometimes necessary to address them directly in the session.

According to Roediger (2025), in externalizing clients, the critical voices are easier to identify because they appear on the front stage (chairs 2A and 2B in Figure 3.5). These voices are expressed outwardly through criticism, attacks, or reproaches toward the partner, thereby directly affecting the relationship.

In contrast, Roediger (2025) points out that in internalizing members, the critical voices are directed toward themselves, taking the form of self-criticism and self-blame. These voices are harder to detect because they are not as evident, operating instead backstage (Figure 3.5) in a more silent and hidden way. The effect of these internal critical voices is that the person becomes trapped in their own judgments, leading to emotional blockage and disconnection, which hinders their ability to communicate and listen to their partner.

Because of these differences, the approach to working with critical voices must vary depending on whether the partner is internalizing or externalizing, as will be explained later.

11.2 Beginning Work with Critical Voices

11.2.1 Identify the Activation of Critical Voices That Interfere with the Session

Whether in internalizing or externalizing clients, when a client has difficulty achieving emotional rebalancing, it is possible that an activated critical voice is triggering an intense emotional response in their child mode, which in turn intensifies their coping mode.

The first step in the intervention is to identify these critical voices, regardless of whether the client is externalizing or internalizing. Once recognized, the therapist validates them and assigns them a name, helping the client perceive them as ego-dystonic elements.

To illustrate this first step, in which the therapist identifies a critical voice that interferes with the rebalancing process, we return to the case of Emmanuel and Valerie, described in Chapter 3.

Emmanuel, 56 years old and Valerie, 54 years old

T: Valerie, I would like you to close your eyes and imagine how Emmanuel would behave if tomorrow he acted the way you wanted.

V: I don't know.

T: What do you think about imagining him coming in and asking how you're doing? Or suggesting you do an activity together as a couple?

V: No.
T: I understand. I'd like you to expand on your answer a little more. What's stopping you from imagining him having these attitudes toward you?
V: I don't deserve it; I'm boring.
T: I'm going to stop the exercise because I think the critical voice is preventing Valerie from getting in touch with her need for assertiveness-autonomy, that is, with her red leg. Does that seem okay to you?
V: Yes.
M: Yes.

11.3 Experiential Work

Once it has been identified that the critical voices are exerting pressure on the client, the next step is to work on them at an experiential level, according to the type of client (externalizing or internalizing) with whom the intervention is being carried out.

The following section presents two ways of addressing these voices depending on the client's profile.

11.3.1 Experiential Work with the Critical Voice in Internalizing Clients

11.3.1.1 Chair Work with the Internalizing Critical Voice

Confronting internal critical voices is generally a difficult process. Those that are directed toward oneself—called internalizing voices—tend to have a negative effect on one's own feelings.

1. **Identifying the irrational ideas of the critical voice:** The client and his or her partner are asked to sit in their respective coping mode chairs and close their eyes; the therapist does this as well (chairs 2A and 2B in Figure 3.5). The client being worked with is then asked the question: "What is the voice in your head telling you right now?" If the client focuses on expectations about his or her partner, the therapist redirects him or her to analyze his or her own self-criticism: "What are the voices in your head telling you about yourself?" The therapist collects three or four of these critical voices, which are usually expressed in the first person, with thoughts such as: "I am responsible for everything," "I have to take care of others," "If my family is not well, it is my fault," or "If my children are not doing well in school, it means I have failed."

2. **Repetition of the messages in the second person:** The therapist takes these messages and returns them to the client in the second person to help them distance themselves and question the validity of their self-critical thoughts. They might say something like: "If I understand correctly, these voices tell you that you should be better, that you are the only one responsible, that you are not a good enough mother, and that if your children don't do well in life, it's your fault." This process allows the client to position the critical voice as something ego-dystonic, that is, as something outside of themselves.
3. **Role-playing the critical voice:** The therapist places an additional chair next to the Vulnerable Child Mode chair (chairs 3A or 3B in Figure 3.5) and next to the therapist's chair (chair 1B in Figure 3.5) to represent the critical voice. The partner of this member sits on the other side of the therapist's chair. The client is then asked to sit in this chair and take on the role of their own critical voice, expressing the judgments and demands they normally impose on themselves towards the chair that represents their own Vulnerable Child Mode (chairs 3A or 3B in Figure 3.5). The therapist sits beside the client, while the other partner remains seated in their chair next to the therapist's chair (chair 1B in Figure 3.5), adjusting it slightly to view the scene from the side. During this exercise, the client must verbalize the "shoulds" and "have tos" that pressure them, attacking their vulnerable side. To facilitate this, the therapist guides them with phrases like: "Now you are the critical voice." Tell your vulnerable side what you pointed out to it a moment ago: "You are the one to blame, you are the one in charge, you are the one who has to do everything." The therapist amplifies the toxicity of the critical voice with provocative questions, helping the client identify its destructive impact: "Who needs a person like that (who needs a person like that who is not giving her best)?" If she is not delivering, who would miss her if she wouldn't be here anymore? This dialogue is maintained for two or three minutes, using three or four sentences, until an intense activation of the schema is induced, allowing the partner to confront the harshness of their own self-demands.

In the previous exercise, the therapist uses a series of questions to highlight the toxicity of the critical voice and how it attacks the client's Vulnerable Child Mode, while the partner remains in the observer role.

To illustrate the use of chair work to represent the critical voice, we continue with the description of the development of the session in the case of Valerie and Emmanuel.

Emmanuel, 56 years old and Valerie, 54 years old

T: Now let's do an exercise. I'm going to ask you to keep your eyes closed, and I'd like Valerie to ask us: "What is the voice in your head telling you right now?"

V: That I'm boring and that I don't deserve people being nice to me.

T: Anything else?

V: Yes, I'm not at all interesting and I can't contribute much to Emmanuel.

T: If I understand correctly, this critical voice tells you that you're uninteresting; that you're boring; and that you don't deserve to be treated nicely. Do I understand correctly?

V: Yes.

T: I'd like to place this chair next to you, which will represent your critical voice. Now, Valerie, I'll ask you to move to this chair and, from there, express all the judgments and demands you mentioned earlier.

V: You are not important, you are not valuable, you do not deserve anyone to make an effort for you, you are boring, you are not interesting.

T: Critical voice, tell me, what does a person like her deserve?

V: Nothing.

T: Do you have the right to ask your partner for something?

V: No.

T: Should your partner make an effort to get closer to you?

V: No, she's not worth it.

Reflection: Why do you think the therapist switches from speaking in the first person to the second person during the exercise?

Therapist's advice: When partners express their head's messages in the first person, it means they are stuck in the submissive coping mode. To help them identify and challenge these messages, they are asked to reframe them in the second person, which allows the critical voice to be externalized. This shift helps the partner begin to perceive these thoughts as coming from someone else (e.g., a parent, coach, teacher, etc.). This process is key because, during childhood, the partner internalized these voices, which reinforced their tendency to adopt a submissive mode, constantly trying to "be a good person" to avoid rejection or disapproval. Rather than working directly with the submissive mode, the therapeutic approach focuses on giving voice to the internal self-criticism, using the empty chair technique to personify and confront it more effectively.

11.3.1.2 Chair Work with the Vulnerable Child Mode of the Internalizing Partner

In this phase, the therapist helps the partners recognize the negative effects of the critical voice on the Vulnerable Child Mode of the partner being worked with. To do so, the therapist may follow these steps:

1. **Identifying the vulnerable child's emotions:** After role-playing the critical voice, the therapist asks the same partner to stand up from the critic-voice chair and move to the Vulnerable Child Mode chair (chair 3A or 3B in Figure 3.5). Once seated there, that partner is asked how they feel about hearing the messages of their critical voice. To facilitate the exploration, the therapist repeats the phrases the critical voice previously told them, for example: "You are responsible for everything," "You have to achieve this," "If you don't achieve this, no one will need you," "You have no right to be here," or "No one will miss you if you are not here." The therapist then guides the partner to delve deeper into their awareness of their emotions, exploring their bodily sensations through questions such as: "How does your stomach feel? Is it expanding or collapsing?" "What is your breathing like? Is it deep or shallow?" "How does your chest feel? Is it expanding or contracting?"
2. **Needs identification:** Once the same partner has identified their emotions, the therapist asks what they need at that moment, using questions such as: "What do you need right now, feeling...?" (the therapist repeats the emotions and body sensations). It is common for the partner to express needs such as help, comfort, validation, or a hug. Once they have become aware of their needs and verbalized them, the therapist asks them to remain in contact with that emotion and need for a moment, allowing them to integrate them before continuing with the intervention.
3. **Identifying the partner's emotions:** The therapist now addresses the other partner and asks the following questions to foster empathy and emotional connection: "Are you in the picture?" "Can you see your partner in that pain?" "How does it feel in your body to observe them like this?" At this point, the partner is expected to experience compassion for the other. If this occurs, the therapist moves on to the next step.
4. **Reconnection:** Once the couple has identified the emotion in the other, the therapist deepens the process by asking, "What is your impulse right now?" The partner's response is often to lean toward the Vulnerable Child Mode chair (chair 3A or 3B in Figure 3.5) of the partner with whom the therapist is working, offering support. At this point, the therapist invites the other partner to hold their partner's hand, hug them, and express their feelings. The therapist then asks the partner being worked with, "How do you feel about hearing what your partner has told you?"

It is important to clarify that the partner of the active member must be in a flexible coping mode in order to reconnect with them; that is, they must already be willing to cooperate by offering comfort and validation (blue leg) to the Vulnerable Child Mode of the active partner.

To illustrate the work done with vulnerable children, focusing on the negative emotions aroused and the needs frustrated by the critical voice, the case of Emmanuel and Valerie is reviewed.

Emmanuel, 56 years old and Valerie, 54 years old

T: Now, Valerie, I'd like you to open your eyes for a moment, move to your Vulnerable Child Mode chair, and close your eyes again. I'd like you to connect with your emotions and bodily sensations to detect how you feel when the critical voice tells you: "You are not important," "You are not valuable," "You don't deserve anyone to work for you," "You are boring," and "You are not interesting."

V: I feel sad; I feel my chest tighten, my stomach drop, and I have trouble breathing.

T: What do you need now that you feel this way?

V: That he hugs me, that I feel valuable, that someone is interested in how I am.

T: I understand. I'd like you to hold onto that emotion of sadness and your need to be seen, appreciated, and embraced while I ask your partner: Have you managed to see the image of Valerie feeling unappreciated?

M: Yes.

T: Can you see the pain little Valerie is feeling?

M: Yes.

T: How does it feel in your body when you look at her like this?

M: My stomach tightens, my chest too, and my breathing becomes labored.

T: Emmanuel, now that you've connected with Valerie's sadness, what's your impulse at this moment?

M: Hug her, tell her that she is important to me, that I do see her.

T: I would like you to do it then.

M: I care about you; I want to know how you feel; I have fun with you; you are very interesting to me.

T: Valerie, how do you feel when you are hugged and hear what Emmanuel is saying to you?

V: Good, now I feel seen.

11.3.2 Experiential Work with the Critical Voice in Externalizing Clients

In the case of working with the critical voice in externalizing clients, the following steps are followed:

1. **Identification of the irrational ideas of the critical voice:** The therapist tactfully interrupts when these voices are attacking the partner. To do this, the therapist first validates the emotion and then points out the possible emergence of the critical voice. The therapist may say something like: "Excuse me for interrupting you; I truly understand your anger. However, it seems to me that behind it there may be an active critical voice, and I think it is negatively influencing the relationship. Would you agree if we place it in this chair to take a closer look at it?" The therapist places a chair next to the Vulnerable Child Mode chair (3A or 3B in Figure 3.5); this chair will represent the externalizing member's critical voice. Then, the externalizing member is asked to sit in the critic's chair while the therapist moves their chair (1B in Figure 3.5) next to them. The other partner places a chair on the other side of the therapist's chair. The therapist then asks, while looking at the empty chair representing the Vulnerable Child Mode of the partner: "When you look at your partner's chair and are completely honest with me, what do you, as the critical voice, think about your partner? Do they really contribute enough to the relationship? Are you truly satisfied with them?"
2. **Representation of the critical voice:** From the critic's chair, the externalizing member directly expresses toward the chair representing their partner's Vulnerable Child Mode the critical ideas identified in the previous step.
3. **Feeling the impact of the critical voice's ideas:** The therapist asks the externalizing member to sit in the chair representing their partner's Vulnerable Child Mode (chairs 3A or 3B in Figure 3.5) while the therapist stands behind them. Then, both are asked to close their eyes. Once in this position, the therapist repeats the sentences previously spoken by the critical voice, inviting the externalizing member to perceive their impact on the body, emotions, and the impulses that arise when experiencing them (such as fighting, surrendering, or fleeing).
4. **Feeling anger toward the critical voices:** The therapist asks both partners to stand up and move to the observer's position (chairs 4A and 4B for the partners and chair 1B for the therapist in Figure 3.5). From this position, the therapist first asks the externalizing member and then their partner what they feel when they see the impact of the critical voices on the partner's Vulnerable Child Mode. After listening to their emotions, the therapist validates them and helps redirect the rejection or anger toward the critical voice rather than toward the partner.

5. **Timeout for the critical mode:** Once both have experienced anger toward the critical voice, they can be in tune with each other. The therapist then asks them to give this critical voice a name, for example, the snake or the toxic smoke. When the voice has been named, the therapist invites them to give it a "timeout" and to send it away. As the clients verbalize this, the therapist symbolically moves the chair, simulating that the critical voice is being removed from the room.
6. **Reconnection:** The therapist asks both partners if they would like to reconnect through a hug.
   Note: If the partner of the externalizing member does not wish to reconnect due to fear of being hurt again by the externalizing member's critical voice, the therapist validates the emotion and explains that the work of therapy focuses on the here and now to improve the relationship. The partner is then invited to express, from their vulnerable side, what they need from the other. If the disconnection persists, the therapist points out that this fear may also represent a critical voice and can restart the exercise, this time exploring the beliefs of the partner's critical voice. When working with the critical voice, this couple therapy approach focuses on the effects that the critical voice has either on oneself or on the partner.

11.4 Closing the Session

11.4.1 Reinforce the Benefits of Partner Support in the Face of Critical Voices

The therapist invites them to reflect on the emotional change they experienced: "How did you feel before the exercise, and how do you feel now?" Finally, the therapist points out that the change of leg is in their hands, emphasizing that practicing this type of interaction can transform the relationship.

To illustrate how the session can differentiate between before and after the critical voices exercise, we review the case of Emmanuel and Valerie.

Emmanuel, 56 years old and Valerie, 54 years old

T: Now reflect on how you feel compared to before doing the exercise. Remember, it's up to you to lean on your blue leg to reconnect with each other. Does this make sense to you?

M: Yes.

V: Yes.

11.4.2 Therapeutic Task: Identifying the Critical Voice

Once the reconnection is complete, the therapist asks the couple to stand and guides them through a reflection with a key question: "Can you feel how these voices are poisoning your life?" They then turn to the partner being worked with and point out that, although these critical voices have been normalized in their lives, it is precisely for this reason that it is necessary to team up with their partner to learn to let go of them, give them less power, and eventually let them go.

The therapist asks if they agree with this idea, and if both do, a mutual support agreement is established: Whenever the partner being worked with starts to be dominated by their critical voices, their partner can signal or say something like, "Hey, I think those are your critical voices putting pressure on you."

This signal can also be used if critical voices begin to affect the partner or children, encouraging greater awareness and support in the relationship.

It is because of the above that they are given the task that every time the partner of the member with whom they worked detects that these voices are activated, they make the agreed signal so that both become aware that it is the critical voices that are speaking and driving the coping modes,

To conclude the exercise, the therapist symbolically removes the critical voice, representing its removal from the session. This act reinforces the idea that the critical voice has no control over the therapy or the couple's relationship. The therapeutic work then resumes from the point where the critical voice had created a blockage, allowing the process to continue without its interference.

Emmanuel, 56 years old and Valerie, 54 years old

T: Well, I'd like to end this exercise with a question: Can you see how these critical voices sabotage the work of therapy?

M: Yes.

V: Yes.

T: I think these voices have become normal for Valerie, so I'd like you both to team up. When you notice these voices activating and causing Valerie to disconnect, you can signal or ask her directly. For example, Emmanuel, you could say something like, "I see you're tuned out today. Have your critical voices been activated?" What do you think of this option?

M: I agree.

V: Me too.

11.5 Resuming Session Work

Finally, if there is time to continue working in the session, the therapist resumes working with the couple where they left off before the critical voice interrupted.

To illustrate how, once the work with the critical voices is complete, the therapist can resume the therapeutic work where they left off.

Emmanuel, 56 years old and Valerie, 54 years old
T: Okay, now I'm going to remove the chair that represents the critical voice, and with that, we'll continue with the work of imagining the best day from where we left off...

To summarize the steps in working with critical voices in couples, the following table is presented below.

Beginning of Work with Critical Voices

- **Identify the activation of critical voices that interfere with the session:** The therapist focuses on those that are directed at themselves with the aim of seeing them as ego-dystonic.

Experiential Work: Chair Work with the Critical Voice

- **Chair Work with the Internalizing Critical Voice**
  - **Identification of the irrational ideas of the critical voice:** Both partners sit in their respective chairs and close their eyes. The focus is directed toward identifying the self-demands or self-criticisms in the client being worked with.
  - **Repetition of the messages in the second person:** The therapist repeats the messages of the critical voice and says them to the partner in the second person.
  - **Representation of the critical voice:** The therapist places a chair to represent the critical voice, and the partner sits in it while repeating the same messages to the chair representing the Vulnerable Child Mode. While this occurs, the therapist asks the critical voice questions that reveal its distorted beliefs.
  - **Identification of the emotions of the Vulnerable Child Mode:** The therapist asks the partner to sit in the Vulnerable Child Mode chair and identifies the emotional effects that the ideas expressed by the critical voice have had on them.

   - **Identification of needs:** The therapist asks the Vulnerable Child Mode what it needs at that moment when it feels that way.
   - **Identification of the partner's emotions:** The therapist asks the partner about their emotional reactions when hearing the emotions and needs of their partner's Vulnerable Child Mode.
   - **Reconnection:** The therapist promotes reconnection between the partners by facilitating physical closeness between them.
- **Chair Work with the Vulnerable Child Mode of the Internalizing Partner**
   - **Identification of the irrational ideas of the critical voice:** The therapist detects and makes explicit the beliefs of the externalizing partner's critical voice directed toward their partner.
   - **Representation of the critical voice:** The externalizing partner, from the critical voice chair, expresses these ideas toward the empty chair representing their partner's Vulnerable Child Mode.
   - **Feeling the impact of the critical voice's ideas:** The externalizing partner sits in the chair representing their partner's Vulnerable Child Mode, while the therapist, standing behind, repeats the messages of the critical voice.
   - **Feeling anger toward the critical voices:** From the observer position, both the externalizing partner and their partner experience anger toward the critical voice for the way it treats the Vulnerable Child Mode of the internalizing partner.
   - **Timeout for the critical mode:** The therapist asks the couple to name the critical mode and give it a timeout each time it appears, symbolically moving the chair out of the scene.
   - **Reconnection:** The therapist invites the partners to reconnect by giving each other a hug.

Closing the Work with the Critical Voice

- **Reinforce the benefits of changing legs:** The therapist points out the differences between before and after doing the exercise.
- **Therapeutic task:** Identify the critical voice: In pairs, you will work as a team to indicate when the critical voice is activated in the member with whom you worked in the session.
- **Continue the session where it left off:** If there is time, the therapist resumes the session where it was interrupted by the critical voice.

Part IV

Reconnection

Up to this point, the previous modules have focused primarily on the process of emotional self-regulation and rebalancing the couple. However, once this rebalancing has been achieved, the specific content of the problems is addressed through the following modules.

In this phase, partners must demonstrate a willingness to find solutions at an emotional level. This state is achieved when both partners have been able to connect from their assertive side (red leg), working through emotions like anger or disgust, to their attachment-connection side (blue leg), related to emotions like sadness or fear, and adopting flexible coping behaviors, such as giving in and cooperating. If the couple has not achieved this emotional flexibility, they are unlikely to be able to solve their problems effectively.

In other words, the goal of the previous modules is to develop flexibility between the "legs" (red and blue), a key skill of healthy adults that reflects the capacity for emotional self-regulation. Once this skill is consolidated, the couple can move toward resolving their problems. According to Valente (in Roediger & Valente, 2025), this change is essential for generating positive results in therapy.

In this phase, we work with joint imagery, involving joint imagery exercises in which one partner visualizes painful events from their childhood or adolescence, while the other enters into their imagination and attempts to satisfy the unmet need or stop the abuse experienced. This strategy aims to help one partner recognize the other's ability to connect with, protect, and comfort their vulnerable child. That is, to help them perceive their partner as someone capable of providing support, affection, trust, and caring, thereby facilitating emotional reconnection.

We also work on partners' ability to express their emotions from their vulnerable side.

Finally, the application of connection dialogues is explained, introducing a technique in which partners must repeat their partner's messages before expressing their own. This exercise, known as "seeing both sides of the phone," allows each partner to understand the other's perspective. By integrating this technique, the brain is encouraged to broaden its perspective of the situation, which fosters a more balanced perspective. When both partners actively participate in this dynamic, a cognitive and emotional reconnection occurs that takes them from "not understanding" to "understanding." At the end of the exercise, their points of view are integrated, allowing both partners to learn something new and expand their mutual understanding, thus strengthening their relationship.

It is important to note that these techniques can be applied at any point during the session, starting with Module IV, without the need to deploy and analyze the mode cycle. The key criterion for assigning this task is that the therapist believes the couple already has the capacity to emotionally reconnect.

While the cases are presented following a structured path (from topic selection to cycle identification), this is intended solely to reinforce the basic process the couple goes through and to provide greater context for what happens within the couple before the reconnection intervention.

Unlike the initial modules of the psychoeducation phase, which must be followed sequentially, and the intermediate modules, which are used optionally if the couple struggles to rebalance, these reconnection modules do not follow a sequential order but are applied as the therapist deems most appropriate, depending on the case and context of the session, with the goal of generating reconnection between the couple. However, it is important to remember that in the exercise of connection dialogues, it is recommended that both partners be clearly balanced.

12

Reconnection with Joint Imagery Exercise (Module IX)

12.1 Introduction

The first stage of the reconnection process aims primarily to foster mutual emotional support between partners. This support is developed through the exercise of joint imagination, in which one partner visualizes significant situations from the past while their partner actively collaborates to meet the unmet emotional needs of the moment. This process, known as reparenting, allows the couple to assume a protective and emotionally supportive role, strengthening the bond between them.

This exercise is based on image rescripting, a technique adapted by Roediger (2025) from schema therapy, which seeks to reconfigure emotionally charged past memories, providing a restorative experience that strengthens the couple's emotional connection.

Reflection: Why do you think this exercise cannot be applied in the first sessions of therapy?

Therapist's advice: It's important to wait with this exercise until the couple has managed to stop the fighting and reconnect in a functional way. Otherwise, you run the risk of the imagery partner becoming hurt and emotionally deprived again. The exercise usually works very well, deepening the partner's understanding of behavioral patterns based on childhood experiences and creating a better emotional connection. Therefore, whenever therapy gets stuck, it's worth trying a little imagery work.

General objective: Promote empathy in the couple and activate the need for attachment in both members.

Specific objectives:

- Test the reparenting capacity of one member toward the other to generate attachment and connection between them.

- Differentiate between the emotions that correspond to negative patterns from the past and the people who generated them and those that correspond to the couple due to the situation that occurred.
- Strengthen the expression of needs and emotions between both members and their ability to offer something in return.
- Increase the couple's use of the blue leg and their ability to feel empathy and compassion for each other.

12.2 Starting the Session: Identifying the Problem to Be Worked On

As in the previous modules, the session begins by inviting the couple to express what they wish to work on in therapy. Since at this stage the couple already demonstrates greater skills in detecting and stopping the mode cycle and rebalancing, the therapist could move directly to the joint imagery exercise during the problem statement (without needing to initiate the mode cycle) to address any of the negative schemas of either partner involved in the situation.

To illustrate the exercise of joint imagination, we return to the case of Isabella and Caroline, described in Chapter 3. Both have faced problems in their relationship due to Isabella's lack of public acceptance of her sexual orientation.

Isabella and Caroline, 34 years old

T: Okay, I'd like to know what you'd like to work on in this session.
I: I would like to address something.
T: Sure, go ahead.
I: Caroline got angry because I let go of her hand while we were walking in the square, and then she didn't want to see us that weekend.
T: Caroline, do you think it's okay if we address this topic?
C: Yes.
T: Perfect, then I ask you to discuss it directly among yourselves.
I: Why don't you understand that it is difficult for me to let other people know that there is something between us?
C: Okay, I understand, but there are people who wouldn't feel uncomfortable holding my hand, no matter who saw them.
I: Tell me, did you go out with anyone this weekend?
C: Why do you want to know? So you can get mad and try to control who I hang out with or not?

T: I'm going to stop the conversation here because I'd like to try an exercise that might help you connect more with each other. Is that okay with you?
C: Okay.
I: Yes.

12.3 Experiential Work

12.3.1 Detect Negative Patterns and Their Origins

During the problem identification phase, the therapist analyzes the possible negative schemas involved in both partners and selects the member who will participate in the "joint imagery exercise".

Typically, the member most activated in the situation is chosen, although another option is to work with the most withdrawn member to encourage their active participation in the session.

Once the analysis is complete and the member is selected, the therapist consults with both partners to see if they agree with the choice. It is clarified that the other partner will have their turn once this intervention is concluded, either in this session or in the next. If both agree, the therapist proceeds to explore the schemas activated in the selected partner's mode cycle.

The initial process with the selected member follows these steps:

1. **Selecting the partner to reparent:** The therapist indicates that an imagination exercise will be conducted and begins by proposing to the couple that they work with one partner first. If both agree, the therapist begins with that partner, clarifying that, once this work is completed, the same process will be carried out with the other partner in the same or a future session.
2. **Sitting in the child mode chair:** The selected partner sits in the chair representing the activated child mode (chair 3A or 3B) related to the issue being addressed with their partner. Meanwhile, the other partner remains seated in their coping mode chair (chair 2A or 2B). The therapist sits close to and slightly behind the partner being reparented.
3. **Imagination of the problematic scene of the present:** The therapist asks both partners to close their eyes and visualize the interaction they just experienced. Then, the therapist guides the partner selected for the exercise to describe the visualization using questions such as: What do you see in this scene?; What do you hear?; Do you perceive any smell or taste?; How does your body feel as you connect with what you're sensing?; What are you feeling in this moment?; What is your partner doing?; As the scene progresses, do your emotions intensify or decrease? Once these questions are answered, the

therapist deepens emotional awareness by asking the partner to replay the most intense part of the experience in slow motion. Then, the therapist invites them to tune into their bodily sensations with questions like: How does that feel in your body?; Does your chest expand or contract?; Is your breathing easier or more difficult?; and Does your stomach expand or collapse?

4. **Floating back:** The therapist builds a bridge between the client's present emotions and those from their past. To do this, the therapist offers the following instruction: "Let this image begin to fade and focus your attention on your feelings and emotions. Now go back in time to your childhood or adolescence. Allow any images to come into your mind. What images are coming up? Try to stay connected to your emotions."
5. **Childhood scene:** The therapist helps deepen the connection to childhood or adolescent imagery by asking questions such as: What is happening in the moment you've remembered?; What are you doing?; What do you feel in your body?; What are you thinking?; What is your impulse?; and What are you feeling? The therapist encourages the client to stay connected to their emotions and to explore where those emotions are coming from. Afterwards, the therapist explains that this scene contributed to the development of the associated negative schema.
6. **Unmet needs from the past:** The therapist guides the partner undergoing the reparenting process to connect with their unmet emotional needs. To facilitate this, the therapist asks questions such as, "What do you need right now?" The therapist then supports the partner in identifying, naming, and validating their active coping mode, recognizing it as an attempt to help meet the needs of the Vulnerable Child Mode.

The case of Isabella and Caroline is then reviewed to show how the therapist implements the necessary steps to select the person to work with first and how the activated schemas are identified along with their origins.

Isabella and Caroline, 34 years old

T: Okay, now I'd like to suggest an imagination exercise. First, we'd focus on Caroline and the events from her past that might be associated with these Child mode emotions. Then, in this or the next session, we'd work with Isabella. Does that sound right?

I: Yes, I agree.

C: Me too.

TD: Alright, Carolina, I'd like you to take a seat in the chair representing your Angry Child mode. Isabel, I'm going to ask you to sit in the chair for your Coping mode. I'll sit next to you, Carolina.

Now that you're both seated, I invite you to close your eyes. Carolina, I'd like you to visualize the situation you just described—the one you experienced with Isabel—and tell me: What do you see in the scene?

C: I see Isabel letting go of my hand while we were walking in the plaza.
TD: What do you hear in this scene?
C: Nothing. There's a heavy silence between us.
TD: Do you notice any particular smells or tastes?
C: It smells like vanilla, and my mouth tastes bitter.
TD: How does your body feel?
C: Tense.
TD: What are you feeling in that moment?
C: A lot of anger.
TD: What is Isabel doing?
C: She's talking to me like nothing happened—as if it doesn't matter that she rejected me like that.
TD: As the scene continues, do your feelings intensify or fade?
C: They intensify.
T: Now I'd like you to go back to the most intense moment in that scene and replay it in slow motion. Can you see it?
C: Yes.
T: How does your body feel now?
C: Hot.
T: Is your chest expanding or contracting?
C: Expanding.
T: Is your breathing becoming easier or more difficult?
C: Easier.
T: Is your stomach expanding or shrinking?
C: Expanding.
T: I see. Now I'd like you to gradually let this image fade while staying connected to your feelings. From this emotional space, I want you to go back in time—to your childhood or adolescence—and allow any images that come to mind to surface. What do you see?
C: I see my dad on the street holding hands with his wife, and I'm standing in front of them with my mom.
T: What's happening in that moment?
C: My mom and I are face to face with my dad, who's walking hand-in-hand with his wife.
T: And what were you doing?
C: I was accompanying my mom to take care of some paperwork.

(Continued)

(Continued)

T: What sensations do you notice in your body?

C: Tension. I could sense my mom's stress. She was my dad's mistress, and his wife didn't know—she didn't even know I existed.

T: What are you thinking?

C: That it's so unfair—what my dad did to my mom. He shouldn't be hiding us. And then, when he sees me, he talks like nothing's happening.

T: What's your impulse?

C: To confront him—to demand an explanation.

T: What do you feel?

C: Powerlessness at not being able to do that, and a lot of anger.

T: I hear you. Stay connected to these emotions and to their roots. Notice how this scene has contributed to your sense of abandonment. Now tell me, what do you need right now?

C: I need to scream—to tell him everything he did to me.

T: It's completely natural to feel that way—and to want to fight for this deep emotional need for unconditional acceptance.

Reflection: Why do you think the therapist addresses the Vulnerable Child Mode from her past directly instead of speaking to her in the third person?

Therapist's advice: According to Valente in Roediger & Valente (2025), addressing the child or adolescent in their memories in the first person allows the partner to connect more deeply with their emotional memory. This approach intensifies the experience of the exercise, generating a more significant impact on the reparenting process. Furthermore, speaking directly helps prevent the partner from falling into a disconnected or avoidant mode, which favors greater emotional involvement and, consequently, better therapeutic outcomes.

To demonstrate the steps outlined in the joint imagery exercise, a script is presented below that can be used during therapy.

Example 12.1 Script to Detect the Schema and its Origins

(in a calm, gentle voice) "I would ask you to choose a conflictive situation from your daily life with your partner in which you felt very emotionally activated. Do you have the image? Now I ask you to play it back in your mind as if you were watching a movie. At what point in that scene were your emotions strongest? Where are you and your partner? What are you doing? What do you see? What do you hear? What do you smell? What do you feel in your body? What thoughts come to mind? What do you feel driven to do?" (The therapist paraphrases the partner's answers). From within these feelings, I'd like you to open yourself up and allow an image from a moment in your childhood and/or adolescence to come to you. Now that you've connected with a scene, I'd like you to tell me: How old is little (person's name)? Now I would like to speak directly to that little boy (child's age), and I would like to ask him: Little (person's name), where are you exactly now? What is happening there? What exactly are you feeling? How does your body feel? What thoughts are you having right now? What would you like to do? What do you need right now? What could help you right now to make you feel better?

Reflection: What do you think should be done when the partner is too emotionally activated during the imagination exercise?

Therapist's advice: When a partner is feeling overactive emotionally, the therapist may choose to stop asking the vulnerable child questions directly and begin speaking to the partner in the third person. Instead of saying, "How do you feel, Little (partner's name), when?" they might say something like, "How does Little (partner's name) feel when?" It is also helpful to stop the imagination before the trauma develops again in the imagination. This way, the vulnerable child can be reparented by preventing the traumatic event from happening in the imagination. To reinforce the sense of control, the therapist may stop what is happening in the imagination by saying something like, "I want you to know that you can stop what is happening in your imagination at any time. That is, whenever you want, everyone will freeze in the memory you are re-experiencing except you."

12.3.2 Joint Imagery Rewriting Work

Once the significant event from the client's childhood or adolescence has been identified, the joint imagination work begins, following the steps detailed below:

1. **Exploring what the partner feels and wants to do:** The therapist begins by asking the partner if they were also able to visualize the image described by the client. The partner then explores the emotions and bodily sensations they experienced when imagining the past event. Questions may include: "How do you feel when you see your partner in that situation? What do you feel in your body when you imagine it? What would you like to say or do for your partner at that moment?"
2. **Comforting the Vulnerable Child Mode:** If the partner of the member being reparented experiences positive emotions and shows a willingness to help, the therapist guides them to enter the past scene evoked during

the imagery exercise using a soft and warm tone of voice. The goal is to comfort and embrace the child mode (now represented in the vulnerable chair) of the partner undergoing reparenting. If appropriate, the partner may also move their chair closer and offer a physical embrace (the partner moves their coping mode chair, chair 2A or 2B, next to the vulnerable child chair, chair 3A or 3B, of the partner being reparented; see Figure 3.5). The therapist might suggest something like: "Move your chair closer to your partner, embrace them, and say something like: I'm here with you, little one (partner's name)." If, at this point (or in subsequent steps), the partner is unable to participate in the reparenting process—perhaps due to being in a detached mode, the activation of negative schemas, or a critical mode expressing judgments toward the partner—the therapist will intervene directly, stepping in to fulfill the role of the reparenting figure themselves.

3. **Confronting the person who contributed to the formation of the negative schema:** Once the partner has comforted the member being reparented, the therapist explains that the next step is to defend them. The partner is invited to confront—within the guided imagery exercise—the person who contributed to the development of the negative schema. This confrontation should be firm yet compassionate, without aggression, and aimed at protecting the inner child. If the partner struggles to find the right words, the therapist can offer suggestions such as: "You can say something like: What you're doing is neither fair nor helpful for little (name of the partner). He/she is a normal child; there's nothing wrong with them. You have no right to treat them this way. You're violating their needs and causing deep harm. They don't deserve to be made to feel this way because of your personal issues. You need to get help to stop hurting them."
4. **Response from the confronted person in the past:** After the confrontation, the therapist asks the partner how they imagine that person from the past would have reacted to those words. Often, such figures respond with avoidance, hostility, or passive-aggressive behavior.
5. **The reparenting partner's response to the reaction of the person who originated the negative schema:** If the person from the past responds in a positive or cooperative way, the therapist can proceed to the next step of the process. However, if the response is dismissive, aggressive, or passive-aggressive, the reparenting partner is invited to firmly confront this reaction, reaffirming

their protective role. If this is difficult for them, the therapist may offer an example such as: "You might say something like: Your reaction shows that you don't understand what a child really needs. You're so absorbed in yourself that you can't take care of this helpless child. I'm not afraid of you, but I'm taking this child away from you—and you will face the consequences of your actions."

6. **The confronted person from the past faces consequences:** The therapist guides the partner through a visualization in which, depending on the case, the figure from the past faces consequences for having contributed to the formation of the negative schema. These consequences can vary—from imagining the person being sent to prison, to receiving psychiatric treatment, offering a sincere apology, and committing to never repeating the behavior. The goal is to restore a sense of symbolic justice and protection for the inner child.
7. **Reparenting the Vulnerable Child Mode:** The therapist then invites the focus to return to the partner's Vulnerable Child Mode, with the aim of validating their emotional experience and offering the nurturing messages they needed to hear. If the partner or their partner is unsure of what to say, the therapist may offer a suggestion such as: "You are a normal child. There is nothing wrong with you. You did the best you could—no one could have done it better. It wasn't your fault. Like all children, you deserve better. We're going to leave this place and go somewhere safe. You're with me now, and I want to be a safe place for you. I want you to know that you can come to me anytime you need protection."
8. **Emotional connection after reparenting:** To conclude the exercise, the therapist asks the reparented partner how they feel after the experience. This may be introduced with a question such as: "How are you feeling now, after going through this exercise and seeing and hearing your partner (or me, depending on the case) respond to you in this way?" The reparented client first shares their emotional response with the therapist, and then with their partner. In turn, the other partner also expresses how it felt to care for and protect their loved one's inner child—first to the therapist, and then to their partner. If both individuals respond in a balanced and emotionally regulated way, the therapist proceeds to the next phase of the therapeutic process.

To illustrate the specific steps of this stage of the strategy, we return to the previously presented case in which Isabella participates in Caroline's imagination to reparent her during the difficult situation she has described.

Isabella and Caroline, 34 years old

T: Isabel, were you able to visualize the image of Carolina's father walking past her and ignoring her?

I: Yes.

T: How do you feel seeing little Carolina, 10 years old, in that situation?

I: It makes me really sad to imagine how she must have felt—and also very angry at her father. How could he act like that? It feels like my stomach is sinking.

T: I'd like you to step into that image now and comfort little Carolina. If you feel ready, you can also move your chair closer and physically embrace her in this moment. Say something to let her know that you're really here. Does that sound okay?

I: Yes. (Isabel hugs Carolina.) I'm here with you, little Carolina.

T: Now I'd like you to confront Carolina's father. What would you say to him?

I: Carolina's father, I want you to know that she is a very valuable little girl, and it's your responsibility to care for her. How could you deny your own 10-year-old daughter?

T: Little Carolina, how does it feel to hear Isabel say that to your father?

C: I feel validated. I wish my mom had done that for me.

T: And how does your father respond to Isabel's words?

C: He doesn't say anything... He just lowers his gaze.

T: Isabel, what would you say to Carolina's father in response to his silence?

I: I'm not sure what to say...

T: How about something like: "Your reaction shows that you don't really understand what Carolina needs. You're so wrapped up in yourself that you can't take care of her. You need to take responsibility, to acknowledge her, and to give her the care she deserves."

I: Sir, Carolina is a wonderful little girl. It is your duty to care for her and recognize her.

T: Very good. Now let's imagine that Carolina's father receives a paternity suit that requires him to legally acknowledge her. He can no longer hide her, and now he must face the consequences of his actions with his wife. Isabel, now I'd like us to shift our focus back to little Carolina. What would you like to do with her?

I: I'd like to hug her and tell her how important she is to me.

T: Wonderful. I'd like you to add something like: "You are a normal little girl. There's nothing wrong with you. It wasn't your fault. Your father should have acknowledged you and never abandoned you. I want to be your safe place now, and I'll be here whenever you need me." Little Carolina, how does it feel to be hugged by Isabel and to hear her say she's here for you?

C: I feel loved and supported.

T: Isabel, how do you feel being there for little Carolina in this way?

I: I feel good... moved.

12.3.3 Link Between Past Experience, Coping Modes, and Child Modes of the Reparented Partner

Once the reparenting process has been completed, the therapist helps both partners become aware of the connection between the activation of the reparented partner's coping and child modes and experiences from their childhood or adolescence. To facilitate this, the therapist may follow these steps:

1. **Connection between the activation of modes and the past experience:** The therapist asks both partners to sit in their coping-mode chairs (which, if the work up to this point has been effective, should now correspond to a flexible coping mode, chairs 2A or 2B in Figure 3.5) and close their eyes again. Afterwards, the therapist sits in chair 1A in Figure 3.5. Once everyone is in position, the therapist establishes a bridge between the childhood or adolescent experience, the development of the negative schema, and the activation of the child and coping modes in response to the current behavior of the partner. This may be explained using a phrase such as: "Do you notice how when you (partner of the reparented member) do (specific coping behavior), it activates in (name of reparented partner) their schema of (schema name), which originated in (past event)? And that's why they feel (active child mode) and respond from (active coping mode)?"
2. **The partner affirms they are not the same as the person from the past:** Once the link between past and present is established, the therapist invites the partner of the reparented individual to affirm themselves as someone different from the person who caused harm and to express their intention to care for their partner and meet their unmet emotional needs. The partner is also encouraged to communicate their own needs and state the flexible coping behavior they would like to see from their partner. If needed, the therapist may offer a suggestion such as: "You might say something like: 'I understand that you feel (activated child mode) when I (behavior that triggers the schema), and that hurts me, because the last thing I want is to make you feel like when (person from the past) did (event). But I would also like you to (desired flexible coping behavior).'"

3. **The reparented partner expresses their current need from a healthy mode:** The therapist guides the reparented partner to express their current emotional needs from a flexible coping mode—either from initiative (red leg) or from vulnerability (blue leg). They may ask: "What would you like to receive from your partner when these memories that activate your (schema name) are triggered? How could you ask for it from a place of vulnerability?" The therapist also encourages the partner to offer something meaningful in return. If necessary, an example might be provided: "I want to share that in my childhood, (person from the past) did (painful event). That's why, when you (current triggering event), I react from (active coping mode) and feel (Vulnerable Child Mode). I know it's my responsibility to face this and try to respond in a more balanced way, but it would help me a lot if you could respond in those moments in a (loving, regulated, assertive, or need-fulfilling) way and have patience with my frustration. I, on my part, commit not to blame you for what others did to me and to work on healing this painful wound." The therapist ensures that the requests made by the reparented partner are specific, realistic, healthy, and achievable.
4. **The partner's response to the reparented partner's request:** The therapist turns to the partner and asks how they feel after hearing their partner's expressed needs. They are then invited to respond with what they would like to offer in return. If the partner shows resistance or difficulty responding positively, the therapist encourages them to make a counterproposal, and the process is repeated until both partners reach a clear and attainable agreement that they can commit to until the next session. In cases where the partner shows a lack of empathy or emotional disconnection, the therapist may use the wound metaphor—for example, imagining that their partner carries an open wound that needs gentle care. Finally, the therapist helps the couple reconnect with the positive emotions that emerged as they reached this agreement.
5. **Emotional and physical reconnection:** Once both partners have emotionally connected (the reparented partner feeling cared for, and the other feeling the reward of providing care), the therapist invites them to engage in physical closeness. They are guided to remove their chairs, sit face-to-face, hold hands, and slowly open their eyes, marking a moment of reconnection and emotional healing.

It is important to clarify that, in the previous exercise, the dialogue between both partners takes place from a flexible coping mode. This mode involves taking the initiative to express one's needs, as well as cooperating or yielding by offering something in return. If the couple experiences difficulties remaining in this mode, the therapist can provide feedback or suggestions to help them stay in or reconnect with it.

Reflection: What do you think the therapist should do when a critical internal voice of the reparenting partner appears in the session?

Therapist's advice: If the partner displays a critical voice or unempathetic attitudes during reparenting, the therapist should stop it, do the reparenting, and address this behavior in another session to explore and work on the underlying patterns that generate it by addressing the internal voice mode (Module IV).

To explore in greater depth how to use the wound metaphor as a way to help the partner of the reparented member gain awareness of what is happening when schemas are activated, the following script is provided as a tool that can be used during the therapy session.

Example 12.2 Script for Explaining the Wound Metaphor

I think one way to explain what happens when your partner's negative schema is triggered by certain behaviors of yours is through the analogy of a physical wound. Imagine that, for some reason, you grab your partner's arm, and she reacts by screaming in an exaggerated way, as if you were hurting her. What you don't know is that, underneath her clothing—right where you touched her—there is a wound that hasn't healed and is still open. Who is at fault in this situation? You, for touching her? Or her, for screaming? The answer is: neither of you. You can't see the wound because her clothing hides it. And she can't help but feel pain—that pain would correspond to her child mode—and scream in the moment—which reflects her coping mode—because the wound is still open. The most responsible thing for the person who is hurt is to show the wound, so the other person becomes aware of it. And for the one who touches the wound, the most responsible thing is to approach it gently, knowing that it will hurt because of past experiences. The same happens with negative schemas. Your partner's job is to tell you how they were hurt and in which areas of their life they feel vulnerable. And your responsibility is to treat them with kindness, understanding that, even if your actions are not inherently harmful, they might still activate the negative schema and cause emotional pain.

To illustrate the specific steps of this stage of the strategy, we return to the previously presented case in which Isabel participates in Carolina's imagery to reparent her during the difficult situation she has described.

Isabella and Caroline, 34 years old
T: I believe there's a connection between that past event—when Carolina's father ignored her as she walked by—the development of her negative schema, and the activation of her angry child mode and active avoidance when Isabel let go of her hand while they were walking. What do you think?

(Continued)

(Continued)

C: I agree.
I: Me too.
T: Now, Isabel, I'd like you to tell Carolina whether it's your intention to do the same thing her father did to her in childhood and whether it matters to you that she not feel abandoned by you.
I: Yes, Carolina, I'm really sorry about what you went through, and I don't like knowing that you felt the same way when I let go of your hand. I want you to know that I want to be with you—I don't intend to push you aside like your dad did.
T: Good. Now tell her what you need from her.
I: I'd like you to understand that my parents don't need to know about my sexual orientation. Aside from them, the people who matter most to me already know you. I'm asking you to be a little flexible as my partner while I work up the courage to tell them.
T: Carolina, what would you ask of Isabel in return?
C: That she faces her fears and tells her parents she has a same-sex partner.
T: Alright. How would you feel about also asking her that, if she's going to let go of your hand, she says something like: "I don't want to make you feel bad, but I'm feeling a little anxious because there are people here who know my parents. Can I let go of your hand? I'm not ready to face this right now."
C: Yes. Isabel, I want you to tell me how you're feeling and ask me before letting go of my hand. That way, I'll feel considered rather than rejected.
T: Very good. Now, what could you offer in return for Isabel's effort to tell her parents about your relationship and to explain her anxiety when she needs physical distance?
C: I'd like to say that, in return, I'll be more supportive with you and stop pulling away from you when I'm angry.
T: Then the agreement is this: Carolina, you commit not to withdraw when you're angry and to show more patience toward Isabel. And Isabel, you commit to working through your fear of introducing Carolina to your parents and to telling her when you're feeling anxious, asking her before creating physical distance. Do you both agree?
C: I agree.
I.: I agree too.
T: Isabel, how do you feel hearing Carolina's requests?
I: I feel good. What she's asking for, and offering in return, feels fair to me.

T: Is there anything else you'd like to ask for or offer in response to what Carolina shared?

I: No

T: And now, to be more concrete: Isabel, regarding your commitment to work through your fear of your parents finding out about your sexual orientation, what specific step are you willing to take between now and the next session?

I: I'm not sure...

T: How would you feel about scheduling or attending an individual therapy session?

I: Yes, I'll commit to having an individual therapy session before our next session to work on my fear of my parents finding out I'm gay.

T: Carolina, how do you feel hearing that commitment?

C: I feel happy.

T: And similarly, Carolina, what concrete step could you take to be more supportive with Isabel and not pull away?

C: I'll also commit to working on my issues with rejection from my father in my next therapy session, so I don't pull away from Isabel when I feel like she's doing the same thing he did to me.

T: Are you okay with that, Isabel?

I: Yes.

T: If you both agree, I'd like to invite you to move your chairs closer together. If you wish, you may share a hug or express the affection you're feeling for each other in this moment. And to close, you can gently open your eyes.

The main objective of this intervention is to facilitate the reparenting process. If the observing partner is able to confront their partner's caregivers in the picture, this can be beneficial, but it is not a prerequisite for achieving a successful outcome. The most important thing is to foster emotional connection and mutual support between the partners.

Reflection: What to do when one of the members doesn't know what to give or offer in return?

Therapist's advice: As a therapist, remember that you model a healthy, balanced adult. If partners are struggling to identify what to give or offer in return, you can intervene by suggesting concrete, practical ideas relevant to their situation. Be sure to guide the conversation to find mutually acceptable options, promoting fair and meaningful agreements.

12.4 Closing the Session

12.4.1 Evaluate the Benefits of Connecting with the Blue Leg

To conclude, the therapist invites both partners to reflect on the differences in their emotions between the beginning and end of the session. He emphasizes that achieving this emotional connection is in their hands, especially when they choose to act from their "blue leg" (needs for connection and vulnerability). This step is exemplified below, continuing with the case of Isabella and Caroline.

Isabella and Caroline, 34 years old

T: How do you feel when you compare how you started the session with how you feel now after this exercise?
C: I feel better with Isabella.
I: I also feel better with Caroline.
T: Remember, it's in your hands to act in support of each other from your blue leg, strengthening the attachment and emotional connection in your relationship. Does this make sense to you?
I: Yes.
C: Yes.

12.4.2 Therapeutic Task: Remind the Partner of Their Reparenting Role, the Vulnerable Child of the Reparented Member, and Carry Out the Agreed Commitment

As homework, the therapist asks the reparented client to recall the partner's reparenting abilities each time their negative schema is activated, reflecting that, although past figures failed to meet their needs, their partner has demonstrated in the exercise their ability to provide emotional support and care. The client is also asked to recall the vulnerable child they reparented during the imagery exercise each time their coping mode is activated in the mode cycle. Finally, the reparented client's partner is reminded of what they committed to doing between now and the next session.

Finally, we present how therapist Daniel explained the therapeutic task at the end of the session, after applying the joint imagery exercise.

Isabella and Caroline, 34 years old

T: Caroline, for homework, I'd like you to remember the exercise we did today every time your negative schema is activated and you feel unworthy or unimportant to Isabella and how it became clear that she truly cares about how you feel. Also, when you feel this way, you could ask Isabella to hug you or share with you the progress and efforts she's making in her therapy to come out about her sexual orientation. What do you think of this suggestion?

I: Sounds good to me.

C: Me too.

T: I'd also like to remind you that between now and the next session, you both agreed to work on these issues in individual therapy. Isabella, your fear of your parents discovering your homosexuality, and Carolina, your father's rejection. Do you agree?

I: Yes.

C: Yes.

Below, as a summary, are the essential steps for putting into practice the joint imagery exercise as a couple:

Beginning of the Session

- **Identification of the problem to be worked on:** The couple talks about the problem to be worked on, while the therapist identifies the patterns that influence emotional activation in both members.

Experiential Work

- **Negative Schemas and Their Origins**
  - **Choosing the partner to be reparented:** The therapist suggests doing imagery rescripting work with one of the partners.
  - **Sitting in the chair representing the activated child mode:** The partner to be reparented sits in the chair representing the activated child mode, while their partner remains seated in the chair of the coping mode.
  - **Imagining the problematic scene from the present:** The therapist asks both partners to close their eyes and visualize the problematic situation they are addressing in the session. The partner to be reparented connects with the emotions experienced during that event.

  - **Floating back:** The therapist builds a bridge between the present emotions and those from the past in the partner being guided through the process.
  - **Childhood scene:** The therapist helps deepen the imagery associated with childhood or adolescence, and awareness is brought to how this contributed to the negative schema activated in the present situation.
  - **Unmet needs from the past:** The therapist helps the partner being reparented connect with their unmet emotional needs.
- **Joint Imagery Rescripting Work**
  - **Exploring what the partner feels and wants to do:** The therapist begins by asking the partner what they would like to express or do for the partner being reparented.
  - **Comforting the Vulnerable Child Mode:** If the partner experiences positive feelings and shows willingness to help, the therapist guides them in comforting and embracing the Vulnerable Child Mode of the partner being reparented.
  - **Confronting the person who contributed to the negative schema:** The partner of the reparented member confronts the person who played a role in the development of the negative schema.
  - **Response of the confronted person from the past:** The person who contributed to the schema responds to the confrontation made by the partner of the reparented member.
  - **The reparenting partner confronts the past figure's response:** If the past figure responds favorably, the therapist may move on to the next step. However, if the response is evasive, aggressive, or dismissive, the reparenting partner is invited to confront that reaction.
  - **The confronted person from the past faces consequences:** Depending on the case, the therapist describes the consequences that the past figure receives for having contributed to the development of the negative schema.
  - **Reparenting the vulnerable child:** The partner of the reparented member validates and nurtures the Vulnerable Child Mode.
  - **Emotional connection after reparenting:** The therapist ends the exercise and asks the reparented partner to share their emotional response to the experience—first with the therapist, then with their partner. Afterwards, the reparenting partner also shares their emotional response—first with the therapist, then with their partner.
- **Link Between the Past Experience, Coping, and Child Modes of the Reparented Partner**
  - **Connection between the activation of coping and child modes and the reparented partner's past experience:** The therapist makes a connection between the situation that occurred in the reparented partner's

childhood or adolescence, the development of the negative schema, and the activation of the coping and child modes in response to their partner's behavior in the present.

- **The partner of the reparented member affirms themselves as different from the person who caused harm in the past:** Once the link between past and present has been established, the therapist encourages the partner to affirm that they are different from the person who caused the original harm. They express their intention to care for their partner and meet the unmet emotional need.
- **The reparented partner expresses their current need to their partner from a flexible coping mode:** The therapist guides the reparented partner to express their present needs to their partner using a flexible coping mode—taking initiative (red leg) and showing vulnerability (blue leg).
- d. The partner's response to the reparented member's requests: The therapist asks the partner how they feel after hearing the reparented member's desires and needs, and encourages them to respond. If the partner is not fully convinced, they may offer a counterproposal.
- **Reconnection:** The couple moves closer and expresses affection physically.

Closing the Session

- **Evaluate the benefits of connecting with the blue leg:** The therapist points out the differences between before and after having done the exercise.
- **Therapeutic task:** Remember the reparenting role of the partner, the vulnerable child of the reparented member, and carry out the agreed commitment.

13

Training the Healthy Adult Mode (Module X)

13.1 Introduction

At this stage, as a result of the work from the previous modules, the couple is now able to connect with both legs, that is, with their need for attachment–connection and assertiveness–autonomy. Once this work is complete, the couple can begin to attempt direct communication with each other.

General objective: To help the couple express their feelings, needs, and desires assertively in moments of activation, connecting with their own (balanced) vulnerability.

Specific objectives:

- The couple receives guidance from the therapist to express their needs in a balanced way.
- Both partners receive guidance on how to express their needs in a balanced way through modeling and shaping.
- Partners are able to see the negative consequences of expressing needs from their dysfunctional coping modes.
- Reconnecting partners after expressing needs in a balanced way and agreeing to meet them.
- Partners are able to express their needs in a balanced way and offer something in return.

13.2 Starting the Session: Identifying the Problem, a Member's Difficulty Speaking from Vulnerability, and Stopping the Interaction

At this stage of therapy, the couple is able to identify and stop the cycle of behavior. They are also able to balance themselves before resuming living together. However, as with any process of change, it is normal for old patterns to reappear.

The couple is asked to identify the conflict to be worked on in the session, whether or not the mode cycle develops when discussing it. When one partner is having difficulty speaking from a vulnerable perspective, the therapist stops the interaction and asks them to stand up so that work can begin from the perspective of the observer team.

This strategy is also applied when, while working with a technique to find rebalancing, one of the members finds it difficult to express themselves in a balanced manner.

To illustrate these initial steps more clearly, we return to the case of Steven and Claire, described in Chapter 3. This couple has faced significant challenges in maintaining both physical and emotional closeness in their relationship.

Steven, 53 years old and Claire, 42 years old

T: I'd like to start by asking you what you'd like to work on in today's session.

C: I want to mention that Steven and I have hardly seen each other this week, and I miss him a lot.

E: We would see each other more if you dedicated more time to the gym.

C: I do want to go.

E: (keeps silent)

C: I already told you that I want to go; don't get mad.

E: I'm not angry.

C: (keeps silent)

T: Okay, I'd like to interrupt here because I notice the mode cycle has been activated between you. Let's analyze what happened from the observer team. We stand up, look down, and observe Steven's and Claire's chairs in this situation.

13.3 Cognitive Work: Observer Team Work: Modeling Expression From Vulnerability

In this stage, the therapist adopts a different approach than that used in previous sessions, where the team of observers focused on identifying active and blocked child and coping modes. In this strategy, the therapist acts as a coach and role model for a healthy adult, guiding the partner to express their needs in a balanced way from a place of vulnerability. This strategy is especially useful when working with externalizing partners.

The following steps are described for the therapist to help the partner express their needs and emotions in a balanced way, from a place of vulnerability:

1. **Needs awareness:** Once the couple and the therapist are standing in the observer positions (position 4A and 4B for the partners and 1B for the therapist in Figure 3.5), the therapist invites the partners to look down at the chairs and speak to them in the third person. Addressing the unbalanced partner, the therapist asks the following: "Become aware of the leg you are standing on right now." The therapist then intentionally seeks to activate the need for attachment by asking questions like: Why do you want a relationship with your partner? What do you really need from him or her?
2. **Expressing needs:** The therapist guides the unbalanced partner to express these needs directly to the empty chair representing their partner's coping mode (chairs 2A or 2B in Figure 3.5) from a place of vulnerability, asking a question such as: "Could you tell your partner's chair, from a place of vulnerability, how you felt when they acted that way?"
3. **Feedback:** If an unbalanced partner expresses needs in a general or unbalanced manner (overly critical, aggressive, or accommodating), the therapist helps them express their needs assertively. To do this, the therapist gently interrupts and offers feedback. This includes pointing out to the unbalanced partner how the message they are sending may be perceived as too "red" (dominant) or "blue" (insecure), rather than balanced and vulnerable. For example, the therapist might say, "You need to be clearer about what you really want from your partner," or "Speaking that way may sound like you're nagging your partner." The partner may also be asked if they agree with this perception.
4. **Modeling:** The therapist suggests and models verbal and nonverbal ways for the client to express their emotions from a vulnerable perspective. For example, the therapist might suggest: "How about saying something like, 'When you behave this way, it triggers painful memories from my life?' Or perhaps you could be more direct and say, 'Even though I find it hard to express

myself because I wasn't listened to in the past, I want to make the effort to tell you that...'" Once the suggestion is presented, the therapist checks to see if the client finds this way of expressing themselves meaningful. The therapist might ask questions like, "How does this way of saying it sound to you? Does it make sense to you? Could you put it into your own words? How would you feel saying this? Do you feel more balanced now?" The partner might also be asked how they would feel if the unbalanced client expressed things to them in this way.

To illustrate the steps needed to provide feedback and model how to express vulnerability to the unbalanced partner, let's return to the case of Steven and Claire.

Steven, 53 years old and Claire, 42 years old

T: Now, Steven, I would like you to stand and look at Steven's chair and tell me, what coping mode are you in? Are you overcompensating, surrendering, or avoiding?

E: He is avoiding.

T: Are you passively avoiding by apologizing and submitting? Or are you actively avoiding by being passive-aggressive or running away?

E: I think actively avoiding.

T: Do you agree, Claire?

C: Yes.

T: Now I would like to ask you, Steven: Why do you want a relationship with your partner?

E: Because I want to be happy, and have a good time.

T: What do you really need from her?

E: That she attends to my needs, that she cares about what I need from her.

T: Could you tell Claire's chair how you felt when she acted that way, trying to express it from vulnerability?

E: Yes. I'm tired of not being happy with you, I'm tired of asking you for things and you not attending to my needs, I no longer expect you to care about what I need from you.

T: I know you feel this way, but I think you're still on the red track. I think it still sounds passive-aggressive. What do you think about what I mentioned, Claire?

C: Yes, that's how I feel "red."

(Continued)

(Continued)

T: Steven, I'd like you to try to tell her things more from the blue side, from a place of vulnerability. Maybe you could say something like: "I want to be happy with you, but sometimes it's hard for me to connect with you when I feel like my life isn't important, and every time you commit to something and don't follow through, it makes me feel like I'm not really important, just like what happened to me when I was a child with my dad, who promised me a lot of things but never followed through." What do you think about saying it this way?

E: Yes. I can try.

T: Perfect, then tell him using your own words from vulnerability.

E: (In an annoyed and dry tone of voice) I want us to be happy, but it is very difficult for me to feel fulfilled with you because, just like my dad, I feel that you promise me things that you do not fulfill.

T: Very well, you've improved a lot; congratulations, but maybe we can go a step further and tell him in a soft voice, connecting with your sadness, something like: (in a soft and sweet voice, repeat the message again). Claire, how would you feel if Steven told you this way?

C: Much better.

T: Steven, would you mind trying it this way in your own words?

E: Yes.

13.4 Experiential Work

13.4.1 Rebalancing

If the partner becomes more balanced, the next phase of the strategy begins: expressing emotions from vulnerability (Section 13.4.2). However, if the partner continues to struggle with achieving a balanced state, the therapist may use one of the following alternatives:

- **Chair work:** This approach is less activating. It consists of the unbalanced partner sitting in the chair representing their partner's Vulnerable Child Mode and, from that perspective, trying to put themselves in their partner's shoes. The goal is to help them reflect on the negative consequences their coping style has had on their partner, helping them become aware of the impact of their behavior.

- **Imagination work:** This method is more activating. In this case, the partner is asked to sit in their partner's vulnerable child chair and, through an imagination exercise, visualize how they are perceived by their partner when expressing things in an unbalanced manner. This allows the partner to understand their partner's perspective and assess how their behavior might be received.

13.4.1.1 Chair Work to Facilitate the Expression of Emotions From Vulnerability

In this first option, designed to help the partner struggling to find balance, they can put themselves in their partner's shoes. The following steps are followed:

1. **Capturing the image of the coping mode:** Both partners and the therapist remain standing. From this observer position (position 4A or 4B for the partners and 2B for the therapist in Figure 3.5), the unbalanced partner is asked to describe their behavior from an external perspective, speaking about themselves in the third person as if observing themselves through a camera. Some useful questions to achieve this goal are: How do they look? How do they speak? What is the volume and tone of their voice? How do their eyes look? What is their energy like? If the client is unable to describe themselves completely or accurately, the therapist may supplement with their own perception and that of the couple.
2. **Sitting in the vulnerable child chair of the other partner:** The therapist asks the unbalanced partner to sit in the chair representing their partner's Vulnerable Child Mode (chairs 3A or 3B in Figure 3.5), while the latter stands in the observer role. Once in the chair, the therapist guides the client through questions such as: "How do you feel (partner's name) when (unbalanced partner's name) tells you (therapist repeats message)?" "Is your chest getting sore?" or "Is your chest getting expanding or contracting?" Is your breathing easy or difficult? Is the feeling in your stomach expanding or collapsing?
3. **Disadvantages of coping mode:** The therapist asks the unbalanced partner to stand again (position 4A or 4B in Figure 3.5) and then asks, "Where is this emotion driving you—toward fight, flight, or submission?" The therapist then helps the partner become aware of the negative consequences of their coping mode by asking something like, "Is this really how you want your partner to feel and act?"
4. **Rebalancing:** To help the client find emotional balance, the therapist guides them toward connecting with their vulnerability by asking questions such as, "What could you do to express things from a more vulnerable place? Do you think you can express this to them again in a balanced way right now?"

To illustrate this first case, in which an unbalanced member fails to express their needs from a vulnerable perspective, we return to the case of Steven and Claire.

Steven, 53 years old and Claire, 42 years old

T: I'd like us, standing as a team of observers, to reflect on how Steven saw himself from his perspective. To do this, I'd like to ask you, Steven: How does that Steven below see himself when he expresses things to Claire in that way?
E: Annoying.
T: What is your way of speaking like?
E: Hard.
T: How loud is your voice?
E: Dry and hard.
T: What do your eyes look like?
E: Resentful.
T: Claire, what do you think about this image that Steven shared with us? Do you agree with it?
C: Yes.
T: Now, Claire, I'd like you to stand. In your case, Steven would like you to sit in Claire's vulnerable child's chair. I'd like Steven, from that chair, being Claire, to tell me how you feel when Steven says the following: "I'm tired of not being happy with you. I'm tired of asking you for things and you not attending to my needs. I no longer expect you to care about what I need from you."
E: I feel attacked and overwhelmed.
T: Is your chest expanding or contracting?
E: It contracts.
T: Is your breathing easy or difficult?
E: It's more difficult.
T: Is the feeling in your stomach of expansion or collapse?
E: It falls apart.
T: OK, once you've identified how Claire feels, I ask you, Steven, to stand up and, from that position, ask yourself: "Where does this emotion drive you to fight, flee, or submit?"
E: To flee.
T: Okay, now I'd like you to stand up, Steven, and I'd like to ask you: Is this what you really want to provoke in Claire—for her to run away?
E: No, I want her to be close to me and my needs.

T: What could you do to express things from a more vulnerable place?
E: I think I should say it more politely.
T: Do you think you can express that to him again in a balanced way at this point?
E: Yes.

13.4.1.2 Imagination Work to Facilitate the Expression of Emotions From Vulnerability

This second possibility to seek balance in the partner follows the following steps:

1. **Imagining their mode of coping:** With everyone standing (positions 4A and 4B for the partners and position 1B for the therapist in Figure 3.5), the therapist asks the unbalanced partner to describe, in the third person, how they communicate with their partner from their coping mode, while looking at the chair representing that coping mode (chair 2A or 2B in Figure 3.5). Some key questions are: How do they look? How do they speak? What is the volume and tone of their voice like? How do their eyes look? What is their energy like? When the unbalanced partner is unable to describe their behavior clearly, the therapist can add information based on their own and the partner's perceptions if the unbalanced partner is unable to accurately describe it.
2. **Sitting in the partner's vulnerable child chair:** The client sits in the chair representing their partner's Vulnerable Child Mode (chairs 3A or 3B in Figure 3.5). The therapist positions themselves beside the client, while the partner sits nearby. The therapist guides the exercise by asking everyone to close their eyes and asks the unbalanced client to try to put themselves in their partner's shoes. They are invited to experience how they feel from the perspective of the Vulnerable Child Mode, observing the image captured in the previous step. Emphasis is placed on becoming aware of the emotions and bodily sensations that arise while visualizing themselves delivering the message in an unbalanced way. To facilitate this process, questions such as: Is your chest expanding or contracting? Is your breathing easy or difficult? Is the sensation in your stomach expanding or collapsing?
3. **Disadvantages of coping mode:** Once the unbalanced client has connected with their partner's emotions and body sensations from the Vulnerable Child Mode, the therapist asks, "From this position, observing the coping mode, what impulse do you feel? Do you want to fight? Do you want to submit? Or do you want to withdraw?" Finally, the therapist asks the unbalanced client, "Is this really what you want from your partner—for them to feel and act this way?"

4. **Rebalancing:** The therapist attempts to reinforce the leg's rebalancing by exploring how much empathy the client has gained with their partner, asking questions such as: "Can you feel like you're in your partner's shoes now?" The therapist also encourages the unbalanced client to find rebalancing by asking questions such as: "What could you do to express things to your partner more vulnerable?" Once balance is achieved, the therapist asks them to open their eyes and proceeds to the next exercise.

Next, the case of Steven and Claire is taken up again to exemplify the same exercise but from the perspective of imagination.

Steven, 53 years old and Claire, 42 years old

T: I'd like us, standing as a team of observers, to reflect on how Steven saw himself from his perspective. To do this, I'd like to ask you, Steven: How does that Steven below see himself when he expresses things to Claire in that way?

E: Annoying.

T: What is your way of speaking like?

E: Hard.

T: How loud is your voice?

E: Dry and hard.

T: What do your eyes look like?

E: Resentful.

T: I agree with you, Steven. I felt the same way. Okay, Steven. Now I'd like you to sit in Claire's vulnerable child chair. I'll sit next to you, and Claire would like you to sit on the other side of me. Perfect. I'd ask you to close your eyes and imagine again how Steven behaved, but as if we were viewing it through Claire's eyes. Do you have the image?

E: Yes.

C: Yes.

T: Now, Steven, I'd like you to imagine that you're watching Steven say to you: "I'm tired of not being happy with you. I'm tired of asking you for things and you not attending to my needs. I no longer expect you to care about what I need from you." He looks stern-faced and annoyed; his gaze is harsh. And tell me, how do you feel seeing Steven like that?

E: I feel overwhelmed, uncomfortable and attacked.

T: Does your chest expand or contract?

E: It contracts.

T: Does your stomach expand, or does it feel like it is collapsing?

E: It falls apart.

T: Is your breathing deep or shallow?

E: It's choppy.
T: What are you inclined to react to: fight, flight, or submission?
E: Flee.
T: Okay, now I'd like to stop our imaginations and ask you, Steven: Is this what you want to achieve in Claire? Do you want her to run away?
E: No.
T: Can you feel like you're in your partner's shoes now?
E: Yes.
T: What could you do to express things to your partner in a more vulnerable way?
E: Make an effort to tell him in a nicer way.
T: Okay now I ask you both to open your eyes.

Once the partner has reached equilibrium, the therapist and partner stand up again as part of the observer team to move on to the next phase.

Reflection: What happens when the partner fails to find balance despite the rebalancing work done by the therapist?

Therapist's advice: If the client continues to struggle to put themselves in their partner's shoes, the therapist may choose to provide empathetic but direct feedback. If the client is overly activated due to their negative schemas, an effective strategy may be to use the joint imagery from Module IX.

13.4.2 Expressing Needs from Vulnerability

In this step, the partner is determined to be unbalanced and attempts to implement the therapist's advice by expressing it directly. To carry out this step, the therapist follows these steps:

1. **Expression of needs:** The therapist invites the unbalanced client to stand and speak from an observer level, addressing their partner's empty chair (chairs 2A or 3B in Figure 3.5), attempting to maintain a balanced tone. During this step, if necessary, the therapist continues to shape and continually adjust the emotional expression to ensure it is empathic and from a place of vulnerability. After the unbalanced client has expressed themselves, the therapist asks the client and their partner how they feel about hearing what the unbalanced client has said from a place of vulnerability.
2. **Chair work:** Once both partners are comfortable with what they have expressed, the therapist asks the unbalanced partner to sit in their active coping mode chair, while the other partner sits in their coping mode chair (chair 2A or 2B in Figure 3.5). The therapist stands next to the unbalanced partner

(chair 1A in the Figure) and asks them to express their thoughts and emotions directly to their partner while looking them in the eye.

3. **Emotional awareness:** The therapist inquires with the unbalanced client about their emotions and bodily sensations after expressing their feelings. Questions such as, "How do you feel about communicating this from a vulnerable perspective?" are key. The client is then asked to maintain this emotional awareness for a moment. The partner is then asked how they feel about hearing their partner speak in a balanced manner: "How does it make you feel when your partner speaks to you this way?"
4. **Rebalancing:** The therapist asks the couple if there was anything they didn't like about what they expressed and if they are willing to respond. At this point, the therapist models and adjusts the couple's responses to what they expect in return to meet the other partner's needs until these are balanced. This process continues until they help them find a healthy solution to the problem addressed at the beginning of the session. If some partners struggle to identify how they want the other partner to behave, the therapist may use the "Best Day" exercise (Module IV) to help them clarify and subsequently help them express these needs assertively.
5. **Reconnection:** To conclude, the therapist asks you to stand up (instead of sitting as in other exercises) and look into each other's eyes and try to reconnect by showing each other physical or emotional affection.

This exercise enables partners to communicate in a balanced, thoughtful, and well-intentioned manner, laying the groundwork for implementing the strategy presented in the next chapter, known as connecting dialogues.

It is important to emphasize that, at the end of the exercise, both partners hug each other while remaining in a flexible coping mode. This moment allows them to reconnect from the sense that their needs have been heard (red leg) and that they are willing to cooperate in responding to the needs of the other partner (blue leg).

To illustrate these steps, we return to the case of Steven and Claire, continuing after the work of imagination described in Section 13.3 of this chapter.

Steven, 53 years old and Claire, 42 years old

T: Good. Now, Steven, I'd like you, standing from this observer's position, to turn to Claire's empty chair and express to her the same thing you just said.

E: (With a sad and soft tone of voice) Claire, I feel sad every time you promise me something and you don't keep it. It reminds me a lot of my dad and how, in reality, to get out of problems, he only told other people what they wanted to hear and never kept it.

T: Excellent! There you have it. Congratulations, Steven; you did very well. How does it feel to say it like that?
E: I like it; I hope Claire can understand it better this way.
T: How did you feel, Claire?
C: I felt good; it helps me connect more with him without feeling afraid.
T: Next, I want to ask you, Claire, to sit in your vulnerable child chair, and you, Steven, to sit in your active avoidance coping chair, and from there, express again what you need from a place of vulnerability.
E: (With a sad and soft tone of voice) Claire, I feel sad when you commit to something and you don't fulfill it. This reminds me a lot of when my dad, to get out of problems, only told me what I wanted to hear and never fulfilled it.
T: Steven, how do you feel about communicating this from a place of vulnerability?
E: Well, I like it.
T: Claire, how does it make you feel if your partner talks to you this way?
C: It helps me better understand how he feels and why he sometimes reacts in that way.
T: Is there anything about the way Steven told you things that you would change or that you didn't like?
C: No, the way he told it to me seems appropriate to me.
T: Okay. Now, I'd like you both to stand up, look into each other's eyes, and give each other a hug or a gesture of affection. How are you feeling about starting the session now?
E: I feel better.
C: I feel calmer.

13.5 Closing the Session

13.5.1 Evaluate the Benefits of Expressing Emotions from Vulnerability

To conclude the session, the therapist invites the couple to reflect on how they felt before and after the exercise, highlighting the changes they experienced. He also reminds them that it's up to them to work on changing legs and continue strengthening their emotional balance.

To illustrate this last step, the case of Steven and Claire will be reviewed, showing how the therapist applied it in the session.

Steven, 53 years old and Claire, 42 years old
T: Do you notice a difference in how you feel now compared to before we did the exercise?
E: Yes.
C: Yes.
T: Remember that expressing things from vulnerability is in your hands and that you can do this for yourself and experience changes in your relationship. Does that make sense to you?
E: For me, yes.
C: For me too.

13.5.2 Therapeutic Task: Try to Change Legs As Much As Possible

The therapist asks both partners to try, to the extent possible, to find balance by expressing their needs from a place of vulnerability. Finally, the therapist returns to the case of Steven and Claire, where the therapist assigns them the therapeutic task to be completed.

Steven, 53 years old and Claire, 42 years old
T: Okay, I'd like to end the session here, and I'd like to leave you with the task of trying to express things from a vulnerable perspective, using the blue leg, as we did in today's session. Is that okay with you?
E: Sounds good to me.
C: Me too.

As a summary, the basic steps that can serve as a guide for the therapist to apply the technique of "modeling expression from vulnerability" are presented.

Beginning of the Session

- **Identification of the problem to be worked on:** Partners present the problem they want to address in the session (the mode cycle may or may not be initiated).
- **Identifying that one of the partners is having difficulty speaking from a vulnerable perspective:** Whether when the couple speaks directly to resolve the problem, in the development of the mode cycle, or in the

application of an exercise, the therapist detects that one of the partners is having difficulty speaking from a vulnerable perspective.

- **Stop the interaction:** Once it is detected that one of the members is having difficulty speaking from a vulnerable perspective, the therapist stops the interaction.

Cognitive Work

- **Work of the observer team:** Model expression from vulnerability: The therapist as a coach guides the partner to express their needs from vulnerability.
  - **Needs awareness:** The unbalanced partner connects and expresses the needs experienced while standing and observing the chair representing his or her partner.
  - **Expression of needs:** The unbalanced member expresses his feelings directly to the empty chair representing his partner.
  - **Feedback:** If the therapist detects that the message is still being expressed in an unbalanced manner (e.g., too aggressively or accommodatingly), he or she politely interrupts and offers feedback.
  - **Modeling:** The therapist suggests and models verbal and nonverbal ways for the partner to express their emotions from a vulnerable perspective. If the partner is unable to appear more balanced, the therapist may apply one of these two strategies:

Experiential Work

- **Rebalancing:** If the partner fails to appear more balanced, the therapist can apply one of these two strategies.
  - **Chair work:** The unbalanced partner sits in the vulnerable child chair that represents his or her partner and, from that perspective, tries to put himself or herself in his or her place (becoming aware of the negative consequences that his or her coping style has had on his or her partner).
  - **Imagination work:** The unbalanced client sits in his partner's vulnerable child chair and, through an imagination exercise, visualizes how he is perceived by his partner when expressing things in an unbalanced way.
- **Expressing needs from vulnerability:** The unbalanced partner applying what was learned during the modeling carried out by the therapist.
  - **Expressing Needs:** The unbalanced client speaks from an observer level, addressing his or her partner's empty chair, while the therapist provides feedback. The therapist asks the client and partner how they feel about hearing the unbalanced client's request from a place of vulnerability.

- **Chair work:** The unbalanced client sits in his or her active coping chair and is asked to directly express his or her thoughts and emotions to the partner.
- **Emotional awareness:** The therapist inquires with the unbalanced client and his or her partner about the emotions and bodily sensations behind the expression of the unbalanced client's feelings.
- **Rebalancing:** The therapist asks the couple if there was anything they did not like about what was expressed and what they would like to respond to the couple (the therapist continues to model and adjust the responses of both partners until they are balanced).
- **Reconnection:** The therapist asks them to stand up (and look into each other's eyes) and try to reconnect by showing physical or emotional affection.

Closing the Session

- **Evaluate the benefits of expressing emotions from vulnerability:** The therapist points out the differences between before and after having done the exercise.
- **Therapeutic task:** Try to change legs as much as possible.

14

Connection Dialogues (Module XI)

14.1 Introduction

When the couple manages to stop the cycles of patterns and find a balance between their attachment–connection and assertiveness–autonomy needs, they can implement a strategy called connection dialogues. The main goal of this strategy is to help the couple work through difficult issues and confront conflicts in a healthy way.

At the beginning, the goal isn't to solve the problem, but rather to listen to the other person and accept their perspective. This step is more important than reaching an immediate resolution to the conflict.

In situations of disagreement or argument, it's common for two opposing points of view to exist. During arguments, partners tend to position themselves more on their red leg, focusing on the other's validation of their perspective (need for assertiveness–autonomy). Instead of actively listening, while one speaks, the other thinks about how to counterargue, giving the impression that the only solution is to accept one side as the only "true" one.

According to Valente in Roediger & Valente (2025), there are two ways of listening in a relationship:

1. **Listening to listen:** This involves active listening with the goal of understanding what's happening and understanding the other person. This is done through the blue leg (attachment–connection).
2. **Listening to respond:** This involves listening while waiting for the other person to confirm your own version of events. This approach is more closely related to the red leg (assertiveness–autonomy).

To address this conflict, it is essential that both partners feel safe expressing their perspectives. Connecting dialogues create this safe space, allowing both partners to present their arguments and be heard respectfully. This dialogue becomes a safe place where each member can understand and value the other's perspective, fostering connection and mutual respect.

This strategy can be implemented at any point during the Reconnection phase, after applying some of the strategies in this stage, as long as it is considered appropriate for the particular session and there is sufficient time to initiate and complete the technique. If used as part of Module XI, the initial sequence will be the same as for any other session.

General objective: To provide partners with a safe framework in which both can respectfully and in a balanced manner express their points of view and needs until they reach an agreement.

Specific objectives:

- The couple opens up to the possibility of hearing two versions of reality through the metaphor of the cell phone.
- Partners apply active listening and paraphrasing to each other.
- Both partners in the couple establish agreements, finding a balance between what they offer and what they ask for in return.
- The couple learns alternative ways of using connection dialogues to establish contact with each other.

14.2 Beginning of the Session: Identify the Problem and Stop the Interaction to Initiate Connection Dialogues

The therapist begins the session by asking the couple about their current issues that day. Once they begin talking and the main issue is identified, they are asked to discuss it among themselves; whether the mode cycle develops or not, the therapist stops the interaction to initiate the connection dialogues.

At this stage of therapy, the couple is able to identify and stop the cycle of behavior. They are also able to balance themselves before resuming cohabitation. The exercise aims to lay the groundwork for negotiation in a safe space where both partners can be heard and their needs taken into account.

To illustrate the application of the connection dialogue technique, we return to the case of Charlie and Joseph, presented in Chapter 3. This couple faces problems in the sexual sphere.

Charlie, 30 years old and Joseph, 35 years old

T: I'd like to start the session by asking you: What are you bringing to work today?

C: I'm really upset because Joseph lost his erection again the other day when we were having sex. And when I asked him what the doctor told him, it turns out he hasn't followed up with him and hasn't made another appointment.

T: Joseph, would you like to discuss this topic in today's session?

J: Yes.

T: Okay, now I'd like you to talk this over directly with each other. Is that okay with you?

J: Yes.

C: Yes. Tell me the truth, are you avoiding having sex with me? Why can't you be more direct and tell me that I'm no longer attractive to you?

J: No, I do like you. It's just that, I don't know, I think I just forgot to go to the urologist.

C: But you were already supposed to go. If you're not going, it's because having sex with me isn't really important to you.

J: Yes, it is important; I just think I forgot.

T: I would like to stop the conversation between you here because I think I can propose an exercise so that you can more effectively address the topic. Do you agree?

C: Yes.

J: Okay.

14.3 Cognitive Work

Once the interaction has stopped and it is the first time that the connection dialogue strategy is going to be used, it is necessary for the therapist to first introduce the idea that there are two realities in a discussion, and an important step to resolve it is for them to be heard and understood before putting them into practice. For this reason, Roediger in Roediger & Valente (2025) presents the cell phone metaphor.

Once the couple can theoretically understand this metaphor, the next step is to explain the rules of connection dialogue so they can apply it correctly during the therapy session while the therapist serves as a guide or coach throughout the process.

14.3.1 Explanation of the Cell Phone Metaphor

Before beginning the connection dialogue exercise, it is essential to help the couple understand that there are two versions of reality and that there is no single absolute truth. To do this, the therapist can use the metaphor of a cell phone.

The steps that the therapist can use to carry out this metaphor are the following:

1. **One partner holds a cell phone:** The therapist asks one partner to take a cell phone in their hands, holding it so that they can see the screen. The couple in front of him will look at the back of the phone, where the cameras are usually located.
2. **Description of what each member sees:** The therapist asks each member to describe what they see on the phone from their perspective. Because the two sides of the phone are different, each member will give a different description.
3. **Reflection on the veracity of both perceptions:** The therapist highlights the differences between the descriptions made by each member and asks: "Which of the two descriptions is true?" He or she then guides the couple toward the conclusion that both descriptions are true because they represent two different sides of the cell phone.
4. **Conclusion on perceptions of the problem:** The therapist explains that, as in the cell phone example, each partner has a valid perspective on what is happening between them. Understanding the other's perspective is essential to avoid having a biased view of reality, that is, focusing only on one of the "faces of the cell phone."

The therapist may encourage the couple to consider two possible approaches (Roediger in Valente & Roediger, 2025):

1. Spending time fighting to impose their vision and prove who is right, seeking to "defeat the other person."
2. Be open to accepting and respecting both realities. This doesn't necessarily mean agreeing with the other's perspective, but rather respecting it as a valid view of what's happening.

Reflection: What should the therapist do if the couple begins to argue, trying to impose their point of view on the other, despite having received the explanation of the cell phone metaphor?

Therapist's advice: When the couple begins to argue during the session, the therapist can take out the cell phone again and place it in front of them to remind them that they are seeing different "sides" of the same reality. If emotions are running high, it may be helpful to stop the argument, ask them to stand, and assume the observer position to describe what is happening from a more neutral perspective.

To illustrate how this step is applied, we return to the case of Charlie and Joseph, in which the therapist explains the cell phone metaphor to them.

Charlie, 30 years old and Joseph, 35 years old

T: I'd like to conduct an exercise so you can pick up the discussion where you left off. But first, I want to emphasize that the really important thing isn't proving who's right, but rather first understanding the other person's perception. To illustrate this, let's do a little exercise. I'd ask you both to sit in your respective chairs and face each other. Charlie, please take out your cell phone and hold it as if you were going to take a picture of Joseph. Perfect. Now, from this position, tell me: What do you see on your phone?

C: A flat screen.

T: Now, Joseph, tell me, what do you see from your perspective?

J: I see the rear cameras of the cell phone.

T: These are two very different descriptions of the same object. So who is right?

C: Both, because we are looking at it from different angles.

T: Exactly! Just as a cell phone has two sides, the problem you're facing also has two perspectives. To better understand it, it's necessary to consider both perspectives, rather than clinging to just one. What do you think about this?

C: I agree.

J: Me too.

T: So, you have to decide: do you want to keep fighting to be right, or do you want to understand and accept the other person's perspective to get a broader view of what's happening between you?

C: I don't want to fight anymore.

J: I want to understand your point of view.

To illustrate the cell phone metaphor in the session, the following reference script is presented below.

Example 14.1 Script to Explain the Cell Phone Metaphor

This thing I'm holding in my hands is a cell phone. You can see one side of it, but the other side, the one I'm seeing, is hidden from you unless I turn it around and show it to you. This metaphor represents an inherent limitation of our perception: each of us is trapped in our own perspective, seeing only part of reality. Therefore, it's essential to learn to accept that there may be a perspective, a side to things that we probably can't see from our position.

14.3.2 Explanation of the Connection Dialogues Exercise

Before starting the exercise, the therapist explains the rules to the couple, which are as follows:

- **Use of the object:** You will be given an object that will determine who gets to speak. The partner holding the object will be the only one allowed to speak. Meanwhile, the other partner must remain silent, focusing on understanding what their partner is saying, without interrupting or trying to take their turn speaking.
- **Paraphrasing the message:** Once the member holding the object finishes speaking, they will pass the object to the other member, who must paraphrase the message received. They should focus solely on repeating what they heard in their own words, without debating or expressing personal ideas.
- **Message correction:** If the speaker feels the message was not understood correctly or that important information is missing, they will repeat their message. The other speaker will attempt to paraphrase it again until the message is clearly understood.
- **Responding to the message:** Once the message has been correctly understood, the other member can respond. This response should be limited to two or three sentences expressing what they feel or think about it.

To illustrate the therapist's explanation of connection dialogues, the case of Charlie and Joseph is described.

Charlie, 30 years old and Joseph, 35 years old

T: Okay, now I'd like to explain the dynamics of the exercise. I'm going to give you this object, Charlie. While you have it in your possession, Joseph won't be able to speak; his only task is to listen. When you finish speaking, you'll pass the object to Joseph, who must repeat the message you sent him, using his own words. If you think Joseph correctly understood the message, you let him know by nodding your head. If he didn't, you ask for the object back and repeat the message, trying to be more clear and concise. Charlie, can you tell me what you understood from what I just explained?

C: What, I'm going to speak, and Joseph has to repeat what I told him?

T: Correct. Furthermore, once the message has been understood, Joseph will be able to respond with two or three sentences expressing what he thinks or feels about what he heard. Joseph, can you tell me what you understood from what I explained?

J: Yes, when Charlie tells me that I understood the message correctly, at that moment he passes me the object, and I can respond with a short message about what I think or feel about what he told me.

T: Exactly. That's the goal. Once you've given your answer, Charlie will take the object again and paraphrase what you said, asking if he correctly understood your message. This process of paraphrasing and responding will alternate between the two of you and be repeated throughout the exercise. The goal is to ensure that both of you feel heard and understood. Was I clear in my explanation?

C: Yes.

J: Yes.

Below is a reference script for the therapist to use in the session to implement the connection dialogue exercise.

Example 14.2 Script for Giving Instructions for the Connecting Dialogues Exercise

We are going to conduct a dialogue exercise using an object. This object can be something simple, like a book, a keychain, or a pencil, and its purpose will be to determine who gets the turn to speak. The partner holding the object will have the exclusive right to speak. The other person must remain silent and not interrupt until they receive the object. Once the person holding the object finishes speaking, they must pass the object to their interlocutor, who must paraphrase what they heard using their own words. When they finish, they must ask the speaker, 'Did I understand what you meant?' and return the object to them. If the speaker confirms that their message was understood correctly, they will hand the object to the other partner, giving them the right to speak. If the message was not understood correctly, the speaker must repeat or rephrase their message for greater clarity, returning the object to the interlocutor so they can paraphrase again. This process will continue until the message is fully understood." Once the message has been understood, the other member gets a turn to speak and can respond using two or three sentences. When they finish, they pass the object to their partner, who must paraphrase what they heard, following the same procedure until they confirm understanding of the message. The exercise will continue alternating throughout the time until we call it a day.

Reflection: How can the therapist ensure that the couple does not forget the rules of the connection dialogue exercise when it is assigned to them as therapeutic homework?

Therapist's advice: To ensure the couple successfully completes the exercise, it is helpful to provide them with a guide with the key criteria, either in print or electronically. This guide should include the steps and rules for the Connection Dialogues exercise, explained clearly and simply, so they can easily refer to them while completing the task at home.

14.4 Experiential Work

14.4.1 Connection Dialogues: Polarization and Contradictions

In this stage, the therapist creates a space for both partners to express their perspectives on a problem. The main goal is to shift from sympathetic activation (a state of stress or defense, common in arguments) to parasympathetic activation (a state of calm and receptivity). This is achieved by listening and repeating the other partner's message, rather than imposing one's own view of the problem. This process of "listening and repeating" helps reduce emotional intensity, relaxing both partners and leading them to operate from their blue leg (vulnerability and connection).

The steps for applying this phase are described below:

1. **Defining the topic and initial turn:** The therapist asks the couple to decide what specific topic they want to talk about and who will initiate the discussion (when this exercise is used in session, it's advisable to continue with the topic discussed at the beginning of the session). They are instructed to talk about the recent situation in a concrete way, without overgeneralizations like "you always do." At this stage, they should focus on the problem, not on feelings or assumptions.
2. **Expressing feelings:** The first partner expresses their point of view and the emotions associated with the topic, using only two or three sentences. The therapist encourages the partner to listen empathetically, without interrupting or reacting immediately.
3. **Paraphrasing:** The partner repeats what they heard, trying to capture the meaning and express it in their own words. The speaker evaluates whether their message was captured correctly. If not, they rephrase their message until the other person paraphrases it accurately. The process does not advance to the next step until the speaker confirms that their message was correctly understood.
4. **Role reversal:** The roles are reversed: now the other partner expresses their opinion, perspective, and emotions on the issue, again limiting themselves to two or three sentences. The therapist can guide by saying something like:

"Now that you understand how your partner defines the problem, you can express your point of view and the associated emotions. Try not to go beyond two or three sentences." The first partner now assumes the role of listening and paraphrasing, following the same procedure until the message is understood.

This process is repeated as many times as necessary until both partners achieve a deeper understanding of each other's perspectives and needs. The exercise encourages active listening and allows each partner to put themselves in the other's shoes, exchanging perspectives without seeking to impose an absolute truth.

To demonstrate the application of the connection dialogue strategy in the therapeutic session, the beginning of the connection dialogue is presented below in the case of Charlie and Joseph.

Charlie, 30 years old and Joseph, 35 years old

T: Okay, if you don't mind, let's get back to the topic you were raising before the mode cycle stopped.

C: Yes. I'm very upset because you keep losing your erection, and you didn't tell me that you had stopped going to the doctor to follow up on the problem.

T: Now pass the object to Joseph.

J: Charlie says he's mad because I lost my erection.

T: Charlie, did Joseph get your message right?

C: No.

T: Joseph, can you pass the object back to Charlie?

J: Yes.

T: Charlie, repeat the message, trying to be clearer this time.

C: Joseph, I'm really angry that you keep losing your erection, and instead of doing something about it, you haven't been going to your doctor's appointments to address the problem.

T: Joseph, it's your turn to paraphrase what Charlie said.

J: He says he's angry that I'm not following up on my doctor's appointments, even though the problem persists.

T: Charlie, did Joseph understand your message correctly?

C: Yes.

T: Good. Now, Joseph, keep the object and tell him a sentence or two about what you feel or think about what Charlie said.

J: It's not that I don't want to go, but I forgot.

T: Pass the object to Charlie. Now paraphrase what Joseph said.

(Continued)

(Continued)

C: He says it's not that he doesn't want to do it, but that he forgot.
T: Joseph, is that what you meant?
J: Yes.
T: Now pass the object to your partner. Charlie, in two sentences, tell him or her how you feel about what Joseph said.
C: I feel like he might not be telling me the truth...
T: Sorry to interrupt you, Charlie, but this time I'd like you to tell him how you feel when you hear this, without judgment.
C: I feel angry because I think he is not being sincere.
T: Okay, pass the object to your partner. Joseph, what did Charlie say?
J: He's angry and thinks I'm not being honest with him.
T: Charlie, did Joseph correctly capture what you wanted to express?
C: Yes.
T: Good. Now, Joseph, pass the object to Charlie and tell him how you feel about what he just said.

In the previous example, the entire connecting dialogue is not presented in order to summarize the intervention, as it tends to drag on. As you can see, this strategy slows down the conversation, making it more leisurely, structured, and seemingly monotonous. This slower pace serves a therapeutic purpose: to reduce emotional intensity and help partners regulate their emotional arousal during the interaction.

Once the opposing positions of both partners have been expressed, listened to, and paraphrased correctly, the next stage of the therapeutic process begins.

14.4.2 Connection Dialogue: Accept, Propose, and Reach an Agreement

In this stage, partners express specific desires and make requests of each other while negotiating what they are willing to accept and what they will ask for in return. This process is repeated until both partners reach an agreement, which must be recorded in writing. The work focuses on the same specific situation addressed in the polarization and contradictions phase. The steps for this stage are as follows:

1. **Expressing wishes to the partner:** The therapist asks one partner to express a wish related to the specific problem being addressed. The other partner should then paraphrase the wish and add their own, without discussing or commenting on the other's wish. The therapist can guide by saying something

like, "Now that we've captured what the other person wants to express, let's ask them for a wish. Our partner will repeat the wish and add their own, without judgment or comment. You don't need to agree at this point."

2. **Proposing suggestions for fulfilling wishes:** Once both wishes have been understood and paraphrased, the therapist guides the partners in suggesting ways they might fulfill the other's wish. The goal here is to provide alternatives to facilitate the successful implementation of possible solutions.
3. **Establishing agreements:** When both partners have found ways to satisfy each other's desires, an agreement is reached. It should clearly describe the expected behaviors of both parties. The therapist may emphasize: "A good compromise is one in which both of you feel you have offered something meaningful. If one of you feels like you are sacrificing too much or if only one party is satisfied, the agreement is probably not well-balanced." Agreements should be put in writing in the form of a contract. The therapist can also explain that violations of the agreement should not be viewed as failures, but rather as starting points for future connection-building conversations.

To illustrate how the session moved from the stage of polarization and contradiction to that of acceptance and agreement, we continue with a description of the case of Charlie and Joseph.

Charlie, 30 years old and Joseph, 35 years old

T: Charlie, now that you've both managed to express what you feel and think about the situation, I'd like you to express a specific wish to Joseph regarding this issue.

C: I want you to tell me if you really still like me.

T: Joseph, what did you understand from Charlie's message?

J: What do you want me to say if I still like you?

T: Charlie, did Joseph get your message right?

C: Yes.

T: Good. Now, Joseph, what would be your wish in this situation?

J: That he trusts me and believes me when I tell him that I still like him.

T: Charlie, can you paraphrase what Joseph expressed?

C: He wants me to trust him when he tells me that he still likes me.

T: Is this what you were trying to say, Joseph?

J: Yes.

T: Perfect. Now let's explore ways you can help each other fulfill these desires. Let's start with you, Joseph. How about suggesting some concrete actions so Charlie can feel like you really still like him?

(Continued)

(Continued)

J: Sounds good to me.

T: What things are you willing to do to express your attraction and affection to Charlie?

J: Tell him I think he's handsome, touch him more intimately, and kiss him more often.

T: Charlie, can you repeat what you understood from what Joseph said?

C: That he will show me more that he likes me by touching me more, telling me that he finds me attractive, and kissing me more often.

T: Joseph, did Charlie get the message right?

J: Yes.

T: Now, Charlie, how about you work on trusting more that Joseph likes you and try to see the problem from another perspective?

C: Yes, but how do I do it?

T: What if, instead of focusing on blaming him, you tried sitting down with him to explore other possible reasons behind his difficulty maintaining an erection?

C: Sounds good to me.

T: So, I would like you to express this to Joseph in your own words, adapting it to your way of seeing it and what you really want.

C: Joseph, I'm willing to believe you when you say you still like me. To do that, I want to shift my focus. Instead of just worrying about what's happening, I'd rather we analyze together what might be causing your difficulty maintaining an erection.

T: Joseph, can you repeat what you understood from what Charlie said?

J: That he is willing to trust me, but that we should sit down together to explore what the cause of the problem may be.

T: Charlie, did Joseph get your message right?

C: Yes.

T: Okay. Now, what do you think of these proposals? Do you agree, or would you like to add anything else?

C: I think it's a good start.

J: Yes, I agree too.

T: Excellent. To reinforce this commitment, I've written an agreement with the points we defined in today's session: Joseph agrees to express his desire for Charlie more through kisses, intimate caresses, and affirming words about his attractiveness. Charlie agrees to trust that Joseph is truly attracted to him and to address the difficulty of erection together from a perspective of exploration and mutual understanding. If you agree, I ask you to sign this sheet as a mutual commitment.

Reflection: What should the therapist do if, during the connection dialogues, the couple fails to reach an agreement?

Therapist's advice: It's important to remember that it's not always necessary for the couple to reach a solution in the first few sessions. The main goal is not only to reach an agreement but also to help the partners de-escalate emotionally, listen carefully to each other, and understand their perspective on the situation they are addressing. This process of listening and empathy is a fundamental step in building the foundation that will allow for solid agreements. At the end of the process, both brains will understand each other's perspective and learn something new.

If the therapist observes that the couple has difficulties in carrying out the connection dialogues, he or she can choose to implement some of the following exercises proposed by Valente in Roediger & Valente (2025):

1. **Cathartic talk:** The session begins by allowing both partners to freely express their feelings in turn, without either partner paraphrasing what has been said. The goal of the talk is to encourage the other partner to listen and the speaker to vent before structuring the connecting dialogue.
2. **Empathic listening:** Regarding a situation unrelated to the couple, one partner discusses an emotional situation. The other partner listens attentively and tries to put themselves in their partner's shoes, confirming whether they understood correctly with questions such as: "Did I understand correctly?" During this exercise, the therapist stands behind the listening partner, offering prompts to guide them. The exercise lasts 15 minutes, after which the roles are switched.
3. **Chair work:** In this variation, both partners sit in two chairs parallel to each other, with the therapist behind them providing support. An empty chair is placed in front of them, representing the person involved in a narrated problem. One partner recounts an emotional situation that does not involve the other partner. The other partner asks empathic questions to gain insight, such as: "What happened to you? What did you feel? What did you think? What did you do?" The listening partner paraphrases the responses, making sure to accurately capture what was said.
4. **Short answers:** Partners sit facing each other. One partner addresses a conflict between them, while the other is allowed to respond only using the following emotional options: "I'm sorry, thank you, I feel sad, I'm scared, I feel angry, or I feel upset."

To illustrate how the therapist can explain the preparation exercise for connection dialogues, below is a script that can be used individually in the therapy session.

Example 14.3 Script for Presenting the Emotion Dialogue Preparation Exercise Called "Short Answers"

Next, one of you will express the situation again to your partner. In response, your partner may only use one of the following options: "I'm sorry," "Thank you," "I feel sad," "I'm scared," "I feel angry," or "I feel upset." The partner speaking will continue to express themselves until they feel they have said enough or until 15 minutes have passed, whichever comes first. After this, we will switch roles.

To illustrate the application of the short-answer strategy, the following describes how the therapist might have implemented it in the case of Joseph and Charlie.

Charlie, 30 years old and Joseph, 35 years old

T: Okay, I'd like to apply a technique that I think can help you prepare for a better dialogue. This technique consists of, first, one of you expressing everything you think and feel about the topic. The other can only respond using one of the following phrases: "I'm sorry," "Thank you," "I feel sad," "I'm scared," "I feel angry," or "I feel upset." We'll talk this way for fifteen minutes, or until the speaker finishes expressing everything they need to say. Then, we'll switch roles and repeat the exercise. Who wants to go first?

C: Me.

T: Do you agree, Joseph?

J: Yes.

T: Okay, Joseph, remember that you can only respond using the phrases I mentioned before: "I'm sorry," "Thank you," "I feel sad," "I'm scared," "I feel angry," or "I feel upset."

J: Okay.

C: I'm really upset that you haven't made the appointment with the urologist.

J: Sorry.

C: Why have you been avoiding it?

J: I'm scared.

C: I think you don't like me anymore.

J: I feel sad.

C: That's all I want to say.
T: Okay. Now let's switch roles. Joseph, it's your turn to express what you think and feel, while Charlie can only respond using the same phrases.

14.5 Closing the Session

14.5.1 Evaluate the Benefits of Conducting Connection Dialogues

The therapist concludes the connection dialogue exercise by highlighting the benefits of this strategy, emphasizing the emotional changes in the partners before and after the exercise, and noting that it is in their power to apply this strategy to strengthen effective communication with their partner.

To show the conclusion of the exercise, the case of Charlie and Joseph is presented again and how they both reflected on the positive changes the exercise generated between them.

Charlie, 30 years old and Joseph, 35 years old

T: Do you notice positive changes between before and after the exercise?
J: Yes.
C: Yes.
T: I'd like you to remember that you can apply this strategy at any time, trying to first connect with what the other person wants to communicate before trying to ask or offer something. Does this make sense to you? Remember that the shift is in your hands and that you can do this for yourself and experience changes in your relationship. Does this make sense to you?
J: Yes.
C: Yes.

14.5.2 Therapeutic Task: Practicing Connection Dialogues

The therapist assigns them the task of addressing the issue directly, rather than postponing the discussion until the therapy session, by applying the connection dialogue strategy when they stop the mode cycle and go to separate rooms once they have attempted rebalancing.

Usually, after a month of practicing connection dialogues, the couple can resume a conversation on their own, giving space to the other member's perspective (the other side of the cell phone), even if they are no longer consciously and intentionally capturing the paraphrasing, opening themselves up to their partner's perspective.

Couples who practice connection dialogues tend to achieve better results in their couples therapy. For this reason, they are assigned a simple therapeutic exercise: each night, one partner will talk for five minutes about their day, while the other simply listens, without interrupting or offering an opinion.

They are also assigned therapeutic homework: schedule a thirty-minute meeting twice a week to practice the connection dialogue strategy. The therapist instructs them to adhere to the following guidelines during these meetings:

- There should be no external interruptions.
- Avoid alcohol consumption.
- Make sure children are not present.
- Do not use cell phones or other electronic devices.
- Physically sitting face to face in chairs or, alternatively, taking a walk together.

The therapist clarifies that if they are unable to reach an agreement on a topic, the therapist recommends leaving it for the time being and returning to it the next day.

To illustrate how the therapist might assign a therapeutic task, the following describes how the session with Charlie and Joseph concluded.

Charlie, 30 years old and Joseph, 35 years old

T: To conclude the session, I would like you, starting today, when you have a discussion and manage to stop the mode cycle, to take a moment to separate into different rooms. When you return, practice the connection dialogues. If, when you reach the agreement phase, you can't find a solution, stop the exercise and try again the next day. Does that seem like a good idea?

J: Yes.

C: Yes.

T: Also, at the end of each day, one of you will speak for five minutes while the other listens, without interrupting or offering feedback. Once that's done, you'll switch roles, allowing the other to speak for the same amount of time with the same active listening dynamic. Do you agree with this practice?

J: Sounds good to me.

C: Me too.

T: Finally, I ask you to schedule two meetings per week to practice the connection dialogue exercise. During these meetings, make sure there are no interruptions: no children, no cell phones, and no alcohol consumption. The conversation should take place face-to-face or, if you prefer, during a walk together. If at any point you can't reach an agreement, let the topic drop for the time being and return to it at your next meeting. Are you in agreement?

J: Yes.

C: Yes.

As a summary, the following are the guiding steps for the therapist to implement the connection dialogue exercise in the session:

Beginning of the Session

- **Identification of the problem to be worked on:** Partners present the problem they want to address in the session (the mode cycle may or may not be initiated).
- **Stop the interaction:** Once the problem is detected (or the start of the mode cycle), the therapist stops the interaction.

Cognitive Work

- **Explanation of the cell phone metaphor:** The therapist explains the cell phone metaphor (reality has two sides).
- **Explanation of the connection dialogue exercise:** The therapist gives the instructions for the connection dialogues (one alternates listening and the other repeats).

Experiential Work

- **Connection dialogues: polarization and contradictions**
  - Define the topic and the initial turn
  - **Expression of feelings:** One member expresses his or her feelings, and the other listens actively.
  - **Paraphrasing:** The partner repeats what he heard.
  - **Role reversal:** Roles are reversed until partners understand both sides of reality.

- **Connection dialogue:** Accept, propose, and reach an agreement.
  - **Express wishes to your partner:** One member expresses their wishes to their partner; the other paraphrases them and adds their own.
  - **Proposing suggestions for fulfilling wishes:** The therapist guides the partners to come up with suggestions on how they might fulfill each other's wish.
  - **Establishing agreements:** When both partners have found ways to satisfy each other's desires, an agreement is reached. This agreement should clearly describe the expected behaviors of both parties.

Closing the Session

- **Reinforce the benefits of conducting connection dialogues:** The therapist points out the differences between before and after conducting the connection dialogue exercise.
- **Therapeutic task: practice connection dialogues**.

Part V

Additional Modules

This section of the modules is designed to complement the couple schema therapy process. It presents a list of therapeutic tasks that the therapist can implement throughout the treatment.

Often, the hardest part isn't changing your partner's behavior but adjusting your expectations of them. Often, the problem lies in people focusing more on what they expect from each other than accepting them as they are. It's as if one partner comes to therapy expecting the therapist to "fix" the other—that is, to turn them into the person they want them to be.

Therefore, it's more effective to help the couple let go of unrealistic expectations and accept the other with their particularities. This doesn't mean resignation, but rather finding a way to live peacefully with reality: recognizing the other person's personality and discovering how to bring out the best in the relationship. Accepting reality generates a shift toward a more relaxed state, even if in some cases it may bring some disappointment. However, if you observe other couples, you'll notice that few achieve the "perfect" relationship. Rather than seeking perfection, the goal is to build a good-enough relationship, one in which both partners can coexist functionally, find compatibility, and, at the same time, develop individually. This flexibility allows the relationship to evolve in a more connected or more accommodating way, depending on the needs of each partner.

It's important to note that in couples therapy, many relationships end not in a deep emotional connection but in a state of disconnection. In these cases, couples may continue living together, but without a true emotional bond. Real change requires an investment of time and effort, although, unfortunately, only a small percentage of couples are willing to do so.

This section of the book describes the procedure to follow when a couple decides to end the relationship, helping them achieve a healthy end to their relationship. The process encompasses the stages of education, rebalancing, and reconnection, which may require a minimum of 10–12 sessions. In these cases, the partners have strong self-reflection and self-regulation skills (healthy adult mode), so only Modules I–IV and IX–XII are necessary. However, for couples who lack these skills and require more practice (Modules V–VIII), the process can extend to 12–18 sessions, depending on the case. Once these stages have been completed, the couple will have received all the tools the model offers, leaving the decision of what to do with their relationship in their hands. If significant change is not achieved within this time, it is possible that one or both partners need individual therapy or that at least one partner no longer truly wants to be in the relationship, and therapy can help clarify this possibility.

15

Homework (Module XII)

15.1 Introduction

It is essential for the therapist to make it clear to the couple, from the beginning of therapy, that changes in the relationship do not only occur during the sessions but also between them. During the session, a shift in perspective is encouraged, psychoeducation is provided, and emotional experiences are generated that serve as a starting point for exploring new forms of interaction. However, what truly transforms the relationship is the application of these lessons in daily life.

For this reason, homework is a key tool that the therapist should assign throughout the therapeutic process. These tasks serve as a reminder that therapy is not limited to the office but also extends into everyday life, where the couple has the opportunity to put into practice what they've worked on in session. It's important that partners don't go home without homework to complete until the next session.

Some of the tasks presented here are not mentioned in the modules described in this text; this is with the objective of giving the therapist the freedom to apply the tasks that according to their therapy style and the case they are addressing in therapy, they believe are pertinent, as long as the general process of the couple of the phases of education, rebalancing, and change in the couple indicated in the couple schema therapy model is respected.

15.2 Tasks for the First Phase of Therapy: Gear Change

These tasks are left to the early stages of therapy: psychoeducation and, if necessary, rebalancing. Therefore, as previously noted, the processes to be established in the couple include stopping the mode cycle and taking a time-out.

Below are the tasks that the therapist can assign during these initial phases.

Module I Onwards

- **Review of explanatory videos of the model:** From the first session, the therapist recommends that the couple review educational materials on schema therapy applied to couples. They are encouraged to consult resources on specialized sites, such as the website: https://www.schematherapy-roediger.org/.
- **Listening to the session recordings:** From the beginning, the therapist instructs the couple to record all sessions on their cell phones. They are then assigned to listen to one recording together each week, alternating responsibility for organizing this meeting.
- **Stopping the mode cycle:** You are instructed that as soon as you detect the onset of the mode cycle during a conflict, both of you should make a conscious effort to stop it and prevent the argument from escalating.

Module II Onwards

- **Filling out the mode cycle card:** The therapist asks the couple to complete the mode cycle cards to identify their own coping modes and child modes, as well as how they interact with each other to form the mode cycle in the relationship.

Module III Onwards

- **Stopping the cycle of behavior, taking a time-out, and restoring communication:** When one partner signals a time-out, both partners should retreat to separate rooms to calm down and regain emotional balance. Once the time-out is over (as determined by the partner who requested the break), they will resume their daily routines with a diplomatic attitude, without resuming the discussion until the next therapy session.

Module IV Onwards

- **Mode cycle analysis during time-out:** While separated, each partner should complete a self-observation exercise. Stand and place two chairs in front of each other. Analyze the mode cycle in your relationship, identifying each partner's emotional leg, along with the predominant emotion and activated coping mode. Record this information on the mode cycle card. Once you have completed this exercise, answer the following reflective questions: What is the purpose of this relationship overall? What is it good for? How will I perceive this situation in 10 minutes, 10 days, 10 months, or 10 years?

- **Couple's pros list:** In this exercise, the therapist instructs each partner to create a list of the positive aspects and advantages of their relationship. They are also instructed that this exercise is intended to help them avoid taking the positive aspects of the relationship for granted over time and seeing them as minimal or expected. Consciously recognizing the value of their relationship fosters gratitude and mutual appreciation. Finally, they are asked to review this list in times of tension or when the couple takes a timeout during a conflict, as it reinforces the meaning of the relationship and reminds them why the bond is worth preserving and strengthening.

15.3 Tasks for the Second Phase of Therapy: Nurturing the Relationship

These tasks are assigned during the reconnection stage, when the couple has already developed the ability to stop conflicts and restore emotional balance.

The main goal of these activities is to strengthen the connection between partners, promoting positive interactions that nourish the relationship and reinforce emotional intimacy.

Module IV Onwards

- **Finding rituals:** The therapist asks the couple to look into each other's eyes when they meet in the morning and say, "Hello, how are you?" Hug each other or give each other a quick kiss, establishing eye contact, for 30 seconds, four or five times a day.
- **Quality time:** The therapist instructs the couple that they should dedicate five minutes of quality time every day, preferably at the end of the day. If they have children, it is recommended to do so after they have gone to sleep. During the meeting, the couple sits together in a relaxed atmosphere, where they take turns asking each other: "How was your day?" Each partner shares their experience for three or four minutes, while the other listens, without interrupting or trying to solve problems. At the end, each partner expresses how they felt about spending this time with their partner.
- **Daily positive feedback:** Every day, both partners should verbally provide positive feedback to the other. This can be recognition of everyday actions, appearance, or shared memories, for example: "The meal was delicious; that dress looks great on you; thank you for washing the car." The therapist can reinforce this activity by using the bank metaphor, where each compliment or positive comment is a deposit into the relationship account.

- **Sharing good memories from the past:** In this exercise, the couple spends time reliving positive moments shared, whether through photographs, videos, or meaningful mementos. These memories of the past, which are evidence of better days, help them change their perception of the relationship, reducing the impact of autopilot on the couple's dynamic and promoting emotional self-regulation.
- **Spend quality time every week:** To consistently nourish your relationship and prevent it from weakening, you need to invest time in it. That's why you should dedicate exclusive time to spending time together at least once a week. During this time, you should avoid external distractions: no children, no phones, no alcohol, no television. The activity can be anything you both enjoy and that fosters connection, for example, going out dancing, going out to dinner together, going for a walk, playing a game at home, or doing a new or recreational activity as a couple.

Module IX Onwards

- **Communication skills training:** Once the couple has learned about communication skills, it is essential that they practice applying them in a structured manner. To do this, they should schedule a connection dialogue at least once or twice a week, lasting 30 minutes. These dialogues should take place in a calm, distraction-free environment, ensuring that both partners are present and engaged in the conversation. Furthermore, these dialogues can be used after a timeout, once the couple has calmed down and entered the reconnection phase.
- **Try to reconnect physically:** Physical touch is a fundamental part of emotional connection in a relationship. That's why the therapist advises couples to make intentional efforts to incorporate more physical contact into their daily routines. This can include simple gestures such as more frequent hugs, holding hands, spontaneous kisses, caresses without specific expectations, and sleeping cuddled or closer to each other. It's not just about sexual intimacy but about creating an environment where physical contact builds trust and strengthens the emotional bond.

It's important to clarify that the tasks don't follow a rigid sequence but should be adapted to each couple's specific needs, the development of the therapeutic process, and the therapist's professional judgment, as long as the phase of therapy in which they are to be applied is respected. For example, if the couple is not in the reconnection phase, leaving out the connection dialogue task would be counterproductive, as the couple hasn't developed the balance between legs necessary to establish a balanced negotiation.

16

Preparing for Separation (Module XIII)

16.1 Introduction

Modules I through XII present the resources of couple schema therapy, designed to strengthen the relationship. Up to this stage, therapy should have helped the couple recognize the benefits of letting go of unrealistic expectations of both themselves and their partner. However, in some cases, external factors or deep-seated incompatibilities may make reconciliation an unattainable goal.

When a relationship faces irreconcilable difficulties, therapy can help the couple establish workable agreements, such as the "living together but separately," or "living separately but together," model. These dynamics allow partners to continue sharing common interests while maintaining independence in areas where their differences are insurmountable.

Not all couples manage to find a balance. In some cases, one partner may come to the conclusion that they no longer want to continue the relationship. When this happens, the therapeutic process focuses on providing emotional support and tools to cope with the separation in a healthy and respectful manner.

General objective: To provide the couple with healthy options to maintain the relationship or separate in a healthy way.

Specific objectives:

- Helping couples end their relationship in a healthy way by facilitating the negotiation process of any outstanding issues.
- Help the couple appreciate the effort made throughout the therapeutic process and how the changes achieved were not sufficient for the proper functioning of their relationship.
- Help the partners weigh the pros and cons of ending the relationship before making a decision.

- Before ending the relationship, the couple considers the possibility of "living together but apart" or having a "living separately but together" as a last resort to see if the relationship can work.
- In the event of a breakup, the couple partners are grateful for all the positive aspects they experienced throughout the relationship.

Stage 1

16.2 Beginning of the Session: Raise the Possibility of Ending the Relationship

The therapist compiles feedback from both partners on the work completed throughout the previous 12 modules, guiding a reflection on the therapeutic process, the lessons learned, and the evolution of the relationship. It is emphasized that, despite implementing the tools of couple schema therapy, reconciliation remains unviable. Given this situation, the therapist raises the possibility of ending the relationship.

If the couple is willing to consider this option, the pros and cons of separation are analyzed. To illustrate how this recapitulation is carried out at the beginning of the Module XIII session, we return to the case of Alfred and Alice, reviewed in Chapter 3 of the book.

Alfred and Alice, 55 years old

T: Alfred and Alice, throughout the therapeutic process, we've worked to understand the dynamics of your relationship. First, we reviewed that we all have two "legs": The red leg, which represents the need for assertiveness and autonomy, is linked to emotions like anger or disgust and negative coping behaviors like overcompensation or active avoidance. The blue leg, which symbolizes the need for attachment and connection, is associated with emotions like fear or sadness and negative coping behaviors like surrender or passive avoidance. Do we agree so far?

ALFRED (AL): Yes.

ALICE (ALI): Yes.

T: We've also identified two main modes in the relationship: coping modes, which are reflected in behaviors, and child modes, which are linked to emotions. In your case, we observed how one partner's coping modes can activate the other's child mode, generating a repetitive cycle.

In particular, we've seen that both partners tend toward active avoidance, which provokes an angry-child reaction in the other. This has led them to seek comfort outside the relationship instead of directly expressing their emotional needs. Am I remembering this correctly so far?

AL: Yes.

ALI: Yes.

T: We've also found that when this cycle is activated, both tend to withdraw and display passive-aggressive behaviors. However, in the therapeutic process, they've learned to recognize these patterns, stop the cycle, and become aware of their own coping and child modes. They've used strategies such as temporarily separating into different rooms and leaning on their "blocked leg" to rebalance themselves.

Is this correct?

AL: Yes.

ALI: Yes.

T: We've worked on strengthening your blue leg of attachment and connection, and you've both experienced each other's perspective through the vulnerable chair exercise. In that process, you've been able to notice how active avoidance creates distance between you and have visualized what your life would be like without the relationship. You've also relived your happiest moments together, identifying the positive aspects of your bond and expressing gratitude and affection toward each other. Are we doing well so far?

AL: Yes.

ALI: Yes.

T: We've also worked on understanding their personal histories. They've managed to connect with their childhood and recognize the unmet needs of that inner child who still seeks attention and affection. In session, they've expressed their vulnerability and learned to ask for what they need from others, offering something in return. They've also developed connecting dialogues, which have allowed them to understand both perspectives and reach agreements. Do you agree with this?

AL: Yes.

ALI: Yes.

T: However, we've identified aspects of the relationship that haven't yet improved. Alfred, although you've managed to reduce your active avoidance, you continue to disconnect from Alice and resort to alcohol consumption when she's not present. Alice, for your part, has secretly created a social network and has continued to seek solace in interacting with others through your posts. Is this correct?

(Continued)

(Continued)

AL: Yes.
ALI: Yes.
T: Given this, would it seem appropriate to discuss the possibility of ending the relationship by reviewing the pros and cons together?
AL: Okay.
ALI: Sounds good to me.

16.3 Experiential Work

16.3.1 Evaluate the Pros and Cons of Separating or Staying Together

Once the therapist has proposed discussing the possibility of ending the relationship, he or she asks the couple to stand and sets up four chairs arranged in pairs: two representing the "pros" of ending the relationship and the other two representing the "cons" (chairs in Figure 16.1). The therapist then explains what each group of chairs represents and guides them through the following steps:

1. **Imagining the pros:** The couple sits in the "pro" chairs and closes their eyes. The therapist guides them through a visualization of what their life would be like six months after the separation. Through questions such as "What positive emotions do you feel after the separation?" "What has changed for the better?" "What is easier in your life now?"
2. **Visualize the cons:** Then ask them to change seats and sit in the "cons" chairs. Repeat the exercise, this time projecting themselves a year after the separation. Ask questions like: "What do you miss about your partner or the relationship?" "How has your life changed for the worse?" "What is more difficult compared to before?"
3. **Reflection and assignment of percentages:** At the end of the exercise, the therapist asks the couple to open their eyes, stand up, and assign a percentage to the pros and cons of the decision. To do this, he or she poses questions such as: "If you had to divide 100% between the pros and cons of ending the relationship, what percentage would you assign to each?" Once the figures are established, they are invited to reflect on their meaning by asking, "What does this result tell you about your decision?" Finally, each partner's individual perception is obtained.

Figure 16.1 shows the arrangement of chairs so that the partners of the couple can see what each chair represents and then sit in their respective chairs to weigh

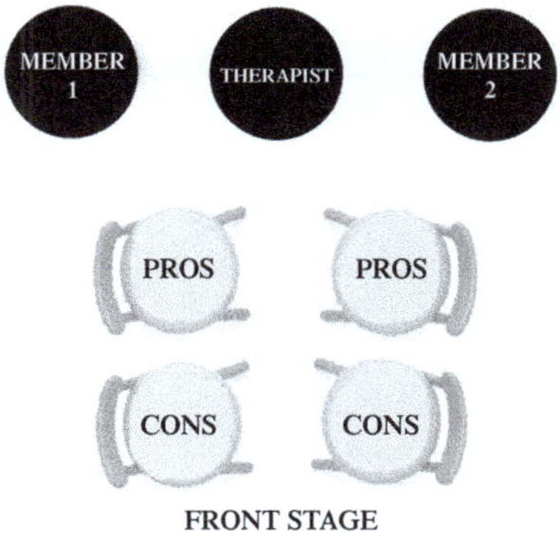

Figure 16.1 Chair work to analyze the pros and cons of ending a relationship. Adapted from Roediger (2025).

the pros and cons in order to evaluate the advisability of ending the relationship in the imagination exercise.

Depending on the case, the therapist can also perform the exercise by analyzing the pros and cons of continuing the relationship. To illustrate this step in the separation process, which consists of analyzing the pros and cons, we continue with the case of Alfred and Alice.

Alfred and Alice, 55 years old

T: I'd like us to stand up, then. I'm going to set up these four chairs. The two on the right represent the "pros" of ending the relationship, and the two on the left represent the "cons." Let's start by sitting in the "pros" chairs, shall we?

ALFRED (AL): Yes.

ALICE (ALI): Yes.

T: Now close your eyes, and I'm going to ask you to visualize what your life would be like six months after separating: How do you feel? What positive emotions do you feel after the separation? What has changed for the better? What is easier in your life now? Okay, now I would like you both to open your eyes and sit in the cons chairs... Close your eyes again, and I would like you to visualize now one year after the separation and reflect: What do you miss about your partner or the relationship? How has your life changed for the worse? What is more difficult compared to before? ... Have you managed to visualize it?

(Continued)

(Continued)

AL: Yes.

ALI: Yes.

T: Okay, now I ask you to stand up again and analyze what happened there in the chairs. And I ask you to divide the total out of 100%, based on what you visualized. What percentage do you assign to the "pros" and "cons"? I'd like to start with you, Alfred. What's your result?

AL: It's 70% "pros" and 30% "cons."

T: What does this result tell you about your decision?

AL: I want to keep trying.

T: Well, in your case, Alice, what was your result?

ALI: 65% "pros" and 35% "cons."

T: What do you conclude from that?

ALI: I'd like to keep trying. (Continued at the end of the session.)

16.4 Closing the Session: Work Plan with Specific Objectives

If both partners decide to try again, a work plan is agreed upon with specific goals for subsequent sessions. The behaviors to be assessed in the relationship should be precisely and specifically described in order to decide the next step. At this stage, what has been learned so far should be put into practice: stopping the mode cycle, separating into separate rooms, returning to a balanced coexistence, and developing the ability to maintain a relationship centered on listening, being clear, asking, and offering.

Once the specific points to be worked on have been established, a specific time-frame is proposed in which to test whether these can generate a functional and satisfactory relationship for both partners, for example, a maximum period of two to three months.

To demonstrate how to conclude the session by establishing a specific work plan, we continue with the description of Alfred's and Alice's case.

Alfred and Alice, 55 years old

T: Well, since both of you are more eager to try than to break up, I suggest we work on a plan to give the relationship three more months and see, if with this, we can resolve the problems that keep recurring.

AL: Yes.

ALI: Yes.

T: So I suggest that you both continue working on your active avoidance coping modes in your individual sessions. Does that seem like a good idea to you?

AL: Yes.

ALI: Yes.

T: Also, commit to fostering positive interactions, meaning two 30-minute connection conversations a week, scheduled as a single date; 5 minutes at the end of the day talking about their day just to listen; and constantly saying what they like about their partner and thanking them. Do you agree?

AL: Yes.

ALI: Yes.

T: I also need Alfred to stop hiding his drinking from Alice. Instead, I'd like you to express how you're feeling from a place of vulnerability. Does that seem like a good idea to you?

AL: Okay.

T: In your case it would be similar, Alice. I would ask you to commit to deleting this social media account and every time you feel like opening a new one or posting something, express to Alfred how you feel from a vulnerable perspective. Do you agree?

ALI: Sounds good to me.

T: Okay, I'm going to write this down in my notebook so it's on record, and I suggest we meet three more times: two more to make adjustments, and the third time to make the decision. Does this proposal make sense to you?

AL: Yes.

ALI: Me too. (End of session.)

However, if the assessment indicates that separation is the best option and neither partner is willing to continue trying, the therapist moves forward with the separation process (point 16.6.1). Below is how the therapist would conduct Alfred's and Alice's session if at least one partner decides it is not a good idea to continue.

Alfred and Alice, 55 years old
T: Okay, now I ask you to stand up again and analyze what happened there in the chairs. And I ask you to divide the total out of 100%, based on what you visualized. What percentage do you assign to the "pros" and "cons"? I'd like to start with you, Alfred. What's your result? AL: It's 30% "pros" and 70% "cons." T: What does this result tell you about your decision? AL: I don't want to keep trying. T: I understand, in your case, Alice, what was your result? ALI: 35% "pros" and 65% "cons." T: What do you conclude from that? ALI: I wouldn't want to keep trying. T: I understand. Before making a decision, I'd like to try one more thing. Is that okay? It would be the last option to see if the relationship can work. AL: Yes, I would like to know what it is about. ALI: Me too... (This session continues at point 16.6).

Stage 2

16.5 Beginning of the Session: Evaluate the Progress of the Work Plan Carried Out

The therapist, together with the couple, analyzes the progress they have made in the specific work over the three months.

16.5.1 Positive Results of the Work Plan

If after this time the coexistence is successful, the work plan is continued and a period of two or three months is allowed again to see if positive changes occur. If this occurs, the partners are discharged with the option of scheduling a follow-up session.

To demonstrate how this first step is worked out in the second phase, we continue with the case of Alfred and Alice in the scenario in which both wanted to keep trying and passed the three months proposed in the therapy.

Alfred and Alice, 55 years old

T: Well, three months have passed since the agreement was made on a specific task to improve the relationship. Would you like to evaluate the results?

AL: Yes.

ALI: Yes.

T: Alfred, how are you doing with avoiding drinking and connecting with Alice instead?

AL: I feel like I've improved; I've stopped drinking, and I've told Alice from a place of vulnerability when I've felt ignored by her.

T: What do you think about this perception of Alfred?

ALI: I agree. I think every time he gets upset, he tells me instead of withdrawing. He's also stopped drinking and has shown me his sadness. I've also seen him very motivated to practice the connection dialogues. I've felt very seen and cared for by him.

T: Very well, congratulations, Alfred, on these changes. And in your case, Alice, how did it go with your coping style of actively avoiding posting and interacting with other people instead of expressing your feelings to Alfred?

ALI: I feel like I've been doing well. I've stopped posting on social media, instead telling Alfred things directly. The conversations have also helped me feel heard. I feel like it's also been easier for me to express my sadness and its source when I don't feel listened to.

T: Alfred, I would like to know what you think about this perception of Alice?

AL.: Yes, I see her as more affectionate and more attentive, and when I tell her how I feel, she is more empathetic with how I feel.

T: Well, I would like you to continue doing this, and if you agree, we will see each other in two months to see if the progress has continued.

ALI: Sounds good to me.

AL: Me too... (End of session.)

16.5.2 Negative Results of the Work Plan

If the work plan is not satisfactory, the therapist suggests the couple make one last attempt before ending the relationship. To illustrate how the therapist addresses this possibility, the case of Alice and Alfred is described further, but in the context of a situation in which the goal of the proposed work plan has not been achieved.

Alfred and Alice, 55 years old

T: Well, three months have passed since the agreement was made on a specific task to improve the relationship. Would you like to evaluate the results?

AL: Yes.

ALI: Yes,

T: Alfred, how are you doing with actively avoiding drinking instead of connecting with Alice?

AL: I feel like I've improved, but Alice hasn't done her part; she's still distant and often tells me she's too busy to do the connecting dialogues.

T: What do you think about this perception of Alfred?

ALI: I don't agree. He's continued drinking. I found a can of beer in the trunk of his car the other time. And he hasn't wanted to do the connecting dialogues either.

T: I'm so sorry things aren't going the way you both hoped. And in your case, Alice, how did it go with your coping style of actively avoiding posting and interacting with other people instead of expressing your feelings to Alfred?

ALI: I feel like I did well. I don't think I have been using social media.

T: Alfred, I would like to know what you think about this perception of Alice?

AL: I don't agree. I've seen her on her cell phone a lot. Also, I haven't felt she's been understanding when I've been vulnerable.

T: Okay. It seems things haven't worked out between you. I think you tried, and it didn't work out. But I'd still like to propose one last option, one last try to see if the relationship can work. Is that okay with you?

AL: Yes, I would like to hear it.

ALI: Me too... (The session continues at 16.6.1.)

16.6 Cognitive Work: Decide Whether to Make a Last Attempt

If the couple decides to separate, either from point 16.3.1, when evaluating the pros and cons, or from point 16.5.2, when evaluating the progress made after the specific work performed, the therapist informs them that there is a final attempt to save the relationship, which consists of choosing one of the following two options:

- **Living separately but together:** In this option the therapist proposes, instead of a definitive breakup, a temporary or trial separation for a defined time in which each member lives in different spaces but with the possibility of continuing the relationship (together but living separately). In this alternative, the needs are still met between the partners, but the only difference is that they live separately. This choice is convenient for couples where one of the partners has a high need for autonomy.
- **Living together but separately:** In this option, the couple decides to live together and satisfy certain needs and desires (most commonly those related to sexuality) with third parties outside the relationship. The advantages of this alternative are that the partners can live together in a relationship with a certain degree of love and cooperation, removing the burden of meeting certain expectations and sharing parenthood in the same space for the sake of the children.

To illustrate how the therapist proposes the options of "living separately but together" and "living together but separately," the following is how the therapist carries out this action in the case of Alice and Alfred in the context in which the plan proposed in the previous session has not yielded results.

Alfred and Alice, 55 years old

T: I'd like to present two options that could help maintain the relationship. The first is to stay together but spend three months apart. During this time, each of you will focus on working through your negative patterns and the aspects that keep you from connecting with the other in individual therapy. If for some reason one of you becomes worried about the other, I can tell you that I, as a therapist, will be in charge of helping you survive on your own; you can leave that to me. If you choose this option, I can see you once a month to review your progress and how you've felt about the separation. Sometimes we need distance to make a more confident decision, whether to miss the other and fight for the relationship or to have the conviction to separate. The second option is "living together but separately," in which you continue living together but try to reach an agreement in which the relationship opens up to third parties who can meet the needs that you can't provide for each other. For example, you, Alfred, can give up talking about politics with Alice, which is the topic she's most distracted about, and find someone else to talk about it with. For your part, Alice, you can give up on Alfred constantly appreciating your looks and find other people who will, as long as certain rules you both agree on are followed. Which of the two options would you prefer?

(Continued)

(Continued)

AL: I would like to try to give us some time apart.
ALI: I could try.
T: Okay, so I'd like to discuss what this "living separately but together" would be like. (Continued at the end of the session.)

Reflection: What do you think the therapist should do if both partners do not choose the same option or one partner is simply not interested in either option and wants to end it?

Therapist's advice: If the partners choose different options, a negotiation can be established between them through a connection dialogue. The therapist can also analyze the pros and cons of each option. If one partner does not want the option their partner is choosing solely because of the activation of schemas (abandonment, self-sacrifice, mistrust-abuse, subjugation, enmeshment, dependency-incompetence, etc.), the critical voice can be worked on in the session. If they cannot agree on the "last option," it may be an indicator of a lack of compatibility. Therefore, the therapist can point out and analyze this perception with the couple and move directly to ending the relationship (point 16.8).

16.6.1 The Couple Decides to Make a "Last Attempt"

If, after the therapist presents the two alternatives for making a "last attempt" to save the relationship, the couple chooses one, the therapist sets the tone for moving on to the closing session, during which specific agreements will be established based on the alternative they have chosen. To illustrate this step, the following review examines the case of Alfred and Alice.

Alfred and Alice, 55 years old

T: Which of the two options would you like more?
AL: I would like to try to give us some time apart.
ALI: I could try.
T: Okay, so I'd like to discuss what this "together but apart" would be like. (Continued at the end of the session.)

16.6.2 The Couple Does Not Decide to Make the "Last Attempt"

If at least one of the partners is not interested in any of these options and wants to withdraw, the therapist should highlight the difference in compatibility, pointing out that, if this perception is true, it is better to separate than to continue, so the session continues from point 16.8.

To illustrate the therapeutic approach in the case where the couple cannot reach an agreement or one or both partners do not wish to pursue some of the options, we illustrate how the session would have concluded in the case of Alfred and Alice.

Alfred and Alice, 55 years old

T: I would like to present two options that could help maintain the relationship [...] Which of the two options would you like more?

AL: None, I would not agree to continue under those conditions.

ALI: Neither do I; I think it would be superfluous.

T: Okay, then it sounds like you both agree to end the relationship.

AL: I feel bad, but it's for the best.

ALI: Yes.

T: Then I'd like you to come to some important points to discuss so we can have a healthy closure between you. (Continued with point 16.8.)

16.7 Closing the Session: Agreements from the Last Attempt

At the end of this second stage, the therapist and the couple agree on the timeframe and rules to be followed, whether they decide to "living together but separately" or "living separately but together." Below are some important points to consider when reaching these agreements, depending on the option chosen by the couple:

- **Living separately but together:** The therapist suggests that the recommended period of living separately but together is two to three months, scheduling couples sessions every four to six weeks. The couple also agrees on how they want to work during this time apart to try to save the relationship, writing down the aspects each partner commits to working on within themselves during the separation. After this time, they reassess whether they want to continue the relationship. The therapist may continue individual therapy with the partner, as negative schemas may be activated as a result of the separation.

- **Living together but separately:** The therapist's role in this approach is to ensure that neither partner is in a surrendered coping or passive avoidance mode. If so, the therapist mediates the negotiation process, identifying which needs should be addressed together and which separately, and under what conditions. For example, if the couple decides to "open up" the relationship and stop being exclusive, they can agree to be discreet and not expose themselves in public or to have purely sexual relationships without romantic feelings and with the rigorous use of condoms, etc. Similarly, two or three months are proposed to evaluate the results of this alternative, scheduling couples sessions every four to six weeks.

To show how therapist Nora closed the stage two session, the case of Alfred and Alice is presented again.

Alfred and Alice, 55 years old

T: Let's agree on the rules of "living separately but together." First, I propose a six-month separation with a follow-up session every two months. After that time, you make a decision: either stay together because it works for you, live together, or end the relationship. Does that sound okay?

AL: Yes.

ALI: I agree.

T: During that time, you can continue with everything as normal: conversations and dates, applying what you learned in therapy. The difference is that you wouldn't be living together. So what's next is deciding who's leaving the house and who's staying.

AL: I propose that Alice stay in the house; after all, it is her parents' house.

T: Do you agree, Alice?

ALI: Yes.

T: During this time, will you be allowed to date other people or have sex with someone else?

AL: Of course not.

ALI: I wouldn't want that to happen either.

T: I understand that you have a pet together. How would you like to distribute the time you spend with it?

ALI: I propose one week each.

AL: I prefer that the dog stay with Alice because I don't know if they accept dogs where I'm going.
T: Do you agree, Alice?
ALI: Yes.
T: (After the couple finishes reaching an agreement) Okay, let's end the session here, and we'll see each other in two months for a follow-up. (Ends the session.)

Stage 3

16.8 Beginning of the Session: Review the Results of the Last Attempt

At the beginning of Stage 3, once the agreed-upon time has passed to try one of the two agreed-upon options (living together but being separated or living separately but together), the therapist and the couple meet to review the progress or setbacks they have experienced in their relationship.

16.8.1 Positive Results of the Last Attempt

If the couple indicates that their interaction has been good during this time and that their relationship has improved, the therapist gives them the option of continuing this agreement indefinitely or trying again to reestablish the relationship as it was before, integrating the lessons learned during this stage. The session ends, and follow-up sessions are scheduled every one or two months to see if the progress is maintained.

Alfred and Alice, 55 years old

T: I'd like us to review how things went for you at the end of these three months of trial separation.
AL: I think things have been going very well. I feel like we're functioning better this way. I feel like we are being more attentive to each other.
ALI: Yes, I agree; I've enjoyed being in this dynamic more, although on many occasions he stays overnight at my house or I stay at his; I think being in different places has been very good for us.
T: And how are things going with your active avoidance behaviors, Alfred?

(Continued)

(Continued)

AL: I feel like I've stopped doing it. I mean, when I'm with her, I don't drink or play on my smartphone. And I think I'm more direct in telling her I'm upset when I feel ignored. Also, I think I can accept that certain topics aren't appealing to her, and she tends to not pay much attention when we discuss them.

ALI: Yes, I agree. I also think I've felt very comfortable with this new dynamic. I think I've felt more cared for by Alfred. I also think that when I'm with him, I'm more attentive and not constantly on social media. If I feel ignored or disregarded, I think it's easier for me to tell him directly, explaining why it's so important to me that he do it and how he can do it.

T: Congratulations. I'm so glad you're making progress. What would you like to do next? You can continue like this for a while; you can decide to stay like this permanently as long as it works for you, or you can live together and try again.

AL: I would prefer to stay like this as long as it works for us, and if for some reason we want to live together again or feel that it's no longer working, make an appointment for couples therapy again.

ALI: I also think the same; at least for a while I would like us to continue the same.

T: How about we schedule a couples therapy session in six months to see how your progress is going and review your relationship? If you need to schedule a session sooner, feel free to write to me and request a session.

ALI: Sounds good to me.

AL: Yes, I agree; six months seems good to me to review how we are doing.

T: So we're done for today, and I'll see you in 6 months. (End of session.)

16.8.2 Negative Results of the Last Attempt

If one or both partners decide not to continue the relationship after this time, they proceed to step 16.9, "ending the relationship." To illustrate the therapeutic approach in the context where a trial separation hasn't worked, we continue with the case of Alfred and Alice.

Alfred and Alice, 55 years old

T: I'd like us to review how things went for you at the end of these three months of trial separation.

ALI: I'm not entirely convinced; I don't feel comfortable; the truth is I think that instead of helping things, it made things worse; I feel that neither I nor he felt more cared for.

AL: Yes, I agree; I think Alice and I both continue to run away when we feel angry, only now that I'm not there she doesn't know if I drink and start gambling, nor do I know if she gets distracted on social media.

T: If I understand correctly, it didn't work for you, is that right?

ALI: Yes.

AL: Yes.

T: I understand, then. I think this is the last option to try to figure out the relationship, so there's no other option but to end it. What do you think about what I'm telling you?

ALI: Yes, even if it hurts, it's the best thing.

AL: Yes, a part of me wouldn't want to, but I'm convinced it's the healthiest thing to do.

16.9 Cognitive Work: Ending the Relationship

If the couple decides to end the relationship permanently and doesn't agree with any of the options the therapist proposes, or if the options they've tried haven't worked, this step is reached. The following steps are followed.

16.9.1 Resolve the Remaining Problems

The therapist helps them agree on how to resolve the outstanding issues. If necessary and the couple agrees, additional couples therapy appointments can be scheduled so they can agree on any issues that need to be resolved related to the separation. The therapist checks to see if any of the partners want to continue therapy, but in individual sessions.

One of the most important agreements concerns childcare and parenting. In this regard, the therapist can propose a "dad days" and "mom days" approach. From this perspective, the partners agree that the children will have two ways of seeing life: "mom's way" and "dad's way." As they mature, they will choose the best of each. To demonstrate how the therapist applied the analysis of the remaining problems, the case of Alfred and Alice is reviewed.

Alfred and Alice, 55 years old

T: I think I've exhausted the options I can offer you through couple schema therapy. I believe either of you (or both of you) have the right, if you so wish, to withdraw from the relationship. So, if you both agree, I'd like to take the rest of the session to sort out some important issues. I remind you that even if you're separated, this doesn't mean you shouldn't continue applying what we discussed in therapy. You'll remain in contact and will have to negotiate some important aspects. I believe that if you apply what we discussed in the process, this can be done in a harmonious and positive way. I'd also like to ask you not to stop making this effort, even if the relationship is no longer in place. I remind you that whatever you haven't been able to develop and resolve in this relationship will very likely carry over into the next. The first point I'd like you to agree on is: Where will each of you live?

AL: I think I'm going to move because it's Alice's parents' house.

T: Do you agree, Alice?

ALI: Yes, I agree.

T: When do you think the deadline for the move would be?

AL: I think no more than a month while I look for a house.

T: And who would keep the pet?

AL: I prefer that he stay with Alice for the time being until I move because I don't know if they accept pets where I'm going.

T: Do you think it's a good idea, Alice?

ALI: Yeah, that's fine.

Note: In the event that the couple comes from a living separately but together (point 16.6.1.1) and it has not worked out, the couple would already be living separately, so the therapist's question would be whether they would continue with the same dynamic or would change something with respect to the move and care of the pet.

T: What other important aspects would you like to agree on here in the session regarding separation?

ALI: I would like to propose to Alfred that he keep the truck with me because I believe I was the one who put up the most money to buy it, and that he keep the car and the living room since he was the one who bought it.

AL: Yes, that seems fine to me, but you better stay with the living room; it's too big; I'll just take the car.

T: Is there anything else you'd like to ask Alfred for now?

ALI: Not at the moment.

T: In your case, Alfred, is there something you would like to ask Alice?

AL: Yes, I would like to stop having shared accounts; I am going to cancel the services that are mine, such as the internet, which is in my name, and the telephone line.

T: What do you think about what Alfred is asking you?

ALI: Okay, but except for the major medical insurance because I don't want to lose my seniority.

AL: So, in that case, I'd like you to speak directly to the insurance agent and manage the payments. For now, I'd like to have zero contact with you—don't take it the wrong way—but the separation will be difficult for me.

ALI: For me too, and that's okay.

T: Is there anything else you'd like to discuss with Alfred right now?

ALI: No.

T: Ok, do you think I should see you in a month to follow-up on how the separation process is going and if any difficulties have arisen during it?

ALI: Okay.

AL: Sounds good to me.

Reflection: What happens if the couple doesn't want follow-up sessions or if problems arise before that session?

Therapist advice: If you do not want follow-up sessions, it is advisable to respect the couple's wishes, pointing out that you can schedule them if necessary. Likewise, the therapist can specify that if anything arises before the scheduled session, the session can be moved up to address the emerging issue within the couple.

16.10 Closing the Session: Farewell to the Couple

If possible, the therapist concludes the meeting with positive feedback from both partners, in which they acknowledge the positive aspects of what they have experienced over the years together, despite present differences and conflicts.

One option is to refer the couple to a mediator for advice on the remaining steps in the separation process. To illustrate how therapist Nora concluded the breakup session, we review the case of Alfred and Alice.

Alfred and Alice, 55 years old

T: I'd like to congratulate you on the effort you put into therapy. I think you've both improved a lot in the use of your two legs. In your case, Alice, I think you've managed to stop running away; I think you've managed to be clearer about what you need from Alfred, offering him something in return. In your case, Alfred, I think that instead of withdrawing, you've also grown in the way you directly express what you need and expose your vulnerability more when doing so. These skills don't go unnoticed; I think they will be very useful in your life and in your interpersonal relationships.

AL: Thank you.

ALI: Thank you very much.

T: Finally, I would like you to stand face to face and look into each other's eyes and thank each other for the positive things that have happened during these years together.

AL: Alice, thank you for the love you gave me and for taking care of me when I was sick; thank you for accepting my pet as if it were yours too. I had some really fun times with you, and it's going to be hard for me; I'm going to miss you a lot.

ALI: Thank you, Alfred, for the support you gave me during all these years and for how well you behaved with my family of origin; they love you very much; also for supporting me and encouraging me professionally and for being a partner to me in many things; it is also very difficult for me to end this, but I think it is the best; for love, I think we have to separate.

T: I'm deeply moved by your words, and I agree with what Alice said: out of love for oneself and for one's partner, sometimes when there's no compatibility, it's better to let the other person go. I'd like to give you the contact information for a mediator. And we'll see each other in a month to see how the separation process is going and if anything has come up that you're having difficulty resolving during that process.

Reflection: Do you think it's a failure when couples therapy ends in separation because they couldn't resolve their difficulties?

Therapist's advice: Due to the therapist's negative schemas, such as self-sacrifice, unattainable goals, and failure, among others, it may be understandable that you feel that it was a failure that the couple did not solve their problems. However, it is important to take into account that the success of the therapy does not depend 100% on the therapist since he or she provides the tools and the couple decides whether or not to use them. Also, couples will not always end up together at the end of therapy since approximately 15% of couples separate at the end of the therapeutic process (Roediger & Frank-Noyon, 2021). Finally, it is important to keep in mind that in many cases there is not much that therapy can offer, since some couples come to therapy at times when the relationship is so worn out and there has been so much violence that it is difficult to establish a reconciliation.

As a summary, the following are the guiding steps for the therapist to implement the "Preparing for Separation" in the session:

Stage 1

Beginning of the Session

- **Raise the possibility of ending the relationship:** The therapist recaps the work done in the sessions so far, highlighting how the disagreements have not been resolved by raising the possibility of ending the relationship.

Experiential Work

- **Evaluate the pros and cons of separating or staying together:** Through an imagination exercise, the therapist has the couple visualize the pros and cons of continuing in the relationship and the cons of ending it.

Closing the Session

- **Work plan with specific objectives**: If the couple has more "pros" than "cons" and decides to keep trying, a plan is made to work on certain specific areas of the relationship, and the couple carries it out for three months. If they do not wish to continue, they move on to the point: "decide whether to make a last attempt."

Stage 2

Beginning of the Session

- **Evaluate the progress of the work plan carried out:** The therapist reviews the progress made with the personalized work plan.

  - **Positive results of the work plan:** If the couple agrees, the plan is maintained, the session is concluded, and a follow-up session is proposed.
  - **Negative results of the work plan:** If the couple does not agree, the process continues to the next step: the last attempt.

Cognitive Work

- **Decide whether to make a last attempt:** If the couple is not happy with the work plan, they will consider some of the following options: Living separately but together: The couple lives separately for six months, but they remain together, and after that time an assessment is made of whether to continue or end the relationship or living together but separately: The couple continues to live together, but they give up the expectations that certain needs will be met by the other member, looking for third parties to obtain them.
  - **The couple decides to make a "last attempt":** If the couple agrees on either option, the session ends by proceeding to the "last attempt agreements" point.
  - **The couple does not decide to make the "last attempt":** If they do not agree to make the last attempt, the therapist proceeds to the point of "ending the relationship."

Closing the Session

- **Last-ditch agreements:** The couple agrees on important aspects of the living separately but together or living together but separately, such as the timing, freedoms, and limitations that each member will have during the duration in which the chosen option is attempted.

Stage 3

Beginning of the Session

- **Review of the results of the last attempt:** The therapist reviews whether the living separately but together or living together but separately has helped them improve their relationship.
  - **Positive results from the last attempt:** The therapist invites them to continue as before for a while longer or indefinitely or to try again to be together under the previous conditions.
  - **Negative results of the last attempt:** The therapist proceeds to the step called "ending the relationship."

Cognitive Work

- **End the relationship:** Resolve the remaining issues: The therapist and the couple discuss and agree on those issues that must be resolved when the relationship ends, such as separation of property, cohabitation with children, etc.

Closing the Session

- **Farewell to the couple:** The therapist thanks them for their efforts in therapy and concludes the process, in addition to providing them with the contact information of a mediator.

References

Ainsworth, M. D. S., Blehar, M. C., Waters, E. & Wall, S. (1978). *Patterns of attachment: A psychological study of the strange situation*. Erlbaum.

Arntz, A. & van Genderen, H. (2009). *Schema therapy for borderline personality disorder*. Wiley-Blackwell.

Arntz, A. & Jacob, G. (2013). *Schema therapy in practice: An introductory guide to the schema mode approach*. Wiley-Blackwell.

Barrett, L. F. (2017). *How emotions are made: The secret life of the brain*. Houghton Mifflin Harcourt.

Baumeister, R. F. & Leary, M. R. (1995). The need to belong: Desire for interpersonal attachments as a fundamental human motivation. *Psychological Bulletin, 117*(3), 497–529. https://doi.org/10.1037/0033-2909.117.3.497

Bennett-Goleman, T. (2002). *Emotional alchemy: How the mind can heal the heart*. Harmony Books.

Berkowitz, L. (1989). Frustration-aggression hypothesis: Examination and reformulation. *Psychological Bulletin, 106*(1), 59–73.

Bliss, T. V. P. & Lømo, T. (1973). Long-lasting potentiation of synaptic transmission in the dentate area of the anaesthetized rabbit following stimulation of the perforant path. *The Journal of Physiology, 232*(2), 331–356. https://doi.org/10.1113/jphysiol.1973.sp010273

Bowlby, J. (1969). *Attachment and loss: Vol. 1. Attachment*. Basic Books.

Bowlby, J. (1988). *A secure base: Parent-child attachment and healthy human development*. Basic Books.

Bracha, H. S. (2004). Freeze, flight, fight, fright, faint: Adaptationist perspectives on the acute stress response spectrum. *CNS Spectrums, 9*(9), 679–685.

Cannon, W. B. (1915). *Bodily changes in pain, hunger, fear and rage: An account of recent researches into the function of emotional excitement*. D. Appleton and Company.

Cannon, W. B. (1932). *The wisdom of the body*. W. W. Norton & Company.

Ceballos, D., & Serrano, N. (2025). *Healing Your Inner Child: Overcome the Schemas That Limit You in Living a Full Life.* CITE.

Chechik, G., Meilijson, I., & Ruppin, E. (1999). Neuronal regulation: A mechanism for synaptic pruning during brain maturation. *Neural Computation, 11*(8), 2061–2080.

Coan, J. A. & Sbarra, D. A. (2015). Social baseline theory: The role of social proximity in emotion and economy of action. *Current Opinion in Psychology, 1*, 40–45. https://doi.org/10.1016/j.copsyc.2014.12.002

Collins, N. L. & Feeney, B. C. (2004). An attachment theory perspective on closeness and intimacy in relationships. In D. J. Mashek & A. Aron (Eds.), *Handbook of closeness and intimacy* (pp. 163–187). Psychology Press.

Damasio, A. R. (1994). *Descartes' error: Emotion, reason, and the human brain.* Putnam.

David, S. (2016). *Emotional agility: Get unstuck, embrace change, and thrive in work and life*. Penguin.

Davidson, R. J. & Begley, S. (2012). *The emotional life of your brain*. Penguin.

Deci, E. L. & Ryan, R. M. (1985). *Intrinsic motivation and self-determination in human behavior*. Springer.

Doidge, N. (2007). *The brain that changes itself: Stories of personal triumph from the frontiers of brain science*. Penguin.

Dweck, C. S. (2006). *Mindset: The new psychology of success*. Random House.

Ekman, P. (1992). An argument for basic emotions. *Cognition & Emotion, 6*(3-4), 169–200.

Ekman, P. (1999). Basic emotions. In T. Dalgleish & M. Power (Eds.), *Handbook of cognition and emotion* (pp. 45–60). John Wiley & Sons.

Erikson, E. H. (1950). *Childhood and society*. W. W. Norton & Company.

Farrell, J. & Shaw, I. (2012). *Group schema therapy for borderline personality disorder: A step-by-step treatment manual with partner workbook*. Wiley-Blackwell.

Farrell, J. & Shaw, I. (2018). *Experiencing schema therapy from the inside out: A self-practice/self-reflection workbook for therapists*. Guilford Press.

Festinger, L. (1957). *A theory of cognitive dissonance*. Stanford University Press.

Fisher, H. (2004). *Why we love: The nature and chemistry of romantic love*. Henry Holt and Company.

Fonagy, P., Gergely, G., Jurist, E. L., & Target, M. (2002). *Affect regulation, mentalization, and the development of the self*. New York: Other Press.

Gilbert, P. (2009). *The compassionate mind: A new approach to life's challenges*. Constable & Robinson.

Goleman, D. (1995). *Emotional intelligence: Why it can matter more than IQ*. Bantam Books.

Gottman, J. M. & Gottman, J. S. (2015). *The seven principles for making marriage work: A practical guide from the country's foremost relationship expert*. Harmony.

Gottman, J. M. & Silver, N. (1999). *The seven principles for making marriage work*. Crown.

Greenberg, L. S. (2011). *Emotion-focused therapy*. American Psychological Association.

Greenberg, L. S. & Paivio, S. C. (1997). *Working with emotions in psychotherapy*. Guilford Press.

Hayes, S. C., Barnes-Holmes, D., & Roche, B. (2012). *Relational frame theory: A post-Skinnerian account of human language and cognition*. Springer Science & Business Media.

Hazan, C. & Shaver, P. (1987). Romantic love conceptualized as an attachment process. *Journal of Personality and Social Psychology, 52*(3), 511–524. https://doi.org/10.1037/0022-3514.52.3.511

Heath, G. & Startup, H. (Eds.). (2020). *Creative methods in schema therapy*. Routledge.

Hebb, D. O. (1949). *The organization of behavior: A neuropsychological theory*. Wiley.

Johnson, S. M. (2004). *The practice of emotionally focused couple therapy: Creating connection* (2nd ed.). Brunner-Routledge.

Kahneman, D. (2011). *Thinking, fast and slow*. Farrar, Straus and Giroux.

Kandel, E. R. (2001). The molecular biology of memory storage: A dialogue between genes and synapses. *Science, 294*(5544), 1030–1038. https://doi.org/10.1126/science.1067020

Kleim, J. A. & Jones, T. A. (2008). Principles of experience-dependent neural plasticity: Implications for rehabilitation after brain damage. *Journal of Speech, Language, and Hearing Research, 51*(1), S225–S239. https://doi.org/10.1044/1092-4388(2008/018)

Lazarus, R. S. (1991). *Emotion and adaptation*. Oxford University Press.

Lazarus, R. S. & Folkman, S. (1984). *Stress, appraisal, and coping*. Springer.

LeDoux, J. (1996). *The emotional brain: The mysterious underpinnings of emotional life*. Simon & Schuster.

Lewis, M. (1993). Self-conscious emotions: Embarrassment, pride, shame, and guilt. In M. Lewis & J. M. Haviland (Eds.), *Handbook of emotions* (pp. 563–573). Guilford Press.

McClelland, J. L., McNaughton, B. L., & O'Reilly, R. C. (1995). Why there are complementary learning systems in the hippocampus and neocortex: Insights from the successes and failures of connectionist models of learning and memory. *Psychological Review, 102*(3), 419–457. https://doi.org/10.1037/0033-295X.102.3.419

McEwen, B. S. (2002). *The end of stress as we know it*. Dana Press.

McKay, M., Lev, A., & Skeen, M. (2012). *Acceptance and commitment therapy for interpersonal problems: Using mindfulness, acceptance, and schema awareness to change interpersonal behaviors*. New Harbinger.

Mennin, D. S. & Fresco, D. M. (2014). Emotion regulation therapy. In J. J. Gross (Ed.), *Handbook of emotion regulation* (2nd ed., pp. 469–490). Guilford Press.

Merzenich, M. M. (2013). *Soft-wired: How the new science of brain plasticity can change your life*. Parnassus.

Miller, E. K. & Cohen, J. D. (2001). An integrative theory of prefrontal cortex function. *Annual Review of Neuroscience, 24*(1), 167–202. https://doi.org/10.1146/annurev.neuro.24.1.167

Mikulincer, M. & Shaver, P. R. (2007). *Attachment in adulthood: Structure, dynamics, and change*. Guilford Press.

Nader, K. & Einarsson, E. Ö. (2010). Memory reconsolidation: An update. *Annals of the New York Academy of Sciences, 1191*(1), 27–41. https://doi.org/10.1111/j.1749-6632.2010.05443.x

Northoff, G., Heinzel, A., de Greck, M., Bermpohl, F., Dobrowolny, H., & Panksepp, J. (2006). Self-referential processing in our brain—A meta-analysis of imaging studies on the self. *NeuroImage, 31*(1), 440–457. https://doi.org/10.1016/j.neuroimage.2005.12.002

Ochsner, K. N. & Gross, J. J. (2005). The cognitive control of emotion. *Trends in Cognitive Sciences, 9*(5), 242–249. https://doi.org/10.1016/j.tics.2005.03.010

Panksepp, J. (1998). *Affective neuroscience: The foundations of human and animal emotions*. Oxford University Press.

Pascual-Leone, A. (2001). *The brain that changes itself: Stories of personal triumph from the frontiers of brain science*. Viking.

Perry, B. D. & Szalavitz, M. (2006). *The boy who was raised as a dog: And other stories from a child psychiatrist's notebook*. Basic Books.

Phelps, E. A. & LeDoux, J. E. (2005). Contributions of the amygdala to emotion processing: From animal models to human behavior. *Neuron, 48*(2), 175–187. https://doi.org/10.1016/j.neuron.2005.09.025

Piaget, J. (1952). *The origins of intelligence in children*. W. W. Norton & Company.

Plutchik, R. (2001). The nature of emotions: Human emotions have deep evolutionary roots, a fact that may explain their complexity and provide tools for clinical practice. *American Scientist, 89*(4), 344–350.

Porges, S. W. (2011). *The polyvagal theory: Neurophysiological foundations of emotions, attachment, communication, and self-regulation*. W. W. Norton & Company.

Rachman, S. (1997). The evolution of cognitive behaviour therapy. *Behaviour Research and Therapy, 35*(7), 697–710. https://doi.org/10.1016/S0005-7967(97)00017-3

Raichle, M. E. & Gusnard, D. A. (2002). Appraising the brain's energy budget. *Proceedings of the National Academy of Sciences, 99*(16), 10237–10239. https://doi.org/10.1073/pnas.172399499

Roediger, E. (2025). *Couples ST-modules overview*. Schema Therapy Roediger. Retrieved April 14, 2025, from https://www.schematherapy-roediger.org/index.php/couples/module-system

Roediger, E. & Frank-Noyon, E. (2021). *Paare bewegen: Schematherapie mit Paaren in der Praxis*. Tübingen, Alemania: dgvt-Verlag.

Roediger, E., Stevens, B. A., & Brockman, R. (2018). *Contextual schema therapy: An integrative approach to personality disorders, emotional dysregulation, and interpersonal functioning*. Context Press.

Roediger, E. & Valente, M. (2025). *Schematherapie—kontextuell, prozessbasiert, interpersonal*. Stuttgart: Schattauer.

Sapolsky, R. M. (2004). *Why zebras don't get ulcers: The acclaimed guide to stress, stress-related diseases, and coping* (3rd ed.). Henry Holt and Company.

Schore, A. N. (2003). *Affect regulation and the repair of the self*. W. W. Norton & Company.

Schwartz, J. M. & Begley, S. (2002). *The mind and the brain: Neuroplasticity and the power of mental force*. HarperCollins.

Selye, H. (1976). *The stress of life* (Revised ed.). McGraw-Hill.

Siegel, D. J. (2010). *Mindsight: The new science of personal transformation*. Bantam Books.

Siegel, D. J. (2012). *The developing mind: How relationships and the brain interact to shape who we are* (2nd ed.). Guilford Press.

Siegel, D. J. & Bryson, T. P. (2012). *The whole-brain child: 12 revolutionary strategies to nurture your child's developing mind*. Delacorte Press.

Simeone-DiFrancesco, C., Roediger, E., & Stevens, B. A. (2015). Schema therapy with couples: *A practitioner's guide to healing relationships*. Wiley-Blackwell.

Stern, D. N. (1985). *The interpersonal world of the infant: A view from psychoanalysis and developmental psychology*. Basic Books.

Stevens, B., & Roediger, E. (2016). *Breaking negative relationship patterns: A schema therapy self-help and support book*. Wiley-Blackwell.

Sweller, J. (1988). Cognitive load during problem solving: Effects on learning. *Cognitive Science, 12*(2), 257–285. https://doi.org/10.1207/s15516709cog1202_4

Tavris, C. (1989). *Anger: The misunderstood emotion* (2nd ed.). Simon & Schuster.

van der Kolk, B. A. (2014). *The body keeps the score: Brain, mind, and body in the healing of trauma*. Viking.

Winnicott, D. W. (1965). *The maturational processes and the facilitating environment: Studies in the theory of emotional development*. International Universities Press.

Young, J. E. (1999). *Cognitive therapy for personality disorders: A schema-focused approach*. Professional Resource Press.

Young, J. E. & Behary, W. (2019). *International training and certification schema therapy program* [Training]. The Schema Therapy Institutes of NJ-NYC-DC.

Young, J. & Klosko, J. (2012). *Reinventa tu vida*. Paidós.

Young, J., Klosko, J., & Weishaar, M. (2015). *Schema therapy: A practitioner's guide*. Guilford Publications.

Young, J., Rafaeli, E., & Bernstein, D. P. (2011). *Schema therapy: Distinctive features*. Routledge.

Index

a

abandonment schema 5, 7, 8, 11, 153, 208, 272
  and critical voice work 272
  imagining partner leaves 153, 157, 159, 160
acceptance 4, 6, 12, 13, 15, 17, 49, 204, 208, 247, 255
Accessing the Assertive Side 180–184, 188, 201
Accessing the Vulnerable Child, see Gaining Access to the Vulnerable Side (Module V)
active avoidance 16, 41–44, 46, 47, 49, 50, 53, 55–59, 88, 89, 91, 93, 106–107, 120, 131, 143, 148, 149, 157, 169, 180, 189, 215, 225, 233, 262, 263, 267, 269, 270, 275
  active avoidance-active avoidance mode cycle 55, 56
  active avoidance-passive avoidance mode cycle 57, 58
  and alcohol/social media in Alfred and Alice case 14, 49, 56, 57, 252, 253, 263, 267, 269, 270, 276, 277
  in externalizing partner 46, 57, 148, 149, 169, 189, 267
  in two-dimensional model 25, 26, 28, 29, 31, 32
active child modes 63–65, 106–108, 125, 128, 131, 177, 213
active dominance-avoidance mode cycle 49, 50
active leg 86, 95, 118, 136, 137, 139, 181
addictions 56, 143, 252, 253, 263, 267, 269, 270
Adult Mode, Healthy, see Healthy Adult Mode
affective regulation 4, 10, 20, 23, 72, 75, 76, 78, 114, 246
agreements 26, 121, 128, 183, 217, 238, 247, 249, 254, 261, 263, 272, 273, 277, 281, 282
  after last attempt 273–275
  connection dialogue 181, 188, 238, 246–250, 252–254
  separation 261, 277–279
Alfred and Alice 56, 262, 265, 266, 268–280
Alice and Alfred, see Alfred and Alice
Amelia 36–39
amygdala 67, 69, 71–73, 78
anger 6, 7, 11, 12, 16, 20–25, 27–36, 38–50, 52–55, 57–64, 88, 90, 92–95, 99, 102–105, 107–111, 118, 119, 130, 131, 138, 143, 148, 153, 156, 157, 160, 161, 169, 172, 177, 178, 187, 189, 196, 197, 200, 201, 204, 206–208, 212, 215, 216, 223, 245, 246, 249, 250, 262, 263, 277
  and Angry Child Mode 11, 16, 41–44, 62–64, 103, 104, 107–109, 111, 131, 148, 157, 161, 169, 177, 206, 215

anger (*Cont.*)
and red leg 11, 30, 31, 33, 40, 42, 46, 53–55, 57, 58, 60, 61, 88, 93–95, 104, 105, 107, 108, 111, 143, 148, 153, 172, 189, 201, 262
Angry Child, see Angry Child Mode
Angry Child Mode 11, 16, 41–44, 62–64, 103, 104, 107–109, 111, 131, 148, 157, 161, 169, 177, 206, 215
anxiety 3, 14, 173, 216
assertiveness 16, 19–22, 27–40, 42, 44–46, 48–50, 53–58, 60–62, 79, 85–88, 90–95, 97, 99, 104, 119, 126, 134, 142–144, 149, 172–174, 177, 180, 181, 187, 189, 191, 222, 237, 262
as flexible behavior 55, 60, 90, 144, 149, 173
speaking from assertive side 158, 172, 173, 180, 183, 184, 186–188, 201
assertiveness-autonomy 16, 19–22, 27–37, 39, 40, 42, 45, 46, 48–50, 53–58, 60, 61, 79, 85–88, 90, 92–95, 97, 99, 126, 142, 143, 149, 172, 177, 180, 181, 187, 222, 237, 262
blocked side 42, 86, 102, 118, 119, 121, 141, 263
attachment 3, 4, 6, 14, 16, 18, 19, 22, 27–32, 34, 35, 38–41, 46, 49, 50, 53–55, 57–61, 76, 79, 85–90, 92–96, 99, 120, 126, 127, 132, 137, 142–144, 152, 153, 157–161, 163, 164, 167, 170–172, 181, 189, 201, 203, 218, 222, 224, 237, 262, 263
attachment figures 4, 6, 76
bond and closeness 4, 18, 19, 27, 28, 54, 61, 133, 143, 159, 168, 185, 189, 203, 223, 255, 259, 260, 263
attachment-connection 16, 18, 19, 22, 27–32, 34, 35, 38–41, 46, 49, 50, 53–55, 58–61, 76, 79, 85–87, 89, 90, 92–96, 99, 120, 127, 132, 137, 142–144, 152, 153, 157, 158, 160, 161, 163, 164, 167, 170–172, 201, 203, 222, 237, 262, 263
need activation 16, 18, 19, 27, 28, 31, 32, 35, 39–41, 46, 50, 53–55, 57–59, 61, 85–90, 92, 93, 120, 127, 132, 137, 142–144, 152, 153, 157–161, 163, 164, 167, 170–172, 189, 203, 222, 224, 262
attachment theory 3
autonomy
see assertiveness-autonomy
and competence 4, 5
high need for autonomy 271
avoidance 6, 8, 11, 14–16, 31, 33, 41–44, 46–51, 53–60, 63, 72–74, 78, 79, 88–91, 93, 99, 106, 107, 120, 122, 131, 138, 143, 148, 149, 157, 169, 172, 173, 176–181, 187, 189, 210, 215, 233, 262, 263, 267, 274, 275
experiential avoidance 13, 14, 74
passive avoidance 16, 41, 43, 44, 47, 48, 50, 53–60, 88, 89, 91, 93, 106, 107, 131, 172, 173, 176–180, 187, 189, 262, 274
schema coping behavior 8
avoidance-avoidance mode cycle 53–58

b

balance 4, 6, 12, 16–18, 21, 22, 34–40, 49, 60–62, 67, 71, 76, 79, 86, 87, 89–92, 97, 99, 104, 105, 109, 114, 115, 118, 119, 121–123, 125, 126, 128, 132, 134, 141–147, 149, 152, 153, 155, 157, 159, 161, 163, 165, 172–174, 181, 182, 186, 188, 189, 202, 211, 214, 217, 222–238, 247, 258–261, 263, 266
between needs 34–40
emotional and behavioral 143, 144
leg balance 147
basic emotions 1, 8, 11, 12, 15, 16, 18, 20–22, 24, 27, 30, 74, 79, 85, 92, 94, 99, 100, 143
anger/disgust 11, 30, 31, 33, 40, 42, 46, 53–55, 57, 58, 60, 61, 88, 93–95, 104, 105, 107, 108, 111, 143, 148, 153, 172, 189, 201, 262
fear/sadness 32, 53, 54, 57, 59, 61, 89, 93, 94, 104, 143, 144, 153, 157, 177, 262
social emotions 11, 16, 21–24, 184
basic needs 3, 18, 19, 22, 27, 30, 31, 34, 35, 38, 60, 79, 85, 93, 99, 126
five core needs 3, 4
two-dimensional model 28–31, 36, 38, 99

Beatrice and Bartholomew 145, 147, 148, 150, 155–159, 161–164, 167, 168
behavioral phase 9, 10
behavioral responses 8, 71, 75, 77
beliefs, maladaptive 3–5, 9
Best Day exercise 133–139
blocked emotions 17, 37, 93, 95, 98, 107, 112, 118, 120, 123, 130, 151
blocked leg 42, 102, 118, 119, 121, 263
blue leg 35–40, 44, 46–50, 52–55, 57–62, 86, 87, 89–97, 101, 103–108, 127, 131–133, 136–139, 141, 143, 144, 147, 149–153, 155, 157, 161, 164, 167–169, 171–175, 177–180, 185–187, 189, 195, 197, 201, 204, 214, 218, 221, 232, 234, 237, 244, 262, 263
  accessing in externalizing partner 143, 144, 152, 157, 160
  and attachment-connection 18, 19, 28, 31, 32, 35, 39, 46, 50, 53, 58, 61, 86, 90, 92, 120, 132, 137, 143, 144, 152, 153, 157, 158, 160, 161, 163, 164, 167, 172, 262, 263
  connecting with 143, 144, 161, 171
  rebalancing toward 218, 221
  switching from red leg to blue leg 144, 171, 188, 200, 233
blue side, see blue leg
bodily sensations 3, 17, 20, 34, 73, 74, 93, 117, 154–158, 160–162, 166, 167, 170, 171, 180, 183, 194, 195, 205–207, 209, 212, 227–230, 232, 236
borderline personality disorder 3
boundaries 4, 6, 20, 33, 39, 52, 68, 70, 82, 153
brain processes 67, 68, 70, 133, 151
breathing 19, 20, 22, 34, 93, 108, 117, 157, 158, 160, 162, 166, 194, 195, 206, 207, 227–230

C

case conceptualization 9
castle metaphor 172, 178, 179
cell phone metaphor 17, 28, 30, 101, 102, 150, 238–241, 252, 253, 258, 270
chair arrangements 64, 65, 93, 107, 128, 264
chair movements 17, 63–65, 73, 82, 85, 89, 91–96, 102, 103, 105–108, 113–116, 119, 122, 125, 127–131, 133, 134, 136, 138, 145–148, 154–158, 160–163, 165, 170, 173, 175, 176, 178–180, 182, 187, 190–197, 199, 200, 205, 206, 210, 212–214, 217, 219, 223–233, 235, 236, 241, 249, 252, 258, 263–266, 268
  for Mode Cycle 63–65, 84, 85, 105, 107, 109
  for pros and cons 264, 265
  vulnerable child chair 210, 227, 229, 230, 233, 235
chair work 17, 64, 65, 191, 192, 194, 199, 200, 226, 227, 231, 235, 236, 249, 265
  critical voices 191–197
  emotion expression from vulnerability 227, 228
  pros and cons of separation 264, 265
  two-chair communication 63–65, 82, 89, 102, 105, 113, 114, 116, 127–129, 134, 145, 146, 173, 175, 190, 191
change phase 8–10
Charlie and Joseph 47, 48, 238, 239, 241, 242, 244–247, 251–253
childhood 3, 4, 16, 20, 22, 23, 33, 61, 74, 193, 201, 203, 206, 207, 209, 213, 214, 216, 220, 221, 263
child modes 10–12, 15, 16, 41–44, 62–65, 73–75, 100, 103, 104, 106–109, 111, 112, 116, 125, 128–131, 138, 144, 146–148, 150, 153, 155–158, 161, 163, 165, 169, 170, 175–178, 187, 190, 192, 194–196, 199, 200, 205, 206, 208–211, 213–215, 219–221, 226, 227, 229, 258, 262, 263
  active and blocked 63–65, 73, 106–108, 125, 128, 131, 176, 177, 213
  chair representation 148, 155–157, 161, 163, 165, 170, 192, 194–196, 199, 205
clinical history 80
closure, healthy 273, 279–283
cognitive debate 9
cognitive fusion 13, 14

cognitive work 63, 84, 85, 87, 89, 91, 93, 95, 99, 103, 105, 107, 109, 111, 114, 115, 117, 119, 125, 128, 129, 131, 133, 138, 146, 147, 149, 151, 164, 169, 175, 177, 179, 180, 187, 224, 225, 235, 239, 241, 243, 253, 270, 271, 277, 282, 283
  advantages and disadvantages 149, 169, 172, 177, 187
  connection dialogues 239–243
  ending the relationship 277–279
  last attempt 270–273
communication 33, 58, 75, 77, 82, 152, 154, 173, 222, 232, 233, 251, 258, 260
  connection dialogues 126, 127, 142, 181, 201, 202, 232, 237, 238, 240, 242–244, 246, 248–254, 263, 269, 270
  functional communication 142
  speaking from vulnerability 153, 157, 158, 223
compatibility 255, 272, 273, 280
compromise 38, 136, 152, 181, 247
conceptualized self, attachment to the (ACT) 14
connection
  emotional reconnection 17, 76, 78, 123, 126–128, 137, 138, 141, 143, 144, 153, 159, 163, 164, 168, 170–174, 181, 186, 188, 194, 197, 198, 200–204, 206, 208, 210, 212, 214, 216, 218, 220, 221, 232, 236, 238, 255, 259, 260
connection dialogues 17, 126, 127, 142, 181, 201, 202, 232, 237–240, 242–246, 248–254, 260, 263, 269, 270, 272
  accept, propose, and reach an agreement 246–250, 254
  cell phone metaphor 150, 239–241, 253
  instructions 243
  polarization and contradictions 244–246, 253
  therapeutic task 251–254
contextual model 1, 3, 4, 6, 8, 10, 12–17
contextual therapies 15, 17
cooperation 18, 19, 27, 40, 47, 49, 50, 53, 60–62, 92, 104–106, 118, 121, 130, 143, 147, 149–152, 160, 170, 176, 195, 210, 232, 271
  and assertiveness 60–62
  flexible coping behavior 47
coping behaviors 8, 10, 15, 17, 25–28, 30–32, 34, 38–41, 43, 44, 46–50, 52–62, 77, 79, 82, 83, 89–92, 95, 98–104, 106, 107, 109, 111, 112, 116, 118–121, 125–127, 129, 132, 138, 144, 148, 149, 164, 177, 201, 213, 262
  fight 15, 25, 30, 35, 42, 88, 119, 129, 150, 156, 196, 203, 240, 241
  freeze 25, 26, 28, 32, 34, 35, 40, 41, 88
  overcompensation 8, 11, 12, 15, 16, 31, 41–48, 50, 52, 79, 88–93, 95, 99, 105–107, 109, 130, 138, 143, 149, 157, 169, 176, 189, 262
  submission 25–29, 32, 33, 35, 38–41, 45, 47, 48, 52, 53, 88, 129, 148, 175, 225
coping modes
  overcompensatory coping mode 95, 148, 149, 152, 153, 158, 159, 161, 164
  surrender 11, 88, 148, 274
coping styles 8–10, 32, 37, 38, 87, 91, 92, 99, 100, 109, 144, 172, 226, 235, 269, 270
Couple Schema Therapy 1, 12, 17, 18, 20, 22, 24, 26–28, 30, 32, 34, 36, 38, 40, 60, 75, 77, 79, 83, 141, 255, 257, 261, 262
  additional modules 255–257, 261
  model overview 1, 15–18, 41
  rebalancing stage 141, 143, 172, 189
  reconnection phase 201, 203, 222, 237
critical internal voices 189–191, 214
critical mode 153, 197, 200, 210
critical voice 12, 76, 189–200, 215, 272
  chair work 191–197
  identification 190, 198
  interference with session 190, 199
  resuming session work 199, 200
criticism 4, 7, 8, 11, 12, 16, 23, 34, 39, 41–43, 52, 76, 153, 161, 177, 189–200, 210, 214, 215, 224, 272

d

dad days and mom days 277, 278
dance metaphor 45, 47
defectiveness/shame schema 5, 8

dependency-incompetence schema 5, 272
depression 3
dialogues, see connection dialogues
dimensional model 1, 15–18, 28, 29, 36, 38, 41, 77, 78, 85, 88, 91, 94, 99, 100, 189
  integration of approaches 15–17
  two-leg metaphor 18, 35, 60, 61, 64, 79, 80, 82, 84–92, 94, 96, 98–100, 280
disconnection 1, 4, 6–8, 11, 13, 14, 26–30, 33–35, 44, 47, 48, 50, 51, 53–59, 72, 73, 83, 88, 90, 91, 105, 117, 123, 126, 137, 141, 157, 172, 176–178, 180, 190, 197, 198, 208, 214, 255, 263
  in couples 1, 6, 33, 48, 55, 58, 59, 91, 105, 180, 214
  schema domain 4, 5
disgust 11, 16, 22, 27–35, 39–42, 45–47, 49, 53–58, 60, 61, 88, 92–95, 99, 103–105, 107, 108, 111, 118, 130, 143, 148, 153, 157, 172, 189, 201, 262
domains of schemas, see schema domains
dominance 6, 11, 14, 44–52, 55, 57, 59, 63, 78, 103
  dominance-avoidance mode cycle 47–50
  dominance-domination mode cycle 45, 46, 103
  dominance-submission mode cycle 51, 52
Dominance-avoidance mode cycle, see dominance
Dominance-domination mode cycle, see dominance
Dominance-submission mode cycle, see dominance

e

early maladaptive schemas, see negative schemas
education stage 8, 9, 16, 18, 76–78, 99, 103, 174, 202, 255, 257, 258
emotional activation 17, 21, 41, 72, 74, 157, 219
emotional closeness 73, 141, 143, 152, 158, 159, 161, 162, 167, 170, 181, 185, 186, 200, 214, 223
emotional deprivation schema 4
emotional inhibition schema 7
emotional memory 9, 10, 71, 73, 74, 208
emotional needs 1, 3, 4, 8–10, 12, 15, 16, 20, 21, 36, 59, 60, 71, 74, 79, 189, 203, 206, 208, 213, 214, 220, 221, 263
emotional protection 4
emotional regulation 4, 20, 72, 75, 76, 78, 114, 121
emotions, see basic emotions; blocked emotions; positive emotions; social emotions; vulnerability
empathy 4, 35, 37, 52, 62, 75, 76, 97, 131–133, 141, 144, 152–155, 172, 194, 203, 204, 214, 215, 230, 231, 244, 249, 269
fostering toward the other 153–156
partner support 197
empowerment 151, 179–182, 184, 187
enmeshment/undeveloped self schema 5, 272
entitlement/grandiosity schema 6
evaluation of benefits 152, 167, 171, 173, 184, 185, 188, 197, 200, 218, 221, 233, 236, 251, 254, 261
executive function 71, 72, 78
experiential avoidance 13, 14, 74
experiential phase 9, 10
experiential work 133, 135, 138, 149, 151–153, 155, 157, 159, 161, 163, 165, 170, 175, 177, 179, 181, 183, 187, 191, 193, 195, 196, 199, 205, 207, 209, 211, 213, 215, 217, 219, 226, 227, 229, 231, 235, 244, 245, 247, 249, 253, 264, 265, 281
  critical voices 191, 196
  externalizing partner 152–154, 157, 158, 160, 163
  internalizing partner 179–184
  joint imagery 205, 206, 209–213
  rebalancing 152, 179, 226, 227, 229

f

failure schema 5, 8, 14, 43, 45, 48, 160, 247, 280
farewell to the couple 279–283

fear 4, 7, 11, 14, 16, 19, 22–24, 27–35, 37, 40–42, 47–50, 53–55, 57–59, 61, 89, 90, 92–95, 99, 103–105, 107, 108, 111, 130, 132, 143, 144, 148, 152, 153, 157, 170, 172, 176, 177, 189, 197, 201, 216, 217, 219, 262
feedback 89, 93, 105, 107, 134, 144, 146, 161, 163, 164, 168, 171, 175, 181, 185, 188, 214, 224, 225, 231, 235, 252, 259, 262, 279
fight coping behavior 15, 25, 30, 35, 42, 88, 119, 129, 150, 156, 196, 203, 240, 241
flexibility 13–15, 17, 34, 40, 47, 49, 50, 53, 55, 57, 59, 60, 62, 71, 77–80, 86, 89–92, 98, 99, 101, 102, 104–106, 112, 116, 118–121, 125–127, 129, 130, 132, 134, 138, 144, 147, 149, 151, 163, 164, 173, 176, 177, 181, 195, 201, 213, 214, 216, 221, 232, 255
flexible coping behaviors 49, 50, 53, 55, 57, 59, 60, 62, 77, 89–91, 98, 99, 101, 102, 104, 106, 112, 116, 118–121, 125–127, 129, 132, 138, 144, 164, 177, 201, 213
flight 11, 20, 25–28, 30, 31, 34, 40, 42, 53, 75, 78, 88, 90, 129, 132, 150, 196, 227, 228, 231
floating back to a honeymoon scene 152, 163–167, 170, 171
four chairs 264, 265
freeze coping behavior 25–28, 30, 32, 34, 35, 40, 41, 54, 88, 209
front stage 64, 65, 190, 265

g

Gaining Access to the Vulnerable Side (Module V) 152–154, 157, 170, 180
Gear Change 257–259
Gestalt therapy 3
gratitude 168, 259, 263, 267
grounding in the body 3, 17, 20, 73, 74, 93, 157, 158, 170, 171, 180, 183, 194, 195, 206, 209, 229, 232, 236

h

Hayes, S. C., 13, 14
Hazan and Shaver 18, 19
Healthy Adult Mode 10, 12, 126, 128, 130, 132, 134, 136–138, 179, 201, 222, 224, 226, 228, 230, 232, 234, 236, 256
  entering after separation 126–128, 130, 132, 134, 136, 138
  training 222–224, 226, 228, 230, 232–236
homework 97, 99, 124, 136, 137, 142, 168, 185, 218, 219, 243, 252, 255, 257–260
  first phase 257, 258
  second phase 259, 260
honeymoon scene, see floating back to a honeymoon scene
human needs, see needs

i

identity 4–7, 17, 49, 67, 86
imagery 9, 10, 74, 153, 160, 180, 183, 187, 201, 203–206, 208–210, 212, 214–216, 218–220, 231
  abandonment imagery 153, 157, 159–162, 170
  best day image 133–139, 199, 232
  joint imagery 201, 203–206, 208–210, 212, 214, 216, 218–220, 231
  miracle imagination 180, 182, 184
  tree-giant imagination 181, 182, 184
imagery rewriting 10, 17, 74, 209
impaired autonomy and performance domain 5
impaired limits domain 6
inactivity, impulsivity, or persistent avoidance 14
individual therapy 116, 141, 142, 152, 189, 217, 219, 256, 267, 271, 274, 277
inflexible attention 14
initiative 39, 40, 54, 55, 60, 71, 89–91, 104, 126, 134, 144, 147, 149, 170, 172, 173, 176, 181, 214, 221
internalizing partners 172–182, 184–188, 191, 194, 200
irrational ideas 191–193, 196, 199, 200

j

John and Rachel 174–186
joint imagery exercise 201, 203–206, 208–210, 212, 214, 216, 218–220, 231
- detecting negative patterns 205–208
- reparenting 9, 43, 74, 75, 203, 206, 208, 210, 211, 213–215, 217, 218, 220, 221
- therapeutic task 218–221

joint imagery rewriting work 209–213

l

last attempt 269–276, 281, 282
- agreements 273–275
- negative results 276, 277
- positive results 275, 276

legs, two, see Two-Legged Dimensional Model
leg switching 37–40, 167, 171, 184, 185, 188, 200, 233, 234, 236
- benefits of 167, 171, 184, 188, 200
- blue to red 180, 184, 185
- red to blue 144, 152, 164, 167

limited reparenting 9, 74
living separately but together 261, 262, 271–275, 278, 282
living together but separately 261, 262, 271, 273–275, 282
Low Self-control/Self-discipline schema 4, 6, 7, 12

m

maladaptive schemas, see negative schemas
Mariana 27–34
mediator 279, 280, 283
metaphors 17, 32, 34–36, 38, 45, 47, 51, 53, 72, 85–87, 100, 103, 104, 150, 172, 178, 179, 214, 215, 238–241, 253, 259
- castle 179
- cell phone 240, 241
- dance 45, 47
- wound 214–216

Michelle 19–21
miracle imagination exercise 180, 182, 184
mistrust/abuse schema 5, 272
mode cycle 41–64, 77, 78, 80, 82–85, 99, 100, 102–116, 118, 120–126, 128, 129, 131, 132, 136–139, 141, 145, 147–149, 169, 174, 175, 187, 202, 204, 205, 218, 223, 234, 238, 245, 251–253, 257, 258, 266
- card 106, 108, 110, 111, 129, 131, 136, 137, 139, 258
- chair display 63–65, 109, 110
- moments 42, 43
- starting 82, 102
- stopping 78, 80, 83, 99, 102, 110–116, 118, 120–125, 128, 132, 136–139, 141, 169, 204, 251, 252, 257, 258, 266

model, simplified two-leg, see Two-Legged Dimensional Model
Module I 79–99
Module II 100–111
Module III 112–125
Module IV 126–139
Module V 143–171
Module VI 163–166
Module VII 172–188
Module VIII 189–200
Module IX 203–221
Module X 222–236
Module XI 237–254
Module XII 257–260
Module XIII 261–283

n

needs
- blocked 86, 118, 121, 141
- frustration of 3, 4, 12, 49, 55, 79

negative emotions 22, 27–29, 92, 101, 144, 157, 160, 161, 170, 195
negative patterns 9, 204, 205, 271
negative schema domains, see schema domains
negative schema modes 10, 11
negative schemas 3–12, 16, 41–43, 74, 116, 160, 170, 189, 204–206, 210, 211, 213, 215, 218–221, 231, 274, 280

Negativity/Pessimism schema 7
neurobiological foundations 13, 66–76, 124, 133
neuroplasticity 66–68
nurturing the relationship 259, 260

o

Observer Team Work 63–65, 78, 84, 85, 99, 103, 111, 114, 125, 128–131, 138, 146, 147, 169, 175, 177, 187, 223–225, 231, 235
  in cognitive work 78, 84, 99, 103, 111, 114, 125, 128, 138, 146, 169, 175, 177, 187, 224, 225
  positions 103, 116, 128, 133, 146, 154, 175, 200, 224, 227, 229, 240
openness 17, 141, 151, 160
overcompensation 8, 11, 12, 15, 16, 31, 41–50, 52, 79, 88–93, 95, 99, 105–109, 111, 119, 120, 129, 130, 138, 143, 147–150, 152, 153, 155, 157–159, 161, 164, 169, 176, 189, 225, 262
  as coping behavior 8, 89, 93, 106, 107, 149, 169, 189, 262
  consequences of 49, 108, 144, 152, 226
  flexible form 55, 149, 173
overcompensatory coping mode 95, 148, 149, 152, 153, 158, 159
overvigilance and inhibition domain 7

p

parasympathetic state 19, 21, 75, 76, 142, 244
partner support 197–199
passive avoidance 16, 41, 43, 44, 47, 48, 50, 53–60, 88, 89, 91, 93, 105–107, 131, 172, 173, 175–180, 187, 189, 225, 262, 274
  dominance-passive avoidance cycle 47, 48
  passive avoidance-passive avoidance cycle 54
pathological environment 3, 4
Peter and Rose 45, 46
play, spontaneity, and pleasure 4
positive emotions 22, 27, 92, 134, 136, 142, 144, 152, 163, 164, 168, 170, 171, 181, 185, 186, 188, 209, 214, 264, 265
positive feedback 144, 168–171, 185–188, 259, 279
precontemplation 150, 151
problem identification 80, 99, 101, 113, 127, 145, 173, 204, 223, 238
pros and cons 261, 262, 264–266, 270, 272, 281
psychoeducation 8, 9, 16, 18, 76, 99, 103, 202, 257
psychoeducation phase 8, 9, 202
Punitiveness schema 7, 8

r

Rachel and John, see John and Rachel
realistic boundaries and self-control 4
rebalancing 16, 17, 76–78, 114, 116, 118, 121–126, 128–130, 132–134, 136–138, 141, 142, 149, 151–153, 155, 157, 159, 161, 163–165, 174, 177, 179, 186, 189, 190, 201, 202, 204, 223, 226, 227, 230–232, 235, 236, 251, 255, 257, 263
  after separation 126–128, 131, 133, 136
  externalizing partner 143, 144, 152, 153, 157, 160, 163, 167
  internalizing partner 172, 177, 179, 180, 184
  training Healthy Adult Mode 222, 226, 227, 229, 231
reconnection 17, 21, 49, 53, 55, 76, 78, 114, 121, 123, 125–128, 133, 134, 136–138, 141, 143, 144, 146, 152, 153, 159, 161, 163, 164, 167–174, 181, 186, 188, 194, 195, 197, 198, 200–204, 206, 208, 210, 212, 214, 216, 218, 220–222, 232, 236, 238, 255, 259, 260
joint imagery 203–205, 209, 218
phase 201–203, 237, 259
red leg 35–40, 44–50, 52–62, 86–97, 101, 103–109, 132, 134, 143–153, 155, 157, 159–161, 163–165, 167, 169, 170, 172, 179, 180, 182, 185, 186, 188, 189, 191, 201, 214, 221, 232, 237, 262

red side, see red leg
reparenting 9, 17, 43, 74, 75, 203, 205, 206, 208–211, 213–215, 217–221
joint imagery 203, 206, 208, 210, 211, 213–215, 217
partner role 218–221
resistance 15, 37, 49, 67, 70, 73, 74, 115, 116, 151, 153, 214
rituals 259
Roediger and Frank-Noyon 281
Roediger and Valente 71–73, 75, 201, 208, 237, 239, 240, 249
Roediger, Eckhard 1, 13–16, 19, 22, 25, 28, 31, 34, 35, 41–45, 47, 51, 53, 63, 71–73, 75, 76, 85, 98, 117, 118, 190, 201, 203, 208, 237, 239, 240, 249, 258, 265, 281

s

sadness 11, 14, 16, 19, 22, 27–32, 34, 35, 37, 39–42, 47–50, 52–55, 57, 59, 61, 62, 89, 90, 92–95, 97, 99, 103–105, 107, 108, 111, 114, 115, 118–120, 125, 130–132, 135, 143, 144, 148, 149, 152, 153, 157–159, 166, 169, 170, 172, 177, 178, 185, 187, 189, 195, 201, 212, 226, 227, 229, 232, 233, 249, 250, 262, 269
Sarah and William 80–82, 84, 87, 91, 94, 96, 97, 99, 101–103, 105, 107, 109, 110, 113, 115, 118, 119, 122, 124, 127, 129, 132, 135, 137
schema-based couples therapy, see Couple Schema Therapy
schema domains 4–7
schema modes 3, 9–11, 15, 18, 43
coping modes 1, 10–12, 15–18, 41, 44, 63–65, 77, 78, 85, 88–92, 97–107, 111, 112, 116–121, 128–130, 134, 138, 141, 143, 144, 146–149, 169, 172, 175, 177, 187, 198, 213, 222, 224, 258, 262, 267
schemas 1, 3–18, 20, 22, 24, 26–28, 30, 32, 34–36, 38, 40–43, 60, 74, 75, 77, 79, 83, 85, 87, 116, 141, 160, 170, 189, 192, 203–206, 208, 210, 211, 213–215, 218–221, 231, 255, 257, 258, 261, 262, 272, 274, 278, 280
18 negative schemas 4
activation 3, 220
schema therapy 1, 3–12, 14–18, 20, 22, 24, 26–28, 30, 32, 34, 36, 38, 40, 41, 60, 75, 77, 79, 83, 85, 87, 141, 203, 255, 257, 258, 261, 262, 278
change phase 9, 10
process 8, 9, 255
psychoeducation phase 9
secure attachments to others 4
self-centeredness 6, 86, 143
self-efficacy 4
Self-sacrifice schema 6, 147, 272, 280
separation 24, 112, 114–116, 118, 119, 121, 122, 124–126, 128–130, 132, 134, 136–139, 142, 155, 168, 186, 251, 252, 258, 261, 262, 264–268, 270–283
sexuality 47, 49, 50, 54, 204, 216, 217, 219, 238, 260, 271, 274
social emotions 11, 16, 21–24, 184
social isolation schema 5
social media 14, 49, 56, 57, 263, 267, 269, 270, 276, 277
spatial representations 63–65
speaking from vulnerability 153, 157, 158, 223, 231, 235
stopping the mode cycle 78, 80, 83, 99, 102, 110–116, 118, 120–125, 128, 132, 136–139, 141, 169, 204, 251, 252, 257, 258, 266
Subjugation schema 6, 272
submission 19, 25–35, 38–41, 44, 45, 47, 48, 51, 52, 55, 78, 88, 90, 117, 129, 147, 148, 173, 175, 185, 225, 227–229, 231
sympathetic state 19–21, 75, 76, 142, 244

t

tasks, therapeutic 97, 99, 110, 111, 124, 125, 136, 137, 139, 168, 171, 185, 188, 198, 200, 218, 221, 234, 236, 251, 252, 254, 255
photos and good times 144, 168, 169, 171, 185–188
therapeutic relationship 9, 10, 152

therapy process 8, 10, 16, 17, 63, 70, 78, 126, 144, 211, 246, 255, 257, 260–263, 281
three key concepts 18, 19, 21, 23, 25, 27
time-out 114–118, 122, 124, 125, 168, 171, 186, 197, 200, 257–260
tree-giant imagination exercise 181, 182, 184
trial separation 114, 261, 271, 273–276, 278, 282
two-dimensional model, see Two-Legged Dimensional Model
Two-Legged Dimensional Model 18, 28, 29, 35, 36, 38, 64, 79, 80, 82, 84–88, 90–92, 94, 96, 98, 99
  basic needs and emotions 18, 21, 25, 28–31

u
unmet needs 10, 22, 29, 30, 88, 201, 206, 220, 263
Unrelenting Standards schema 7

v
Valente, Matias 71–73, 75, 201, 208, 237, 239, 240, 249
values alteration 14
ventral vagus nerve 75, 76
violence 4, 177, 281
vulnerability 5, 11, 12, 16, 32, 41–44, 61–64, 74–76, 103, 104, 107, 108, 111, 131–133, 136, 138, 141–144, 147–165, 169, 170, 173, 176–180, 187, 192, 194–197, 199–201, 206, 208–211, 214, 215, 218, 220–236, 244, 263, 267, 269, 270, 280
  expressing emotions from 224–227, 229, 233–236
Vulnerability to Harm/Illness schema 5
Vulnerable Child, see Vulnerable Child Mode
Vulnerable Child Mode 11, 12, 16, 41, 43, 44, 62–64, 74, 75, 103, 104, 107, 108, 111, 131, 138, 144, 148, 150, 153, 155–158, 161, 163, 165, 169, 170, 176–179, 187, 192, 194–196, 199–201, 206, 208–211, 214, 218, 220, 221, 226–230, 233, 235
  chair work 194, 200, 210, 227, 229, 230, 233, 235
  in critical voice work 194–196
  in joint imagery 203, 205, 208, 213, 214, 218

w
withdrawal 20, 28–30, 46, 47, 50, 51, 55, 57, 117, 147, 205, 216, 229, 263, 269, 273, 278, 280
work plan 266–270, 281, 282

y
Young, Jeffrey 1, 3, 4, 8–12
Young Schema Questionnaire (YSQ) 9